DATE			

★FELLOW WORKERS and FRIENDS★

Recent titles in
Contributions in American History
Series Editor: **Jon L. Wakelyn**

Edited by PHILIP S. FONER

★FELLOW
WORKERS
and FRIENDS★

I.W.W. Free-Speech Fights
as Told by Participants

Contributions in American History, Number 92

GREENWOOD PRESS
WESTPORT, CONNECTICUT • LONDON, ENGLAND

Copyright Acknowledgment

"On the Wobbly Train to Fresno" by E. M. Clyde originally appeared in *Labor History*, 14 (Spring 1973): 264-90. Reprinted by permission.
"Free Speech in Montana" by Elizabeth Gurley Flynn originally appeared in Elizabeth Gurley Flynn, *The Rebel Girl* (New York: 1973), pp. 103-5. Reprinted by permission of International Publishers.

Library of Congress Cataloging in Publication Data
Main entry under title:

Fellow workers and friends.

   (Contributions in American history ; no. 92
ISSN 0084-9219)
   Includes bibliographical references and index.
   1.   Industrial Workers of the World.   2.   Liberty of
speech--United States. I.   Foner, Philip Sheldon, 1910-
HD8055.15F44   323.44'3'0973   80-23621
ISBN 0-313-20660-0 (lib. bdg.)

Library of Congress Catalog Card Number: 80-23621
ISBN: 0-313-20660-0
ISSN: 0084-9219

First published in 1981

Greenwood Press
A division of Congressional Information Service, Inc.
88 Post Road West, Westport, Connecticut 06881

Printed in the United States of America

10 9 8 7 6 5 4 3 2 1

Contents

Preface

The exciting story of the Industrial Workers of the World
(I.W.W.) has been well told. It is no longer possible to say, as
did Paul F. Brissenden in his pioneer study of the I.W.W., published in 1919: "The public still knows little about the organization or its members." I, Melvyn Dubofsky, Patrick Renshaw,
Robert F. Tyler, and Joseph R. Conlin have compiled com-
prehensive histories of the I.W.W. Joyce L. Kornbluh has
edited an I.W.W. anthology made up of articles, songs, poems,
cartoons, and photographs, and Deborah Shaffer and Stewart
Bird have produced "The Wobblies," a documentary film on
the I.W.W. As a result, the public is aware that the I.W.W.
made valuable contributions in the campaign to organize the
unorganized (particularly unskilled, foreign-born, women,
and black workers), spearheaded the fight for free speech, and
pioneered in the battle for industrial unionism.

A number of I.W.W. leaders have published their autobiog-
raphies. In addition, many Wobblies, rank-and-filers as well as
leaders, presented accounts of their experiences. This is especially true of the men and women involved in the great I.W.W.

free-speech fights. While the story of these battles is part of most histories of the I.W.W., the present volume represents the first time that it has been told by the participants themselves. As these accounts make abundantly clear, the I.W.W. free-speech fights are among the most spectacular of labor activities in the first two decades of the twentieth century, and rank high in the history of the civil liberties movement. The deprivation of the right of I.W.W. members to free speech foreshadowed the repression of antiwar dissenters during the First World War and was reflected in the Espionage and Sedition Acts of the federal government.

In presenting this early form of what may be called "Oral History," I have retained the spellings and punctuations of the original, despite the occasional inconsistencies. In the preparation of this volume, I have had the kind assistance of numerous libraries and historical societies. I wish to thank the staffs of the Kansas Historical Society, State Historical Society of Wisconsin, Library of the U.S. Department of Labor, Library of the Department of Labour (Canada), Washington State Library, Library of Congress, National Archives, Labadie Collection (University of Michigan Library), Tamiment Institute Library of New York University, the public libraries of the following cities: Denver, Everett and Spokane (Washington), Fresno and San Diego (California), Portland (Oregon), and the libraries of the following universities: California, Chicago, Columbia, Duke, Harvard, Iowa, Kansas, Michigan, Missouri, Nebraska, Oregon, Pennsylvania, State University of South Dakota, State College of Washington, Washington State University, Wayne State, Wisconsin, and Yale. I wish also to thank the Langston Hughes Memorial Library of Lincoln University, Pennsylvania, for valuable assistance in obtaining material through interlibrary loan. My brother Henry Foner read the manuscript and helped in preparing it for publication.

Philip S. Foner
Emeritus Professor of History,
Lincoln University, Pennsylvania
Visiting Professor of History,
Rutgers University, Camden

★FELLOW WORKERS and FRIENDS★

Introduction by Philip S. Foner

By the summer of 1904, many progressive leaders in the
American labor and socialist movements were convinced of
the need for a new national labor organization, one that
"would correspond to modern industrial conditions, and
through which they [organized workers] might finally secure
complete emancipation from wage slavery for all wage workers."[1] It was this conviction that led to the formation of the
Industrial Workers of the World. Under the impetus of the
Western Federation of Miners, which had recognized the im-
possibility of converting the conservative American Federation
of Labor (A.F. of L.) into the type of organization that would
achieve real benefits for the majority of workers, these leaders
agreed to establish a labor organization that could effectively
organize and unite the working class. With their democratic
proclivities and dislike of elitist craft unionism, they supported
industrial over craft unionism as one of the basic principles of
the I.W.W.

On June 27, 1905, more than two hundred delegates, representing close to one hundred fifty thousand workers, met in

Chicago to establish a new industrial union movement. On the stage of Brand's Hall in Chicago were William D. ("Big Bill") Haywood of the Western Federation of Miners, Eugene V. Debs of the Socialist Party, Daniel De Leon, leader of the Socialist Labor Party, Mother Jones, beloved organizer of the mine workers and other unions, and Lucy Parsons, wife of Albert R. Parsons, one of the Haymarket martyrs. Haywood, as the representative of the Western Federation of Miners, which was the key organization behind the new I.W.W., acted as chairman. In opening the convention, he declared:

> This is the Continental Congress of the working class. We are here to confederate the workers of this country into a working class movement that shall have for its purpose the emancipation of the working class from the slave bondage of capitalism. . . . What we want to establish at this time is a labor organization that will open wide its doors to every man that earns his livelihood either by his brain or his muscle. . . . There is no man who has an ounce of honesty in his make-up but recognizes the fact that there is a continuous struggle between the two classes, and this organization will be formed, based and founded on the class struggle, having in view no compromise and no surrender, and but one object and one purpose and that is to bring the workers of this country into the possession of the full value of the produce of their toil.[2]

The organization that emerged from the convention was essentially a reaction against the A.F. of L. During the five days of the convention, three main charges were directed at the federation:

(1) Its adherence to craft unionism limited union membership to a small minority of the working class, the skilled "aristocrats of labor"; helped to stimulate "union snobbery"; created the "union scab," who would continue to work at a particular trade even if workers in an allied trade in the same industry were on strike; and left most of the working class helpless on the industrial battlefield.

(2) Its assumption of an identity of interest shared by employer and employee and its denial of the existence of the class struggle, with its leaders becoming labor lieutenants tied up closely to the captains of industry.

(3) Its denial of the necessity of achieving socialism, its refusal to lead the working class towards united political action, and its domination by a small clique of dictatorial bureaucrats hindered the development of effective unionism.[3]

In contrast to the policies of the A.F. of L., the new movement advocated a militant stance on the economic and political fronts. The preamble to its constitution affirmed such militancy:

> The working class and the employing class have nothing in common. There can be no peace so long as hunger and want are found among the millions of the working people and the few, who make up the employing class, have all the good things of life. Between these two classes struggle must go on until all the toilers come together on the political, as well as on the industrial field, and take hold of that which they produce through an economic organization of the working class. . . .[4]

The name "Industrial Workers of the World" was adopted. It later became known as the "Wobblies" because of the way in which its Chinese-born members pronounced the letters "I.W.W."[5] The organization's motto was "An Injury to One Is the Concern of All." Only wage-earners were eligible for membership in the new organization. Race, creed, color, and sex were no bar to membership, and any immigrant with a valid union card could join. At the meeting ratifying the work of the convention, Haywood declared that although unions affiliated with the A.F. of L. discriminated against a Negro or foreign-born worker, to the I.W.W. it "did not make a bit of difference whether he is a Negro or a white man. It does not make any difference whether he is American or foreigner."[6]

Initiation fees and dues were set very low in order to facilitate, in one delegate's words, "the up-lifting of the fellow that is down in the gutter."[7] "I do not care the snap of my

finger whether or not the skilled workman joins this industrial
union movement at this time," Haywood declared. "When we
get the unorganized and unskilled laborer into this organization, the skilled worker will of necessity come here for his
own protection."[8]

Under the I.W.W. organization plan, the industries of the
United States were divided into thirteen major industrial
groups on the basis of the products manufactured. All were
to be organized on an industrial union basis, which meant that
all the crafts within a shop would belong to the same local.
Thus, in the mining department, all the men working in and
around a mine as well as the clerks in that particular mine
office would be organized, not just the skilled workers.[9]

Among the resolutions adopted by the founding convention of the I.W.W. was one which hailed the "mighty struggle
of the laboring class of far-off Russia against unbearable outrage, oppression and cruelty and for more humane conditions
for the working class of that country." It pledged support for
the Revolution of 1905, underway in Russia. Among the other
resolutions adopted was one to establish an educational bureau,
composed of a literature and lecture section, "to show the
workers that their interests are common in every part of the
world . . . that the earth and all that the earth holds are theirs."
Another resolution condemned militarism as an evil force
antithetical to the interests of all workers and denied membership to anyone who joined the state militia.[10]

The founding convention of the I.W.W. set a constitutional
limit on dues of fifty cents a month and on initiation fees of
$5.00 sliding down to $1.50 (the exact sum to be set by each
industrial union). These limits were never exceeded and often
were lowered. (When workers joined in large groups, there was
rarely an initiation fee.) Twenty-five cents a month for dues
and initiation fees of a dollar were common, and these were
sometimes overlooked during an organizing drive.[11]

Printed in tens of thousands of copies, the constitution of
the I.W.W., with its fiery first sentence, "The working class
and the employing class have nothing in common," heralded
the birth of a militant organization of American workers.[12]

The constitution and resolutions were designed to attract and meet the needs of specific groups of workers. One important group was the Western migratory workers—the seasonal laborers of logging camps and lumber mills, mines and construction projects, orchards and agricultural fields—who, after 1908, constituted the majority of the I.W.W. members in the West and made up the core of the organization in that region.[13]

It is important to recognize that by the time the I.W.W. was founded a dispossessed, homeless proletariat—the migratory workers—had been created throughout the West. It was a roaming army of several million, who were not attached to any particular locality or to any special industry. They made possible the operation of the lumber, railroad construction, mining, and agricultural industries of the West. Young (the typical age was under 25), wifeless, homeless, semiskilled or unskilled, they moved about from job to job in empty boxcars, or "sidedoor coaches," as they called the freight cars. In the main, they followed seasonal occupations, harvesting wheat, logging, maintaining the grades for the great transcontinental railroads, or mining silver, lead, copper, and tin in the Rocky Mountains mining regions.[14]

These men built America's railroads and highways, felled the timber in the forests, plowed the land, threshed the crops, husked corn, and picked apples. Their reward was to be treated as "scum" when they were employed and as dangerous "parasites" when they lacked visible means of support. Forced to live under unspeakable conditions in the "jungles" and labor camps while working, they received extremely low pay and labored from sunup to sundown.[15]

In a grim assessment of the situation made a few years before the outbreak of World War I, Samuel Gompers asserted that "The lot of the migratory worker in the United States today is worse than slavery."[16] The A.F. of L. had made a feeble attempt to organize these workers before concluding that it was impossible. Its excuses were many. The migrants lacked stability. It was too expensive to keep track of them. The problem of organizing thousands of workers who were constantly on the move seemed insurmountable. Then again,

even though the majority of the migratory workers were na-
tive Americans, there was a significant percentage of foreign-
born workers of different nationalities whom employers mixed
together to make the task of organizing them more difficult.[17]

These obstacles did not faze the I.W.W., whose policy and
tactics were designed to overcome them. The I.W.W.'s refusal
to differentiate among workers because of race, color, nation-
ality, or religion appealed to the migratory workers, who
mingled freely while traveling on boxcars. Low initiation fees
and dues were ideal for a group of workers with meager in-
comes. Interchangeable membership cards permitted them to
remain in the organization even when they made frequent job
changes. Moreover, wherever the migrant worker turned, he
found the I.W.W.—on the freight trains, in the jails, in the bunk-
houses, and in the "jungles"—its gospel spread by fervent converts who were themselves workers and who followed the
transients on and off the job.[18]

For migrants, affiliation with the I.W.W. served a number of
important purposes. The I.W.W.'s mutual protection associations were a safeguard against fraudulent employment agencies
which charged for jobs that were hundreds of miles away and
were either nonexistent or not what the agency had described.
The migrants also needed and received protection from boot-
leggers, boxcar robbers, gamblers, highjackers, and train crews
which preyed upon them. A paid-up dues card in the I.W.W.
usually provided admission to freights carrying migrants from
job to job, and even hostile brakemen learned to respect the
I.W.W. card.[19]

These workers appreciated the I.W.W.'s militant philosophy,
which provided an outlet, meaning, and dignity to the migrant
group, rootless and poverty-stricken in a land of plenty, despised and exploited by society, and unwanted by any other
labor organization. A man considered a "bum" by most members of society was accepted into the I.W.W. and even glorified
as "a real proletarian" without whom "the farms would not
be cultivated, the logs cut or the mines mined" and who would
lead the working class toward the establishment of the in-

Introduction

evitable cooperative commonwealth.[20] Is it any wonder that these workers flocked into the I.W.W.?

Much the same reasons account for the I.W.W.'s attraction for the unskilled and semiskilled immigrant workers in the East and Midwest. Like the immigrant workers, they found the I.W.W. a congenial organization. The policy of low initiation fees and dues appealed to these workers as much as it did to the migrants. Again, like the migrant workers, the immigrant industrial workers, whose foreignness was ridiculed in the commercial press with terms like "Hunks," "Bohunks," and "Dagoes," found dignity and status in the I.W.W. The I.W.W. took pride in its appeal to immigrant workers. An extensive foreign-language press was organized specifically to attract the foreign-born. *Solidarity* and the *Industrial Worker*, the I.W.W.'s English-language organs, contained frequent articles about the immigrant worker, suggested ways in which he should or should not be approached by I.W.W. organizers, and warned them never to regard the foreign-born worker as inferior because he could not understand English.[21]

Most I.W.W. organizers took this advice to heart and quickly won a reputation among the foreign-born. Regarding the I.W.W. as their spokesman and champion, the immigrant workers flocked to it, often without being asked. "This country has an obligation to these strangers who furnish so much of its labor force," one paper editorialized piously, after describing the foreign-born as being "like children." "It owes them the duty of protection against such an organization like the I.W.W. . . ." The I.W.W. agreed that the country did owe these workers an obligation—but an obligation to reward them for the wealth they had produced so that they were not forced to live in dire poverty. It insisted that the nation had an obligation to protect these workers when they struck against unbearable conditions, not to assist employers in defeating their struggles.[22]

In general, the I.W.W. operated chiefly among the workers whom the A.F. of L. would not and did not reach—the migratory workers of the West and the unskilled industrial workers of the East. As one contemporary journalist succinctly summed up: "The I.W.W.'s deepest strength lies in the fact that it extends the red hand of fellowship to the lowliest of workers, that it has made itself the special champion of those who are paid the least and work the hardest."[23]

Between 1905, when it was born, and 1908, the I.W.W. was wracked by intense factional feuds which resulted in several splits. The first split occurred in 1906 at the second convention, when President Charles O. Sherman was forced from office by a faction led by William E. Trautmann, Daniel De Leon, and Vincent St. John. Viewing Sherman and his followers as conservatives out to use the I.W.W. for personal gain, the Trautmann-De Leon-St. John faction pushed through the convention a proposal to abolish the office of president and elected Vincent St. John as chairman. At first Sherman and his followers held control of I.W.W. headquarters, but they were forced to surrender as a result of a court order which upheld the convention and its actions and declared that Sherman's acts "were illegal." For a brief period, Sherman headed a separate I.W.W. in Joliet, Illinois.[24]

On June 6, 1906, at its fourteenth annual convention, the Western Federation of Miners had gone on record as being an integral part of the I.W.W. and announced that it would "do everything to build up the I.W.W. throughout the country."[25] The majority of the W.F. of M. membership condemned the 1906 split and charged that it had been deliberately provoked by Daniel De Leon to gain control of the new industrial union and convert it and its affiliated unions into an appendage of the Socialist Labor Party. In an effort to revive unity in the I.W.W., the 1907 W.F. of M. convention invited "the contending factions" to meet with the Western Federation of Miners "for the purpose of re-establishing and strengthening the Industrial Workers of the World." But this effort at reconciling the two factions in the I.W.W. came to naught. The I.W.W. dismissed the call, condemned the W.F. of M. Executive Board for addressing the invitation "to officers of both factions of the I.W.W.," and insisted that "there is but one I.W.W. in existence now or at any time that has claim to the name."[26]

The W.F. of M. dropped the plan for unification, and at its

sixteenth annual convention in 1908, participation in the
I.W.W. was broken off.[27] At the same time an increasing number of industrial unionists from the Socialist Party began to
leave the I.W.W. Even former Socialist founders of the I.W.W.,
like Eugene V. Debs, turned cool to the organization as the
antipolitical, anarcho-syndicalist forces headed by Trautmann
and St. John increased their influence.[28]

There are many definitions of syndicalism. William Z.
Foster, an outstanding authority on the subject, defines it as
follows:

> In its basic aspects, syndicalism, or more properly anarcho-
> syndicalism, may be defined very briefly as that tendency
> in the labor movement to confine the revolutionary class
> struggle of the workers in the economic field, to practi-
> cally ignore the state, and to reduce the whole fight of
> the working class to simply a question of trade union
> action. Its fighting organization is the trade union; its
> basic method of class warfare is the strike, with the gen-
> eral strike as the revolutionary weapon; and its revolu-
> tionary goal is the setting up of a trade union "state" to
> conduct industry and all other social activities.[29]

One effect of the departure of the W.F. of M. was to reduce
the influence in the I.W.W.'s Western branches of large, well-
established unions with more stable membership and increase
that of the shifting migratory workers, the very members who
were to play an important role in the free-speech fights. Furthermore, the departure of many Socialist Party members strengthened the influence of the direct-action, anarcho-syndicalist
elements in the I.W.W. At the 1908 convention, the migratory
workers (dubbed the "Overalls Brigade") joined with the direct-
action I.W.W. leaders, Trautmann and St. John, to gain complete control and to force out Daniel De Leon and his followers.[30] With the De Leonites out of the way, St. John,
Trautmann, and the "Overalls Brigade" eliminated from the
I.W.W. preamble all reference to political action and emphasized primarily economic, direct action in the class struggle.

Vincent St. John was elected general secretary-treasurer, and
the I.W.W. remained under his guiding hand until 1915.[31]

No sooner had the 1908 convention adjourned when the
Industrial Union Bulletin, the I.W.W. official organ, predicted
that the future of the organization was linked inextricably
with the Western element. "The outstanding thing about the
fourth convention," it observed, "is the spirit that actuated to
an unusual degree those delegates who, lacking the means of
transportation, had to cover hundreds of miles on foot, travel
by freight and in boxcars in order to participate in the convention. . . . With such men in the ranks, the I.W.W. may confidently hope that success will crown their persistent efforts
towards industrial emancipation."[32]

It was with "such men in the ranks" (and women too) that
the I.W.W. set out in 1909 to organize the unorganized. In the
process the Wobblies became involved in the greatest free-
speech fights in American history. The I.W.W. captured national attention as Wobbly after Wobbly was yanked off soapboxes by police in scores of cities and marched off to jail,
after uttering these four challenging words,"Fellow workers
and friends," the salutation that usually prefaced the speech
of an I.W.W. soapbox orator. In the years between 1909 and
the First World War, these four words came to be associated
with some of the most spectacular attempts to put the Bill of
Rights into practice which the country has ever seen—"the
struggle for the use of the streets for free speech and the right
to organize" (the I.W.W.'s description of a free-speech fight).

It was essential that the right to speak on the streets be
protected, because this was the method the Wobblies relied on
to gather new recruits among the itinerant workers who
poured into the cities of the West every winter. "The street
corner was their only hall," wrote an I.W.W. organizer, "and
if denied the right to agitate there then they must be silent."
At street-corner meetings they could distribute newspapers,
leaflets, and pamphlets, all carrying the message of industrial
unionism to the unorganized. The importance of this educational process was explained in the *Industrial Worker*'s account

of the free-speech fights: "We have little desire to enter into these scraps, neither will we stand idly by and see our only hope taken from us—the right to educate the working class. When we lose that we have lost all our hopes and ambitions so take care what you are playing with when you try to throttle Freedom of Speech."[33]

Street-speaking was important for still another reason. Because of suppression or distortion by the commercial press of the workers' position in a strike, the most effective way that the Wobblies could get their story to the public was the open-air meeting. Being colorful speakers, the Wobblies usually attracted large audiences, and they not only aroused sympathy for the strikers but helped build a much-needed strike fund by selling literature and taking collections.

By passing ordinances suppressing the I.W.W.'s right of free speech on the streets, city officials, acting for lumber, agricultural, and mining interests and other employers, were convinced that they could crush the organizing drives and destroy the movement. At the same time they would rid the community of men who, in the eyes of "respectable elements," were the antithesis of the American ideal. They were "only tramps and hoboes who rejected home-life, one of the foundations of the American nation."

For the I.W.W. the issue was clear: the right to speak meant the right to organize. The Wobblies rallied their strength across the continent to break the attempt to stifle this right, convinced that they were upholding the constitutional rights of all people in their battles to smash gag laws.

The practice of speaking in spite of official bans was not associated only with the Wobblies. It had long been followed by progressive groups, trade unions, and radical political parties before the emergence of the I.W.W. Even specific aspects of the strategy followed by the I.W.W. in their spectacular free-speech fights had been used before. For example, in the fall of 1907, during the administration of Mayor W. H. Moore, Socialists in Seattle, led by Dr. Herman F. Titus, challenged a city ban against their speaking in the streets. One after another, they mounted the soapbox, were dragged down by

the police, carted off to jail, denied bail, fined, and imprisoned. Police Chief James Wappenstein threatened to throw
all Socialists into jail "as regularly as they spoke." After Dr.
Titus threatened from jail a mass invasion of free-speech
fighters if Seattle did not stop arresting and imprisoning
Socialists, the police backed down, permitted street meetings,
and released the men and women in jail.[34]

In 1908 the Socialist Party, the Socialist Labor Party, and
the I.W.W. jointly waged an effective free-speech fight in Los
Angeles after deliberately violating a city ordinance forbidding
street meetings without police permits for all organizations except religious groups. When a speaker was arrested for speaking without a permit, "his place was speedily filled upon the
soap box." Speaker after speaker, men and women, black and
white, mounted the soapbox, were arrested, and jailed. "The
Jail Is Our Weapon," the free-speech fighters of Los Angeles
announced late in June. "We are going to jail in numbers.
That is the way the fight has been won wherever it has been
really won."[35] Free-speech fighters so crowded the jail and
clogged court calendars that the City Council was forced to
repeal the objectionable ordinance. "Free Speech Is Won"
was the headline in *Common Sense*, organ of the Socialist
Party of Los Angeles, after six months of struggle.[36]

The I.W.W. was the first labor organization to present its
major free-speech fights so dramatically and to organize and
publicize the battle for freedom of speech so effectively.
The I.W.W. worked out a pattern of free-speech fighting which
enabled it to make the most use of its scattered members and
created the impression that ten men existed when there was
only one. Vincent St. John explained the strategy: "Whenever
any local union becomes involved in a free-speech fight, they
notify the general office and that information is sent to all
the local unions . . . with the request that if they have any
members that are footloose to send them along."[37] In response
to these calls, Wobblies would converge on a town or city
that prohibited street meetings. Though denied a license,
Wobblies, one after another, would mount the soapbox to
address "Fellow workers and friends," ringing out their defiance

of police edicts. As soon as a Wobbly was marched off to jail, another one would mount the soapbox. He, too, would be hauled down by police only to be replaced by still another Wobbly. The "four-word speech" would continue all evening as the Wobblies were yanked off the soapbox. " 'Afraid of getting arrested? Hardly! We want to get arrested. We'll flood the jail, and the county farm and any other place they want to send us to.' That's what a member of the Industrial Workers of the World involved in the free-speech fight said yesterday to this reporter [for the *Kansas City Star*] at their headquarters."[38]

Thus the free-speech fighters invited arrest, cheerfully allowed themselves to be marched off by the police, and crowded eagerly into the jails, bull pens, old schoolhouses, abandoned hospitals or any other available building, supremely confident that, as one of the songs proclaimed:

> There is one thing I can tell you
> And it makes the bosses sore.
> As fast as they can pinch us,
> We can always get some more.[39]

The pattern of speeches, arrests, and overcrowding in jails created a burden for each city in which a free-speech fight occurred, and the costs were borne by the taxpayers. In addition Wobbly strategy called for making further demands on a city's resources. Each Wobbly in jail demanded a separate trial by jury to clog the courts and administrative machinery. Inside the jails, the free-speech fighters would sing rebel songs. "In jail we had one lively time. Rebel Red songs from the I.W.W. song books were sung almost continuously. . . . We spoke for the benefit of the police, loud enough for them to hear. We burned the stuff called food. Then we sang some more."[40] Working through an elected committee, the free-speech fighters in jail decided all questions of defense tactics. An outside committee publicized the struggle and rallied support for the imprisoned men. Usually no money was spent (or, as Wobblies put it, "wasted") on legal fees. All funds were used to take care of the men pouring into the community, to supply tobacco and, if possible, food to those in jail, and to get the widest publicity.

By this pattern, the Wobblies hoped to win the support of liberal sympathizers outraged by the violation of a basic constitutional guarantee and, in alliance with progressive-minded citizens, to force the authorities to grant them the right to speak. In many communities the I.W.W. did win such support. University professors, political leaders like Senator Robert M. La Follette, liberals of all types, Socialist Party members, A.F. of L. local unions and city central bodies supported the free-speech fights, and this support was often crucial for the I.W.W.'s victory.

The technique of the free-speech fights evolved gradually. It was born in Missoula, Montana, in 1908, it was dramatized and further developed in Spokane and Fresno some months later, and it reached its peak in the most widely publicized of the I.W.W. free-speech fights—the one in San Diego, California, which began in 1912 and continued for more than eighteen months.

There were numerous aspects to the free-speech fights, and many comical situations have been recorded by old-time I.W.W.'s that have become part of the Wobbly lore. One story tells about the harvest hand who dropped off at Sioux City, Iowa, during a free-speech fight, and finding no one in the corner, he decided that the Wobblies were all in jail and that he had better speak himself. Climbing onto the box, he began: "Fellow workers and friends." Nothing happened. He paused and started again: "Fellow workers and friends." Again nothing happened. Finally, in an aggrieved tone, the would-be free-speech fighter demanded: "Say, where's the cop?"[41] There are many stories in the tradition of the bragging, fighting, "miracle men" tales of American folklore, full of Wobbly humor.

But there was nothing humorous about the brutal methods used to smash the I.W.W.'s right of free speech. The police were often vicious even at the beginning of a free-speech fight, and as the battle continued—for days, weeks, and months—their brutality increased. In addition, private individuals, organized as vigilante committees, worked hand-in-hand with the police, and together they inflicted unspeakable cruelties on the Wobblies and their sympathizers. Almost every month during the period of the epic free-speech fights, the I.W.W. papers carried stories and pictures of the victims of police and vigilante brutalities, men murdered, maimed, beaten, and starved.

Some I.W.W. leaders had long protested against the free-speech fights, declaring that they led to "fighting the bull instead of the boss." In December 1911, John Pancner, one of the best I.W.W. organizers, urged that the free-speech demonstrations be dropped because they were destructive to the organization; defense money for those jailed took funds better spent on constructive organization on the job, and the jailings, beatings, and bread-and-water diets were ruining the cream of the movement. Free speech should be employed on the job: "Organize the wage slave, not the bourgeois, the street moocher and the saloon soak."[42]

Others felt that the entire strategy of passive resistance used in the free-speech fights, with special care being taken by the Wobblies that no act of violence be committed by the free-speech fighters, put the membership at a terrible disadvantage. "The free-speech fighters are restricted by these tactics to the *very weakest weapon* in the arsenal of Industrial Unionism— passive resistance," *Solidarity* complained as early as 1910.[43] No effective substitute for passive resistance was, however, developed. In the midst of the San Diego battle, the Wobbly press declared that "new methods" were needed to resist "police and vigilante thugs," and that the free-speech fighters should begin "*to actively protect themselves from these thugs,*" but when Walker C. Smith recommended that "ammunition" be shipped to the free-speech fighters in San Diego, the *Industrial Worker* denounced the suggestion. It recommended an ounce of sabotage.[44]

Still another objection to the free-speech fights was that while they attracted widespread attention and even aroused sympathy among many who were hostile to the doctrines and

activities of the I.W.W., they interfered with the effective conduct of strikes. Wobbly organizers objected that strikes were
lost because they were allowed "to degenerate into a free-
speech fight," and charged that this was precisely what the
employers wanted. Free-speech fights, it was further charged,
did not result in any organizational growth in the community
affected. For one thing, agitation and "soapboxing" were
viewed by these critics as a limited means of reaching the mass
of the workers, the majority of whom did not congregate at
street-corners. Furthermore, free-speech fighters scattered as
soon as they were released from jail, and some of the most
competent organizers, like Frank Little, left to participate in
other free-speech battles. The purpose of the free-speech conflicts—to organize the unorganized—was forgotten in the hour
of victory. "Having won the free-speech fight," the Wobblies
were reminded, "the work of the Fresno I.W.W. has just begun. It is now up to them to do what they started out to do
when they first came here—to organize the unskilled workers."[45]
But by the time this advice was published, many of the Fresno
free-speech fighters were en route to another battle. The following account in the Spokane *Spokesman-Review*, early in 1912,
describes the aftermath of a free-speech victory in a Washington community that was frequently repeated:

> Having been granted the privilege of speaking in the
> streets . . . and having no more "worlds to conquer" in
> this section, one hundred members of the Industrial
> Workers of the World are preparing to shift the scene of
> their activities to San Francisco, where public-speaking
> rights have been denied members of their order.
>
> The leaders of the contingent, many of whom came here
> from St. Louis, declare that they do not care to speak
> where the privilege has been extended, but prefer to
> promote their campaign in those localities where the
> right is denied or curtailed.[46]

As Melvyn Dubofsky pointed out, too often the free-speech
fights "brought no improvement in working conditions and

added few members to the IWW." Still, he added, the I.W.W.
found that "street speaking continued to be the most effective
means for spreading the IWW gospel and for winning new recruits to the organization."[47] Certainly these battles publicized
the I.W.W. as a national organization dedicated to preserving
a basic principle of American democracy—freedom of speech.
American workers are indebted to the free-speech fighters, who
brought about the repeal of undemocratic ordinances and
opened the gates to unionism (branded "un-American") in
many communities.

The free-speech fights, of course, demonstrated that business
interests would violate constitutional liberties and would resort
to force and violence to keep unorganized workers from unioni-
zation. The vigilantes, historians Selig Perlman and Philip Taft
pointed out, were "to be classed with the fascist formations in
Italy and Germany."[48] Moreover, the "respectable elements"
were often the most vicious. A shocked citizen of Minot, North
Dakota, recorded the following conversation with Judge Davis,
a leading light in the community and a magistrate in the city
courts:

> "Judge, Can't you do something to prevent the beating
> down of innocent men?" I asked.
>
> "Prevent Hell. We'll drive the G--D---Sons of B-----s into
> the river and drown them. We'll starve them. We'll kill
> every damned man of them or drive them together with
> the Socialists from the city," he thundered back.

A similar appeal to an official of the Second National Bank
of Minot brought this reply: "There ain't no use in threatening
those fellows with kindness. The only thing to do is to club
them down. Beat them up. Drive them out of the city."[49]

In the courts, the free-speech fighters received no judicial
assistance in upholding their constitutional liberties. As the
Industrial Worker aptly put it: "A demonstration of working
men in the interests of the constitutional right of freedom of
speech is judged a 'riot' by the courts; but violence and terror-

ism on the part of the capitalists and their tool is 'law and order.' "[50]

The free-speech fights may have contributed little to building an organization, but they did build within the movement a spirit of unity in action. They were also significant in cementing solidarity among I.W.W., Socialist Party, and A.F. of L. members. In several communities, these three groups worked together in conducting the free-speech fights, and in most others, where the Wobblies carried the brunt of the battle, they received support from local S.P. and A.F. of L. officials. During the entire period of the free-speech fights, however, there was not a single reference in the *American Federationists*, the official national A.F. of L. organ, to these battles!

The I.W.W. free-speech fights are part of the great American tradition. Writing in *Pearson's Magazine* on the subject of "Free Speech in the United States," Courtenay Lemon paid a glowing tribute to the I.W.W. and praised it for taking "the lead in the fight for free speech":

> Whether they agree or disagree with its methods and aims, all lovers of liberty everywhere owe a debt to this organization for its defense of free speech. Absolutely irreconcilable, absolutely fearless, and unsuppressibly persistent, it has kept alight the fires of freedom, like some outcast vestal of human liberty. That the defense of traditional rights to which this government is supposed to be dedicated should devolve upon an organization so often denounced as "unpatriotic" and "un-American," is but the usual, the unfailing irony of history.[51]

In 1945 an I.W.W. member referred to a struggle in Toronto in the summer of 1906 as "the first free-speech fight of the I.W.W. . . . . It was a small affair and its outcome is not known to the writer."[52] The reference was to the fact that the Toronto locals went into court when the police interfered with their street-corner meetings. "Against this denial of our *right*," the Canadian industrial unionists announced, "we as revolutionary wage workers intend to fight."[53] There is no report of what happened in this fight.[54] Nevertheless, it launched the I.W.W. struggle for free speech. The exact number of these battles is impossible to determine. Paul F. Brissenden, the first historian to study the I.W.W., listed twenty-six free-speech fights, twenty of which occurred between 1909 and 1913 alone, and all but one of which took place between 1909 and 1916. His list ends with the bloody battle at Everett, Washington, in November 1916.[55]

During the various free-speech fights, the I.W.W. and Socialist journals and newspapers carried the participants' accounts of their experiences. Then on September 19, 1914, both *Solidarity* and *Industrial Worker* published the following announcement over the heading "Information on Free Speech Fights Wanted":

> We have been requested to furnish the United States Industrial Relations Commission with information about the free speech fights in which the Industrial Workers of the World has been involved.
>
> Believing that the publicity to be gained is worth the work it will entail, we have concluded to gather all available data of occasions where police authorities have interfered with free speech, free press, free assembly and where the writ of habeas corpus has been denied.
>
> Facts in regard to these important issues will make a permanent propaganda document of great value.[56]
>
> This report should include every city and town where a free speech fight has occurred, wherever possible giving names of mayor, chief of police, sheriff, policemen, deputies, detectives, also names of politicians, members of Citizen Alliance and other thugs.
>
> The locals that have been involved should make a general statement. The individual members that have taken part in free speech fights anywhere in this country are requested to write the facts in detail, covering their personal

experiences. Write your story in your own way, giving
dates, if you can, manner of arrest, prison treatment, trial
sentences, etc., etc.

Send in any circular pamphlets, bulletins or reports bearing on the fights for free speech. Send all communications
to General Headquarters, 307 W. Washington St., Chicago,
Ill.

                                    Vincent St. John[57]
                                    General Sec'y-Treas.

                                    Wm. D. Haywood[58]
                                    General Organizer

Just how many replies this notice produced cannot be determined, but in the files of the Commission on Industrial Relations housed in the National Archives, Washington, D.C., there
are several letters describing the writers' experiences in free-
speech fights. They are included below with other accounts by
participants in these battles. These firsthand accounts constitute a "document of great value," portraying the determination,
enthusiasm, and hardships associated with these epic battles.
They also provide insight into the varying political views of the
men and women involved, the conflicts among them, and their
unifying desire to make the Bill of Rights a reality.

Free-Speech Fight in
Missoula, Montana, 1909

Introduction

Elizabeth Gurley Flynn was born in 1890 and was named
after her family's doctor, Elizabeth Kent. Annie Gurley Flynn,
Elizabeth's mother, was an advocate of equal rights for women,
and her four children were delivered by women doctors.
Elizabeth's father was an Irish rebel, and she grew up amidst
Irish revolutionaries, feminists, socialists, and anarchists. In
public speeches at age fifteen, she asserted that full freedom
for women was impossible under capitalism and that the
government should undertake financial support of all children
so that women would not become dependent on men. Her
first public address, entitled "What Socialism Will Do for
Women," discussed how socialism supported the abolition of
prostitution, the economic independence of women, the social
care of children, and the women's right to an education, participation in government, and entry into the arts, sciences, and
professions. A New York paper headlined her address, "MERE
CHILD TALKS BITTERLY OF LIFE." The novelist Theodore
Dreiser, after hearing her first speech, described her as "an
East Side Joan of Arc." She actually lived in the Bronx in New
York City.

First arrested at sixteen with her father for blocking traffic and speaking without a permit, she was brought to trial. During the trial, her lawyer proclaimed her the "coming Socialist woman orator of America." She was pardoned and immediately returned to the soapbox.

Elizabeth Gurley Flynn (or "Gurley" as she was now called) joined the I.W.W. in 1906 as a member of Local No. 179 in New York City. Her first strike experience was in Bridgeport, Connecticut, during the summer of 1907 with the Tube Mill Workers, after which she was elected a delegate to the I.W.W. convention. During a speaking tour for the I.W.W. in the West, she met and married a fellow I.W.W. member, Jack Jones, and went with him in the fall of 1908 to organize migrant workers in Missoula, Montana, where the first important free-speech fight erupted.[1] Missoula was not only an industrial town of some importance but also a gateway to numerous lumber camps and mining towns, and migratory workers regularly passed through. With the aim of organizing these transient workers, Gurley and her husband had been sent to Missoula. They opened an I.W.W. hall in the basement of the leading theater and began to recruit migratory workers at street-corner meetings. The migrants responded eagerly to Gurley Flynn's vigorous attacks on the employment agencies that fleeced workers by collecting fees in advance and sending them to fake jobs from which they were fired after collecting their first wages. The employment agencies in league with employers, with whom they shared the fees, pressured the City Council to pass an ordinance prohibiting street-speaking.[2] Elizabeth Gurley Flynn's account of the workers' defiance of the prohibition is followed by an anonymous diary of the free-speech fight in Missoula published in the *International Socialist Review*.

Free Speech in Montana
By ELIZABETH GURLEY FLYNN

. . . My first participation in an I.W.W. free-speech fight and my second arrest occurred in this little place, which was not an industrial town but was a gateway to many lumber camps and mining areas. It was surrounded by mountains, the air was clear and invigorating. It was a clean and attractive little place, the site of a State University. We held street meetings on one of the principal corners and drew large crowds, mainly the migratory workers who flocked in and out of town. We had rented as an I.W.W. hall a large roomy space in the basement of the leading theatre and were rapidly recruiting members into the organization. The store-keepers objected to our meetings, especially the employment agencies, which we attacked mercilessly. Under their pressure the City Council passed an ordinance making street speaking unlawful. We decided to defy this ordinance as unconstitutional, a violation of the first amendment guaranteeing freedom of speech. There were only five or six of us in town at that time. One was Frank Little,[3] who was lynched in Butte, Montana, eight years later, during World War I. When we tried to hold meetings, two were arrested the first night, who were dismissed with a warning not to speak again. Four were arrested the second night, including my husband, Jones,[4] Frank Little, and a stranger to us, Herman Tucker. He was employed by the U.S. Forestry Department, which had an office in a building overlooking the corner. He rushed downstairs when he saw a young logger dragged off the platform for attempting to read the Declaration of Independence. Tucker took it over, jumped on the platform and continued to read until he was arrested. (A few years later this young man, an aviator of World War I, lost his life in San Francisco Bay, while distributing "Hands Off Russia" leaflets[5] from the air over the city.) Our Missoula free-speechers were sentenced to fifteen days in the county jail. Those of us who were left, planned the mass tactics which were advocated in free-speech fights, of which Missoula was one of the first examples.

We sent out a call to all "foot-loose rebels to come at once—to defend the Bill of Rights." A steady stream of I.W.W. members began to flock in, by freight cars—on top, inside and below. As soon as one speaker was arrested, another took his place. The jail was soon filled and the cellar under the firehouse was turned into an additional jail. But the excrement from the horses leaked through and made this place so unbearable that the I.W.W. prisoners protested by song and speech,

night and day. They were directly across the street from the
city's main hotel and the guests complained of the uproar.
The court was nearby and its proceedings were disrupted by
the noise. People came to listen to the hubbub, until finally
all I.W.W.'s were taken back to the county jail.

The fire department next turned the hose on one of the
meetings, but the townspeople protested vigorously against
this after several people were hurt. College professors at the
University took up the cudgels for free speech, especially
when another woman, Mrs. Edith Frenette, and I were arrested.
We were treated with kid gloves by the Sheriff and his wife,
although my husband had been badly beaten up in the jail by
this same Sheriff Graham. Senator La Follette spoke at a public
forum in the theatre over our hall.[6] One of our members gave
him a copy of a fighting paper defending our struggle, the
Montana Socialist, published by a woman, Mrs. Hazlett, in
Helena, Montana. He made a favorable comment in his speech.
Butte Miners Union No. 1, the biggest local in Montana, passed
a strong resolution condemning the local officials for "an un-
American and unjust action in preventing men and women
from speaking on the streets of Missoula," and commending
"our gallant fight for free speech." They sent it to the Missoula
papers, stating that my arrest had caused them to investigate
the matter and adopt the resolution.

There were some humorous aspects to our efforts. Not all
the I.W.W. workers were speakers. Some suffered from stage
fright. We gave them copies of the Bill of Rights and the Declaration of Independence. They would read along slowly, with
one eye hopefully on the cop, fearful that they would finish
before he would arrest them. One such was being escorted to
jail, about two blocks away, when a couple of drunks got into
a pitched battle. The cop dropped him to arrest them. When
they arrived at the jail, the big strapping I.W.W. was tagging
along behind. The cop said in surprise: "What are you doing
here?" The prisoner retorted: "What do you want me to do—
go back there and make another speech?"

Eventually, the townspeople got tired of the unfavorable
publicity and excitement. The taxpayers were complaining
of the cost to the little city. They demanded that it be reduced.

An amusing tussle then ensued between the I.W.W. and the authorities as to who should feed our army. We held our meetings early so the men would go to jail before supper. The police began to turn them out the next morning before breakfast, forcing us to provide rations for the day. Finally, the men refused to leave the jail although the door was thrown wide open. They had been arrested. They demanded a trial, and individual trials and jury trials at that! At last, one man "broke solidarity." He was married and he sneaked out to see his wife. But when he returned the door was locked. He clamored to get in—he did not want the fellow workers to think he was a quitter. The cop said: "You're out. Now stay out!" The townsfolk, gathered around, roared with laughter.

Finally, the authorities gave up. All cases were dropped. We were allowed to resume our meetings. We returned to our peaceful pursuit of agitating and organizing the I.W.W.[7]

Elizabeth Gurley Flynn, *I Speak My Own Piece,*
Autobiography of "The Rebel Girl" (New York, 1955),
pp. 92-94.

Free-Speech Fight Diary, Missoula, Montana

Oct. 3   Elizabeth Gurley Flynn, organizer of the Industrial Workers of the World, was arrested here tonight for persistently attempting to hold an advertised open-air meeting in the business section.

The plan of action outlined by Elizabeth Gurley Flynn was to select leaders of small squads and distribute them about town, giving each a chance to gather a crowd before the police might become cognizant of the movements of the I.W.W.

At the police station Mrs. Flynn said the I.W.W. could not be suppressed and that the work would be carried on as outlined if 10 men are jailed every day.

Oct. 6   Attempts on the part of the police to quell the incendiary speeches of the members of the I.W.W.

on the public streets have thus far proven utterly unavailing and the situation becomes daily more tense, with the authorities seemingly unable to cope successfully with the conditions.

Tonight the police were kept busy for two hours arresting and escorting I.W.W. orators to jail and when the 35th man had been taken in charge the multitude surrounded the authorities and jostled them all the way to jail.

Mrs. Charles Frenette, a Spokane woman member of the I.W.W. and a member of the advisory board, was arrested last night and while being escorted to the station the multitude which followed, threw stones at the police, severely injuring Officer Hoel about the body.

Oct. 8th   From Spokane. — The Industrial Workers of the World, who went from this city to Missoula to assist Elizabeth Gurley Flynn in the street speaking contest, are returning in large numbers. A large delegation arrived early this morning via the "limited."

The men report that they have won a complete victory at Missoula, and that they now have the privilege of the streets. J. P. Thompson,[8] who has been serving as a local organizer for some time, returned from Missoula yesterday.

C. L. Filigno, the secretary of the local I.W.W. organization, stated yesterday that the membership of the new union at Missoula had been increasing rapidly during the street speaking controversy.

"Sixteen new members joined on Saturday night and eight on the next day," said Mr. Filingo. "The membership there has been increasing rapidly."

At the trial the cases were all dismissed.

International Socialist Review, November 1909.

Free-Speech Fight in
Spokane, Washington, 1909-1910

Introduction

"The I.W.W. storm center for the West just now appears to be Spokane, Wash.," the *Industrial Union Bulletin* of February 20, 1909, reported. Here, in the largest Western center of the migratory workers, the I.W.W. conducted its most successful membership drive and built the biggest local union in the organization. One reason for such success was its campaign to remedy the most pressing grievance of the "floaters" shipping out of Spokane—the fraudulent employment agencies or, as the Wobblies bitterly labeled them, the employment sharks. The sharks, in alliance with unscrupulous employers, fleeced the "floaters" of thousands of dollars by sending applicants to jobs that did not exist. Not only did the men lose the fee, paid in advance, but also the railroad fare to and from the job. The foremen split the fees with the employment sharks. The vicious system provoked the grim joke that the sharks had discovered perpetual motion—"one man going to a job, one man on the job, and one man leaving the job." One Wobbly reported that a single firm employing only 100 men at a time hired and fired 5,000 men during the season.[1]

In the fall of 1908, I.W.W. speakers began to attack the system on Spokane streets near the employment agencies, exposing their practices and citing hundreds of cases where workers
had been cheated by their trickery. The I.W.W. called for a
boycott of the agencies and demanded that the employers hire
through the union. The "Don't Buy Jobs" campaign of the
I.W.W. so frightened the sharks that they formed the Associated Agencies of Spokane, and at its instigation, the City
Council passed an ordinance in October 1908 prohibiting "the
holding of public meetings on any of the streets, sidewalks or
alleys within the fire limits" after January 1, 1909.[2] The osten-
sible reason for the ordinance was to prevent traffic conges-
tion. The I.W.W. was informed that the Wobblies could hold
their meetings in the public parks and vacant lots, but these
were blocks away from the scene of the struggle against the
sharks.

During the winter months the I.W.W. violated the ordinance
and again held meetings in front of the employment agencies.
But the organization received press commendation for preventing indignant workers from using violence against the
sharks. A report in the *Spokane Spokesman-Review* of January 18, 1909, described how 2,000-3,000 workers were about
to wreck the offices of the Red Cross Employment Agency
"when James H. Walsh, organizer of the Industrial Workers
of the World, mounting a chair in the street, stemmed the ris-
ing tide of riot and pacified the multitude. In the opinion of
the police had it not been for the intervention of Walsh a riot
would surely have followed. . . . Walsh discouraged violence
and summoned all workers to the I.W.W. hall where he warned
the crowd against any outbreak." This report is significant in
view of the fact that when the recently-enacted ordinance was
amended to exempt religious bodies like the Salvation Army,
the I.W.W. was refused exemption on the ground that it encouraged "violence and riots."[3] This rank discrimination
touched off the free-speech fight.

On the evening of November 2, 1909, when James P.
Thompson, local organizer for the I.W.W., took the platform
at a street-corner meeting, a policeman yanked him down,

arrested him on a disorderly conduct charge, and hauled him off to jail. Other Wobblies swarmed to take his place on the stand. One hundred and fifty, including three women, were arrested and jailed for defying the ordinance. Late in the evening, the police raided the I.W.W. hall, arrested four I.W.W. leaders, closed the offices of the *Industrial Worker*, Western organ of the I.W.W., and announced that the source of "violence and conspiracy" had been eradicated.[4] The tactics, developed by the Wobblies in the free-speech fight in Missoula, were apparently unknown to the law enforcement agencies in Spokane. Before the men arrested had been locked in their cells, word was sent Spokane to all parts of the Pacific Coast and as far east as Chicago: "Big free-speech fight in Spokane; come yourself if possible, and bring the boys with you!"[5] I.W.W. unionists answered by catching the next freight to Spokane. The evening of November 3 saw I.W.W. tactics bearing fruit. The next morning's Portland *Oregonian*, which gave the battle complete coverage, told how a police officer had arrested the first "red-ribboned orator. . . . No sooner had the officer placed the first man under arrest than another took the stand. It was necessary to arrest nine of the offenders before the crowd quieted down. The prisoners were led to the city jail without giving resistance."[6] Thirty new arrivals talked their way into jail the second evening, and the press reported that 1,000 men were on their way to Spokane in empty freight cars to join their I.W.W. brothers. By November 5, the city jail was filled to overflowing. "Still they come, and still they try to speak," the local press wailed.[7]

In an effort to halt the mounting conflict, delegates from the A.F. of L., and the Socialist Party petitioned the City Council to repeal the ordinance and permit unrestricted use of the streets. A hearing was held on the petition, but the move to repeal the ordinance failed. Meanwhile, the Court upheld James Thompson's conviction in municipal court, thus giving the police the signal to proceed with the arrests and jailings.[8]

And proceed they did! The city jails overflowed, and the crowding of prisoners in cells was characterized by one reporter as "monstrous." (Twenty-eight men were forced into a

cell seven by eight feet in size.) The Spokane authorities put
the overflow into an unused, unheated building, the Franklin
School. Still the Wobblies poured into town on every freight,
mounted soapboxes, were arrested and sent to the city jails or
the temporary cells in the school building. The Wobblies carried on the struggle even while imprisoned by singing rebel
songs night and day. "The singing and shouting service of the
I.W.W.'s in jail continues at night; a veritable bedlam being
created," the *Oregonian* reported.[9]

The police attempted to stop the flood of prisoners with
brutality, bread-and-water rations, and atrocious jail conditions. Food at the Franklin School was "one-third of a small
baker's loaf twice a day." The prisoners went on a hunger strike,
but the authorities refused to change the bread-and-water diet.
When they protested, hoses were turned on the prisoners,
who were drenched with icy water. Packed into small cells,
the steam heat was turned up to "sweat" the prisoners. Many
fainted during this treatment, and only the pressure of closely-
packed bodies kept them from falling to the floor. After the
"sweating," the guards returned the prisoners to their cold
cells.[10]

Three times a week the police shuttled the prisoners from
the school, eight at a time, to the city jails for baths. Guards
stripped the prisoners, pushed them under a scalding spray
followed by an icy rinse, and brought them back to their
freezing quarters in the school. Three Wobblies died in the completely unheated Franklin School. Many prisoners developed
pneumonia and other ailments. One month, 334 prisoners were
hospitalized; another month, 681.[11]

The free-speech prisoners were jailed for 30 days; when
"liberated," they immediately attempted to speak again. Two
youths of eighteen years, arrested a second time, were offered
a suspended sentence by Judge Mann if they would promise
not to speak again and leave town. Both refused and were
sentenced to another 30 days in jail and a fine of $100, to be
worked out on the rock pile.[12]

On November 16, the press reported the arrival of "Elizabeth
Gurley Flynn [who] addressed a meeting in the Municipal

Courtroom and after roasting the newspapers, police judges and
city authorities, took up a collection of $25."[13] Since she was
pregnant, the Wobblies decided that the "rebel girl" should not
speak on the forbidden streets but only in I.W.W. halls and
clubs and before organizations willing to let her speak to raise
defense funds. But the condition of "the beauteous, black-
haired firebrand" did not concern the police. On November 31,
the police arrested the second group of I.W.W. leaders, among
them Gurley Flynn, and threw them in jail.[14] In flaming head-
lines, the Wobbly press flashed the news of the imprisonment
of the "Joan of Arc of the I.W.W." Circulars were issued announcing that "Elizabeth Gurley Flynn, a girl organizer only
19 years old, soon to become a mother, was arrested, charged
with criminal conspiracy, confined in jail with prostitutes and
insulted by an officer of the law." (The last was a reference to
Gurley Flynn's charge that an officer approached her in her
cell and attempted to take improper liberties with her.)[15]
The Wobblies west of the Mississippi, now more aroused than
ever, poured into Spokane in increased numbers. In a special
circular, the Spokane I.W.W. Free-Speech Committee set
March 1, 1910, as the day "to begin again a new full scale invasion to fill Spokane jails and bull-pens. We will never surrender
until we gain our constitutional right to speak on the streets of
Spokane. The right to organize must be protected."[16]

It became too much for the citizens of Spokane. With 500-
600 Wobblies in jail, all of whom announced that "we will
serve 30 days on bread and water, and when we get out we will
immediately be arrested," with 1,200 arrests on the books, and
with fresh delegations arriving from points as far as McKees
Rocks, Pennsylvania, Canada, Mexico, and Skowhegan, Maine,
it was obvious that the town had been vanquished. Moreover,
the I.W.W. had instituted damage suits for $150,000 against
the city and individual officials, and threatened to carry them
to the Supreme Court if necessary.[17]

On March 5, 1910, the city officials surrendered and made
peace with the I.W.W. on the following terms: (1) street-speaking would be permitted; (2) all I.W.W. prisoners would be released; (3) the I.W.W. hall would reopen and remain undisturbed;

(4) the *Industrial Worker* would be free to publish; (5) all I.W.W. damage suits against the city would be dropped; (6) the I.W.W. would refrain from speaking on the streets until the prohibitive ordinance was repealed. The City Council unanimously repealed the law on March 9, 1910. The great victory was made complete by the City Council's revocation of the licenses of nineteen of the city's employment agencies and the promise to compel the employment agencies to repay some of the losses suffered by defrauded workers.[18]

The Spokane free-speech fight was front-page news throughout the country. But the most vivid account came from Elizabeth Gurley Flynn, who published three articles on the great battle in the *International Socialist Review* and one in *The Workingman's Paper* of Seattle (formerly *The Socialist*) under the heading, "Story of My Arrest and Imprisonment." These are followed by a letter by Agnes Thecla Fair, a Spokane Socialist imprisoned for participating in the free-speech fight, which described an attempt to rape her while she was in prison, and which, when published in *The Workingman's Paper*, almost caused it to be shut out of the mails. Next is an account by William Z. Foster, who came to report the free-speech fight for *The Workingman's Paper*, and was arrested and imprisoned. Upon his release, Foster joined the I.W.W. Foster's account is followed by that of Robert Ross, participant in the free-speech fight; Ross's account was sent to Vincent St. John to be forwarded to the Commission on Industrial Relations. The last piece is by John Pancner, who described his experiences in the free-speech fight many years later.

The Free-Speech Fight at Spokane
By ELIZABETH GURLEY FLYNN

I

The working class of Spokane are engaged in a terrific conflict, one of the most vital of the local class struggles. It is a fight for more than free speech. It is to prevent the free press and labor's right to organize from being throttled. The writers of

the associated press newspapers have lied about us systematically and unscrupulously. It is only through the medium of the
Socialist and labor press that we can hope to reach the ear of
the public.

The struggle was precipitated by the I.W.W. and it is still doing the active fighting, namely, going to jail. But the principles
for which we are fighting have been endorsed by the Socialist
Party and the Central Labor Council of the A.F. of L.

The I.W.W. in Spokane is composed of "floaters," men who
drift from harvest fields to lumber camps from east to west.
They are men without families and are fearless in defense of
their rights but as they are not the "home guard"[19] with per-
manent jobs, they are the type upon whom the employment
agents prey. With alluring signs detailing what short hours and
high wages men can get in various sections, usually far away,
these leeches induce the floater to buy a job, paying exorbitant rates, after which they are shipped out a thousand miles
from nowhere. The working man finds no such job as he expected but one of a few days' duration until he is fired to make
way for the next "easy mark."

The I.W.W. since its inception in the northwest has carried
on a determined, relentless fight on the employment sharks
and as a result the business of the latter has been seriously im-
paired. Judge Mann in the court a few days ago remarked:
"I believe all this trouble is due to the employment agencies,"
and he certainly struck the nail on the head. "The I.W.W. must
go," the sharks decreed last winter and a willing city council
passed an ordinance forbidding all street meetings within the
fire limits. This was practically a suppression of free speech
because it stopped the I.W.W. from holding street meetings in
the only districts where working men congregate. In August
the Council modified their decision to allow religious bodies
to speak on the streets, thus frankly admitting their discrimination against the I.W.W.

The I.W.W. decided that fall was the most advantageous time
for the final conflict because the members of the organization
drift back into town with their "stake" to tide them over the
winter.[20]

A test case was made about three weeks ago when Fellow
Worker Thompson spoke on the street. At his trial on November 2nd the ordinance of August was declared unconstitutional
by Judge Mann. He made a flowery speech in which he said
that the right of free speech was "God given" and "inalienable,"
but with the consistency common to legal lights ruled that
the *first ordinance* was now in vogue. Members of the Industrial
Workers of the World thereupon went out on the street and
spoke. They were all arrested and to our surprise the next morning were charged with disorderly conduct, which came under
another ordinance. It looked as if the authorities hardly dared
to fight it out on the ordinance forbidding free speech. From
that time on, every day has witnessed the arrests of many
members of the Industrial Workers of the World, Socialists
and W.F. of M. men.[21]

On the third of November the headquarters of the I.W.W.
was raided by Chief of Police Sullivan and his gang. They
arrested James Wilson, editor of the Industrial Worker, James P.
Thompson, local organizer, C. L. Filigno, local secretary, and
A. E. Cousins, associate editor, on a charge of criminal conspiracy. E. J. Foote, acting editor of the *Industrial Worker*,
was arrested out of the lawyer's office on the next day.[22]
The idea of the police was presumably to get "the leaders,"
as they are ignorant enough to suppose that by taking a few
men they can cripple a great organization. The arrest of these
men is serious, however, as they are charged with a state offense
and are liable to be railroaded to the penitentiary for five years.

The condition of the city jail is such that it cannot be described in decent language. Sufficient to say, that the boys
have been herded twenty-eight to thirty at a time in a 6 x 8
cell known as the sweat box. The steam has been turned on
full blast until the men were ready to drop from exhaustion.
Several have been known to faint before being removed. Then
they were placed in an ice-cold cell and as a result of this inhuman treatment several are now in so precarious a condition
that we fear they will die. After this preliminary punishment
they were ordered to work on the rock pile and when they
refused were placed on a diet of bread and water. Many of the

boys, with a courage that is remarkable, refused even that. This is what the capitalist press sneeringly alluded to as a "hunger strike." The majority has been sentenced to thirty days. Those who repeated the terrible crime of saying "Fellow Workers" on the street corner were given thirty days, one hundred dollars' fine and costs. The trials have given additional proof to our much-disputed charge that justice in the United States is a farce. Fellow Worker Little was asked by the Judge what he was doing when arrested. He answered "reading the Declaration of Independence." "Thirty days," said the Judge. The next fellow worker had been reading extracts from the Industrial Worker and it was thirty days for him. We are a "classy" paper ranked with the Declaration of Independence as too incendiary for Spokane.

A case in point illustrates how "impartial" the court is. A woman from a notorious resort in this city which is across the street from the city hall and presumably operated under police protection appeared and complained against a colored soldier charged with disorderly conduct. The case was con-tinued. The next case was an I.W.W. speaker. The Judge with-out any preliminaries asked "were you speaking on the street?" When the defendant replied "Yes" the Judge sternly ordered thirty days, one hundred dollars' fine and costs.

Fellow Worker Knust, one of our best speakers, was brutally beaten by an officer and he is at present in the hospital. Mrs. Frenette, one of our women members, was also struck by an officer. Some of the men inside the jail have black eyes and bruised faces. One man has a broken jaw, yet these men were not in such a condition when they were arrested.

Those serving sentence have been divided into three groups, one in the city jail, another in an old abandoned and partly wrecked schoolhouse and the third at Fort Wright, guarded by negro soldiers. These outrages are never featured in the local leading papers. It might be detrimental to the Washington Water Power-owned government. The usual lies about the agitators being ignorant foreigners, hoboes and vags are current. Assuming that most of those arrested were foreigners, which is not the case, there are 115 foreigners and 136 Americans,

it would certainly reflect little credit on American citizens that
outsiders have to do the fighting for what is guaranteed in the
American constitution. Most of the boys have money. They
are not what could be called "vags," although that would not
be to their discredit, but they do not take their money to jail
with them. They believe in leading a policeman not into tempta-
tion. They are intelligent, level-headed working men fighting
for the rights of their class.

The situation assumed such serious proportions that a committee of the A.F. of L., the Socialist Party and the I.W.W.
went before the City Council requesting the repeal of the present ordinance and the passage of one providing for orderly
meetings at reasonable hours. All of these committees, without qualification, endorsed free speech and made splendid talks
before the Council. Two gentlemen appeared against us. One
was an old soldier over 70 years of age with strong prejudices
against the I.W.W. and the other president of the Fidelity
National Bank of Spokane; yet these two presumably carried
more weight than the twelve thousand five hundred citizens
the three committees collectively represented. We were turned
down absolutely and a motion was passed that no further action
would be taken upon the present ordinance until requests came
from the Mayor and Chief of Police. The Mayor, on the strength
of this endorsement by a body of old fogies who made up all
the mind they possess years ago, called upon the acting governor
for the militia. His request was refused, however, and the acting governor is quoted as saying that he saw no disturbance.

The "Industrial Worker" appeared on time yesterday much
to the chagrin and amazement of the authorities. Perhaps they
now understand that every member in turn will take their place
in the editorial chair before our paper will be suppressed.

The organization is growing by leaps and bounds. Men are
coming in from all directions daily to go to jail that their organization may live.

The fight is on to the finish and we rely upon the active co-
operation of our fellow-workers everywhere. We must have
funds. The legal defense of the men who are charged with penitentiary offenses will be an expensive one. Resolutions of sym-

pathy are very encouraging but they will not pay expenses or fill jails. Our plan is to make this difficulty as expensive for the taxpayers of Spokane as possible. Let them cry quits to their Mayor and police force if they do not relish it. We can keep up the fight all winter.

Coeur D'Alene district of the W.F. of M. has passed splendid resolutions boycotting Spokane as a scab city. Pressure brought to bear upon the pocket book of the average small business man is the only plea that will ever touch him.

I hope that the readers of the International Socialist Review will realize the seriousness of the situation. It is a fight for life as far as the I.W.W. is concerned. Men and women here are willing to sacrifice everything. Surely it is not asking too much if you endorse our stand, to dig up part of your daily earnings. "An injury to one is an injury to all."

*   *   *   *   *   *

And now, from almost every state in the union, socialists are on the way to help their comrades in Spokane. Comrade Tom Lewis writes us from Portland, Oregon, that in response to the telegrams sent out by the I.W.W. and Socialist Party headquarters calling for men, the Portland friends arranged a meeting to call for volunteers.

"At that meeting forty men lined up. A collection was taken and handed to the little band to be used for 'Coffee-and-' while the men were en route. At this time the rainy season is on and it requires men of the real stuff to volunteer to go, especially since nearly all of them will have to make their way jumping freights. Where would we be without such material!"

"As the time for the men to depart approached, those who were unable to go, gave up their sweaters and overcoats to their comrades. It was an inspiring sight. Finally the word was given. 'Boys, forward,' and the little army of proletarians made their way through the streets of Portland in silence, while the rain splashed in the gutters. The passers-by looked and wondered where the determined-looking marchers were going and the

police followed them. Doubtless they expected the men to
jump the freights in Portland, but we decided it would be
better for them to walk to the ferry, cross to Vancouver, Wash.,
and at 12:30 midnight, board the 'Workingmen's Flyer'—the
freight. These are the men we need in our organization, men
who are not afraid of the truth, men who will fight, men who
have nothing to lose, but a world to gain. Strange as it may
seem none of our 'reformer' friends joined the band going to
Spokane. But—as I have said—the night was a rainy one, and
the reformers care only to lead and be looked up to. It would
be well if these would-be saviors of the party got out and
allowed it to become a wage-workers' organization."

II

On December 3rd Prosecuting Attorney Pugh thundered,
in his attack upon the Industrial Workers of the World: "Let
them feel the mailed fist of the law," amply justifying our
definition of government as "the slugging committee of the
capitalist class." This threat was presumably made in a full
appreciation of what a roaring farce "constitution," "justice,"
"rights" constitute in Spokane—city of the Washington Water
Power Company and the employment sharks.

Since last writing for the Review we certainly have individ-
ually and collectively felt the mailed fist.[23] Workingmen may
come into this fight with respect for and faith in American
institutions, but they will come out with every vestige ruth-
lessly destroyed by official acts and judicial decision. Free
speech, free press, free assembly and the right of foreigners to
avail themselves of the "benefits of our glorious government"
(whatever that is) are non-existent in this western town. Outrage upon outrage has been heaped upon us—men, women
and children—until the depths of indignation are reached and
words fail to adequately express our intense feeling.

Every day men have gone upon the streets in numbers ranging from six to twenty-five and thirty, have said "Fellow
workers" and have been railroaded for thirty days with a
hundred dollars fine and costs. Ordered to work on the rock

pile, and refusing, they have been given only bread and water in meagre rations. Bread and water for a hundred and thirty days means slow starvation, means legal murder yet even on Thanksgiving day, the only exception made to the rule was to give smaller portions of more sour bread. The good, Christian Chief of Police Sullivan sneeringly remarked, when asked if the turkey and cranberry dinner applied to all: "The I.W.W. will find the water faucet in good order." As a result of this diet the boys have become physical wrecks and are suffering with the scurvy and other foul diseases. Once a week a day is appointed as "bath day" by the authorities, and the boys are brought from the Franklin School into the city jail in the interest of cleanliness. The newspapers have repeatedly informed the public that the I.W.W. men object to baths, and many a reader has turned away in horror, I suppose, from the dirty hoboes. The gentle and beneficent bath has been described as follows by a man who endured it: "First they strip your clothes off by force, then turn a stream of hot water over your head and shoulders scalding and blinding you at once, and then a stream of ice cold water." This alternating process would probably be enjoyed as much by the critical editor of the *Spokesman Review* as it is by the I.W.W. boys.

As the prisoners were being taken from the school to the jail the I.W.W., Socialists and sympathetic onlookers lined up along the streets and threw sandwiches, fruit and tobacco into the wagon. Officer Bill Shannon, in charge, took a fiendish delight in kicking this food away from the starving rebels. With face and form like an African gorilla, showing no sign of either human compassion or intelligence, he held back the weakened men that they might not catch the fruit thrown. When one man got a sandwich and held on with hands and teeth, strengthened by desperation, Shannon grabbed him by the throat and choked him till he dropped the food. Mrs. Frenette with others lined up near the school and sang "The Red Flag"[24] to encourage the prisoners. She was arrested and tried for disorderly conduct, the Chief of Police and six other officers testifying against her. They swore that she acted as if she were drunk, that she had carried on in a disorderly manner on the

streets since this trouble started, and one said she acted like
"a lewd woman." Testimony showing that she had stood on a
private porch and had taken part in an orderly meeting was to
no avail. She was requested to recite "The Red Flag" and did
so with such dramatic force that the Judge was horrified at
its treasonable and unpatriotic sentiment. She was sentenced
to thirty days, one hundred dollars fine and costs, and Judge
Mann recommended to the Prosecuting Attorney that a further
charge of participating in an unlawful assemblage—a state
charge—be filed against her. She was held for two days in the
foul city jail, supplied with only the coarsest and most unpalat-
able foods and subjected to rigorous cross examination every
little while. Bonds were put up by two local Socialists and she
was released in a weak and starving condition.

Between three and four hundred men have now been sentenced for speaking on the street. At first the court room in
which they were tried was open to the public, and spectators
to the number of two hundred could be accommodated. But
they didn't show a proper amount of respect for the official
lights. One afternoon Attorney Crane was conducting his own
case, wherein he was charged with disorderly conduct—speaking from his office window. In cross examining Chief of Police
Sullivan he unexpectedly asked: "How much had you been
drinking on the day of my arrest?" An irresistible burst of
laughter swept over the entire court room, including the Judge
and the Chief, but the excuse had now been found and the
court room was ordered cleared. A partition was erected over
night and the court is now so small that only a bare handful
may be admitted. All the other public courts in Spokane that
I have yet attended are of like character and the public are
practically debarred from these "star chamber" proceedings.
For additional precaution a bailiff is placed at the doorway,
and I have seen him admit well-dressed lawyers and detectives
while refusing to admit the wife of one of the men in jail,
gruffly stating: "There are no seats."

The Spokane Chamber of Commerce, after a vituperative
address by Mayor Pratt, passed resolutions unanimously de-
nouncing the I.W.W. City Comptroller Fairley has announced

that the free-speech fight is taking a thousand dollars a week out of the city treasury. We can well understand the reason for our condemnation. The I.W.W. has unanimously denounced the Chamber of Commerce. We are lined up on different sides of the class war, and the feeling of opposition is mutual.

Members, presumed by the police to be influential, have been arrested as they quietly walked along the street and thrown in jail, sometimes for several days before a charge was filed. For the protection of some of these, writs of habeas corpus were demanded of Judge Hinkle. He refused absolutely at first, stating that he did not care to have his court tied up with a lot of labor cases. This flagrant abuse of an old Anglo-Saxon right caused a roar of protest in the public press and throughout the labor organizations. The Judge, after a few hours of serious "thought," recanted and gave two writs, one dealing with a vagrancy case, the other with a disorderly conduct case as tests. The reason for his reversal can probably be found in the fact that fees of four dollars apiece were demanded before the City Clerk would file the papers. This practically means if you have money you can protect yourself before the law; if you have not, you can stay in jail till you rot. Prominent lawyers in the city gave their opinion that such a hold-up was without precedent.

This same Judge Hinkle had made himself infamous in connection with the juvenile cases. Perhaps the most disgraceful affair of many connected with the Spokane free-speech fight was the raid on the hall December 1st, resulting in the arrest of eight little newsboys. Simple on the surface, it is a subtle attempt to undermine the right of a parent to teach a child ideas different from the established order. The children were taken to the chief's office and put through a severe cross examination, after which they were locked up for the night. "The third degree" on youngsters ranging in years from eight to sixteen is quite a credit to the Spokane detective force. Couldn't you get evidence from grown-ups, Captain Burns, throwing light on the "secrets" and "conspiracy" of the I.W.W. without scaring it out of a lot of little boys? "The I.W.W. hall is no fit place for them," said Prosecuting Attorney Pugh of these poor,

ragged, little urchins who trudge the streets in their thin little
shoes going in and out of saloons and cheap resorts all hours
of the day and night. The parents of the boys with that innate
respect for law came in fear and trembling to say that they had
not sanctioned the children joining. One woman said she was
too poor to buy her boy a necktie so let him wear the red one
that a man gave him. The parents knew nothing of the I.W.W.
and the little youngsters were rather deserted by the very ones
who ought to know what's wrong with conditions that force
them to send their little ones on the streets this frosty weather.
One by one the youngsters succumbed and promised not to
sell the I.W.W. paper or go near the hall. One notable exception
was little Joseph Thompson. This little man bore himself with
all the moral courage of a revolutionist straight through, refusing to retreat an inch. Over this boy the hardest conflict raged.
Evidence was produced to show that Mrs. Thompson was in
full accord with the I.W.W. and accompanied the boy to the
hall. Judge Hinkle then remarked that, from his personal experience, "the I.W.W. Hall is no fit place for a woman and no
good woman frequents it." "Besides," he remarked, of this
clean, healthy, little youngster, "he looks dirty and uncared
for." Language becomes inadequate and a horsewhip looks
reasonable in face of this cowardly, scurrilous statement. If
the condition of the judge's red and bloated face is indicative
of his mode of life one may safely assume that his reputation
as a notorious drunkard is not overdrawn, yet he is the guardian
of juvenile morals, the critic of working women!

The next day, the cases being postponed for two days, Mrs.
Thompson and her boy came to the court room where Mr.
Thompson was expected to be tried. The probation officer
called the boy out and his mother followed. He asked what the
boy was doing there and she replied that she was accustomed
to taking him with her everywhere she went. The officer retorted: "You are not a fit person to take care of the boy," and
ordered the boy to go home.

In 1817 Shelley was deprived of his three children because
he was an atheist.[25] Is the time coming in this United States
when Socialists are to be deprived of their children because

they are Socialists? There is no insult too gross, no trick too low, no act too heartless for these brutal representatives of law and order to resort to. Who is to fix the standard of what constitutes proper care for children and correct ideas to teach them—shyster lawyers, drunken judges and ignorant, illiterate police officers?

But Judge Hinkle overstepped the bounds when he said no good woman frequents the I.W.W. hall. Saturday, December 4th, saw his court room lined with men and women who visit the hall regularly, and many of the women were not in a pleasant frame of mind. The judge blustered around, tried to make amends and then summarily dismissed the juvenile cases. The whole affair, however, is but a straw to show the trend of modern capitalism. It will happen again and we must be prepared.

The conspiracy cases have been increased to eleven within the last month and we are continually reminded by the prosecuting attorney that more are to follow. Fellow-Worker Filigno was given a preliminary hearing before Judge Mann and bound over in the Superior Court under two thousand dollars bond. Fellow-Worker John Pancner was adjudged guilty and sentenced to six months in the county jail. A change of venue was demanded on the strength of the judge's admitted prejudice and was granted for the conspiracy cases, but the street-speaking cases remained in the hands of a judge who stated that "the right to speak is God-given and inalienable" but that he "would sentence any man for disorderly conduct who spoke or attempted to speak." The conspiracy cases are now being tried before Judge Stocker, with progress up to the present as follows: E. J. Foote, James Wilson and James P. Thompson have been sentenced to six months in the county jail and A. E. Cousin to four months. Still to be tried are George Speed, Louis Gatewood, Charles Conner, William Douglass and Elizabeth Gurley Flynn.[26] Appeals have been taken in all cases up to date and as the rest of us will probably get the same sentence appeals will be taken to a higher court and a jury trial.

I am certain the readers of the *Review* will appreciate for themselves the enormity of this injustice.

The Mullen case, one that should be heralded from coast to coast, is as follows: The court room was crowded one day and Officer Shannon was appointed to keep further spectators from coming in. A little fellow by the name of Mullen, not an I.W.W. man, presumably did not understand that the court room was closed and started in. Shannon instead of telling him the circumstances, grabbed him, kicked him and beat him continually down the stairs and through the hallway to the booking office of the jail, where he struck the man's head against the desk. The business in the court room was completely interrupted for at least ten minutes while the man's shrieks and agonized cries for mercy rang through the building. The judge suavely thanked the spectators for their orderly behavior during "the disturbance." Mullen was kept in jail for three or four days, probably that he might recover his normal looks, and then was tried with the result that he was sentenced to thirty days, one hundred dollars fine and costs, in spite of the fact that four non-partisan witnesses testified to the man's quiet behavior and Officer Shannon's intense brutality.

Shannon is an old man on the force, has a reputation for being "a tough proposition" and is now so near his time for retirement that no matter what he does he will be retained on the force that he may draw his pension.

That such inhuman conduct is not uncommon among the police of Spokane is shown by the attack of Officer Miller made upon a harmless drunkard a few weeks ago when he beat him into unconsciousness before a crowd of indignant citizens. Ernest Untermann[27] was a witness to this incident. The citizens complained so strenuously to the Police Commissioner that Miller was dismissed, but if he had attacked an I.W.W. man he would probably have been given a gold medal.

The *Spokesman Review* was very much excited over the fact that the I.W.W. "jail birds" insulted the Salvation Army. Of course their indignation turns to unctuous praise when Prosecuting Attorney Pugh designates James Wilson as a coward, a sneak and a liar, trying to whine out of his responsibilities. The Salvation Army has not the courage to continue its street meetings, but must come down to the city jail to talk to starving men who cannot get away. They did not put in an appearance on Thanksgiving day to feed the hungry or give drink to the thirsty, but like the hypocrite in the bible when asked for bread, "they offered a stone." The insult was not that the I.W.W. boys howled at them and jeered them out of the place, the insult was that they ever dared to come at all. The Industrial Workers are interested in a live issue of better things for this world. As Mr. Pugh so aptly put it we are a modest aggregation "who, after they win the free-speech fight, intend to come back after the whole works."

Needless to say people who advise us to be contented and humble and look for our reward in heaven are not very popular when we're starving and suffering that we may get a little less hell on earth.[28] If we are, as Mr. Pugh says, "the hoboes, tramps and ne'er-do-wells," then it is up to us to change our status right here and now.

The A.F. of L. Central Labor Council and the Socialist party are working earnestly on the initiative petition and it is progressing splendidly from all reports. The miners of Butte have followed up the action of the Coeur D'Alene district in boycotting Spokane and all her products. Damage suits have piled up against the city, many filed by indignant citizens who were drenched by the hose of the fire department, others filed by members of the I.W.W. who have been assaulted by officers both in and out of jail. Needless to say all of these different activities have their result upon the opinions of the taxpayers and the business men. We can appeal to their pocketbook far more effectually than to their intelligence or sense of justice.

The newspapers have gloated over the fact that the switchmen's strike is helping to cripple the I.W.W. To a certain extent the influx of I.W.W. volunteers is certainly being delayed[29] but the fight can never be lost when starved and beaten men will come out of jail and voluntarily offer to go back that the fight may not be lost. Such courage and endurance as the rebels have shown in this fight is almost beyond the comprehension of the average citizen. Particularly are they surprised

at the "non-resistant" attitude,[30] at the self-control and
splendid discipline under circumstances that would try the
average man to desperation.

The hunger strike was called off by the unknown fighting
committee for the reason that they felt the I.W.W. boys were
practically committing suicide under the surveillance of a police
force that were glad to see them do it. In a war there is no
sense in doing what the enemy want you to do. Some of the
boys have gone on the rock pile and from now on others will
probably go without being considered either traitors or cowards
by the organization. The reason is that they can in this way
get three square meals a day and fresh air to keep them in good
fighting condition. As for work that will be rather a minus
quantity, a sort of graceful shifting, of shovel or pick from one
hand to the other.

This fight is on to the bitter end. It will never be settled for
us until it is settled right. They may send us all to jail, but that
will not stop the agitation for free speech. They may deport
the I.W.W. men but the battle will not be crushed. Let sympathizers on the outside help to spread the news of this brutal
conflict and express their sympathy in the coin of the realm.
The great need of the hour is financial assistance. Readers of
the *Review* are invited to contribute their share.

III

The agitation of the I.W.W. and free speech fight in Spokane,
Washington, if it brought no other effects has been valuable
in that it has forced the officials to take action against the employment agencies. In the beginning of the difficulty they were
admitted by Judge Mann to be the cause of all the trouble.
Since that time Mayor Pratt has frankly admitted refunding
thousands of dollars to workingmen who had been sold ficti-
tious jobs by the employment agencies. There were about
thirty-one in the city of Spokane but the licenses of all but
twelve of these were revoked.

The following statement from Mayor Pratt explains this
action: "On the whole we have found that the larger agencies

have not been causing so much trouble. Some of the larger
men have made a study of the business, understanding human
nature, and have been successful. In some cases we find that
men who do not understand the business have engaged in it
nevertheless and have made a little money and have held on
to every dollar that has come into their possession whether
they were entitled to it or not."

The institution of job-selling has by no means been abolished.
Simply the smaller ones have been weeded out and the larger
ones, which are practically the labor-furnishing departments
of the lumber trusts and railroad corporations, have been permitted to remain. Legislation was suggested in the city council
to the effect that employment should be furnished free to
workingmen and all fees should be borne by the employer.
The Northern Pacific and Great Northern Railways thereupon
publicly announced that upon the passage of such legislation
they would boycott Spokane and secure their labor in the
east and in the coast cities. The threat had the desired effect
upon the city council and the proposed legislation was summarily dropped. (Such a threat upon the part of the I.W.W.
would be characterized as criminal conspiracy.)

A further effect of publicity in connection with the free-
speech fight is the enforced resignation of at least three members of the police force. Scores of affidavits have been furnished
by I.W.W. men alleging extreme brutality on the part of the
police. Officers Shannon and Miller were mentioned by name
in these affidavits and their acts specified. Shannon is 63 years
of age, already three years past pension time. The Board of
Police Commissioners accepted his resignation by a unanimous
vote although he stoutly protested against rendering it. His
reward for years of service as a police officer consists of
$47.50 per month and a position as night watchman and house
detective for the Spokane Hotel. Miller was also requested to
resign from the force against his individual protest, to be at
once re-employed by the Washington Water Power Company.
Both the Spokane Hotel and the Washington Water Power
Company believe in the policy of "rewarding our friends." It is
needless to say, perhaps, both of these men have a record in

connection with the recent imprisonment of the I.W.W. men
that will hardly bear the light of public investigation and their
sudden removal from the police force, but further justifies us
in this conclusion.

Another of the incidental but beneficial effects of the ever-
increasing publicity is the agitation of the appointment of a
matron in the city jail.[31] The Woman's Club and various organizations of a non-partisan character have taken up the fight.
The city council voted at one meeting to appoint a matron and
with the trickery common to all politicians killed the motion
in the finance committee on the grounds of expense. The city
of Spokane is in a peculiar financial condition. She can afford
to suppress the Constitution of the United States, yet cannot
afford a matron in her city jail.

Since last writing for the *Review* all of the I.W.W. con-
spirators have been disposed of as follows: Roe, 90 days in the
county jail; Amundsen, 15 days in the county jail; Fisher, 30
days in the county jail; Brazier, 5 months in the county jail;
Gatewood, 4 months in the county jail; Douglass, 30 days in
the county jail; Reese, 15 days in the county jail; Whitehead,
Speed, Justh, Foss, Grant and Shippy, 6 months in the county
jail. The trial of the latter has been well characterized in a
western Socialist paper as *"Six business men sentenced six
workingmen to six months in six minutes."* The time element
was really but a few seconds over this.

Attorney Symmes of Chicago was associated with Attorney
Fred H. Moore[32] in the defense of these cases, but the "expense to the county" was held up in such appalling terms by
the prosecuting attorney's office that the able defense of our
lawyers was powerless to counteract the economic fear of these
little tax-payers.

One of the most humorous documents yet foisted upon the
innocent public is a letter of Mayor Pratt to Prosecuting Attorney Pugh, published on January 8th, wherein he compliments
the prosecuting attorney on his "able, energetic and willingly
given assistance during the recent I.W.W. demonstration against
the laws of this city which contributed in a great degree to the
victory over the conspiracy to defeat the enforcement of law
in this community."

Leonard D. Abbott,[33] a well-known Socialist in New York, addressed the Mayor in regard to the treatment accorded myself and others in the county jail. His vigorous protest was characterized by Mayor Pratt in an open letter on January 7th as "impudent criticism." The letter read as follows: "It may surprise you to be informed that Miss Flynn was never confined in the Spokane city jail; that inasmuch as the charge preferred against her was conspiracy under the state law she was confined in the Spokane County jail over which this city and its authorities have no jurisdiction. However, those having charge of that jail, while admitting that Miss Flynn was confined therein, deny decisively the wild and hysterical inferences and conclusions drawn by Miss Flynn."[34]

"A man's reputation is dear to him, and if based upon true character he deserves that his good name should not be unjustly attacked as a mere incident to a hysterical and lawbreaking conspirator. We who know him [Bigelow, the officer who approached Flynn in her cell, and tried to take liberties with her] know that his character is so high and his daily conduct so well ordered that Miss Flynn's charge against this man refutes itself and discloses the prejudice and hysterical character of her letter."

Chief of Police Sullivan is quoted as follows: "I have been on the force 20 years and I have never heard a complaint from any female prisoner against her treatment here until the charges of Elizabeth Gurley Flynn. I think them of the same brand of lies as those against the police department. If there is a spark of decency left in them the women do not go to jail but are provided for otherwise."

Prosecuting Attorney Pugh is quoted as follows: "The only complaint ever registered was by Elizabeth Gurley Flynn, the I.W.W. leader who made charges against the jailers that were false and made out of whole cloth."

Readers of the *Socialist Review* will remember that the "Industrial Worker" was suppressed by the forcible confiscation of 7,000 copies in the office of the Inland Printing Company. Chief of Police Sullivan justified this drastic action by saying that he would proceed at once under the criminal libel law. This story was published in the confiscated issue of

the "Industrial Worker," yet almost two months have elapsed
and no legal action has been taken to substantiate the chief's
claim.

Upon the publication of the Mayor's letter he was openly
challenged to take action under the criminal libel law or to
apologize for his statements in regard to the condition of my
mind. He did not have the courage to take a decided stand on
either ground. Thereupon the attorneys for the I.W.W. started
suit against the three officials quoted above for the sum of
$10,000 each. Needless to say with the sort of jury we are
able to draw in Spokane we hardly expect to collect $30,000
for *"spending money,"* but we certainly intend to force these
officials, who so commonly brand one as hysterical and
libelous, to prove their assertions.

Since the release of the majority charged with disorderly
conduct, suits have been entered amounting to $120,000
against Chief of Police Sullivan, Captain of Detectives Burns,
Captain Miles and Officers Shannon, Warner, Nelson and Jelsett.
These suits are based upon the treatment the men received in
the sweat box and the Franklin School. Every man injured will
certainly cost the city of Spokane thousands of dollars before
the fight is settled. The tax payers seem to have no sense of
justice or humanity, consequently an appeal to their pocket-
books as a last resort will be the most effective. The I.W.W.
have already been forced to spend hundreds of dollars from
the defense fund caring for sick and disabled members as they
were discharged from custody. At the present time one man,
George Prosser, is ill at the Kearney Sanitarium, two others,
Ed. Collins and M. Johnson, are confined in local hotels with
extreme cases of rheumatism, and Frank Reed is in the Washington Sanitarium illl with erysipelas. This little fellow who,
by the way is one of Uncle Sam's ex-soldiers, went through
the hunger strike at Fort Wright and but a few days after his
release was re-arrested and charged with criminal conspiracy
and desecrating the flag. When he was taken ill he was allowed
to remain for 48 hours without medical treatment and in a
terrible delirium. County Physician Webb excused this ill-
treatment by saying that Reed had been left in charge of a
trustee, in other words—a fellow prisoner. He was put under

the care of a special nurse and during the first 48 hours he was in an extremely critical condition. The cost to the I.W.W. for the first two days alone amounted to $166.00. This is not reported in any mercenary sense for dollars are of course not to be considered in the balance with the life of a revolutionist, but the extreme character of his suffering and the costly treatment that it required is a severe reproach to the standard of civilization attained in the Spokane County jail.

Governor M. E. Hay has put himself on record with the following statement: "The I.W.W.'s do not seem to be able to understand the idea of our form of government. A large percentage of them are nonresidents, many of them foreigners, and no small percentage absolutely illiterate. They desire no laws that interfere with their way of thinking. If we were all of that opinion we would soon have no law but anarchy and that is the law of might." There are laws in the State of Washington forbidding cigarette smoking, forbidding tipping, demanding open screens before saloons; forbidding playing cards, forbidding the exercise of one's "God given and inherent right" to free speech, but it certainly is the last straw to have the Governor criticize those who *desire no laws that interfere with their way of thinking.* " Not only are we deprived of free speech, free press, free assembly, but it seems we must now submit a schedule of our thoughts for official approval, and this is "Free America."

The Chamber of Commerce of Spokane have appointed a military committee to devise schemes for getting recruits for the militia, and have decided to give as a premium military brushes and gold watches to all militia men who bring in a substantial number of recruits. The inevitable result will be a strong well-armed force of ignorant, brutal men, practically under the control of the Chamber of Commerce, to be used in defense of their "economic" interests in further I.W.W. demonstrations. These, in conjunction with the negro soldiers at Fort Wright, are certainly typical of the *"Slugging committee of the capitalist class."*[35] The workers will feed them, clothe them, house them—to be murdered by them when they fight for their rights.

In view of the recent developments the contention of the

officials that the I.W.W. can "have a hall" becomes not only
an absurdity, but an insult. The Socialist Party Local has rented
the Oliver Hall for six years, but on January 17th, after a talk
by myself on "Industrial Unionism," they were notified that
they could no longer secure the hall. Application was made by
both the Socialist and the I.W.W. to a number of owners of
halls as well as to theatrical managers, exorbitant rents were
offered, but the same curt refusal was general everywhere. But
one hall is open to the I.W.W. to-day. The police notified the
Turner society[36] that they would have to quit renting their
hall for free speech meetings, and the latter body (ignorant
foreigners, the Chief would probably call them) voted to rent
their hall to us whenever it was not otherwise engaged and
demanded that the police take legal action if it were objectionable to them.

The Turner Society is certainly to be congratulated. They
are the only people in Spokane who have the courage to take
a stand against a popular prejudice in favor of the right. The
I.W.W. are holding splendid lecture meetings every Wednesday
and Sunday nights at this hall. Organizer James P. Thompson
has been released on $2,000 bond and he is now doing the
speaking, although in a very weak condition, having lost 25
pounds as a result of 90 days in jail.

One of the most noticeable features of the entire fight is the
splendid liberality of the rank and file of the American Federation of Labor.[37] Local after local upon receiving an appeal for
financial assistance have emptied their treasury to us, express-
ing the regret that they did not have more to offer.

I addressed the convention of the Shingle Weavers at Marys-
ville, Washington, on January 3rd, and they passed a strong
resolution of endorsement, and also a motion donating
$100.00 to the defense. A recent trip through British Colum-
bia netted splendid financial results from the locals of the
W.F. of M., this in spite of President Moyer's recent attack
upon the free speech fight and the I.W.W.'s, wherein he characterized "the so-called I.W.W. as an absolute failure," and
prophesied that they would be a "thing of the past in less than
12 months from to-day."[38] He prophesied that the Butte

Miner's Union would be carried down to destruction in this crash if it continued to assist the I.W.W., but the threat did not seem to have greatly worried either the miners of Butte or B. C. They probably believe that a man who would have been throttled on the scaffold by the capitalist class had it not been for the organized labor throughout the United States is certainly not one to criticize a revolutionary and militant labor organization.

The trial of myself and fellow worker Filigno commenced Wednesday, February 9th, and at date of this writing the jury has been finally completed. A change of venue was requested on a basis of intense prejudice created by the *Spokesman-Review* and the *Evening Chronicle*, but the motion was denied by Judge Kennan. One hundred and twenty-six names were produced in court as signers to a protest against a change of venue, one of whom was the Reverend Dr. Hindley. Yet one prospective juror after another admitted intense prejudice on the basis of increased taxation or newspaper articles and had to be excused by the court. The further progress of the trial and the ultimate decision will be reported in next month's issue of the *Review.* [39] Here's to the ultimate victory of the toilers.

Elizabeth Gurley Flynn, "The Free-Speech Fight at Spokane," "The Shame of Spokane," and "Latest News from Spokane," *International Socialist Review* 10 (December 1909): 483-89; (January 1910): 610-19; (March 1910): 828-34.

Story of My Arrest and Imprisonment
By ELIZABETH GURLEY FLYNN

On Tuesday morning, Nov. 30, at about 8 o'clock, I was walking toward the I.W.W. hall. As I reached the corner of Stevens and Front avenue I was accosted by Officer Bill Shannon, with the demand: "Are you Miss Flynn?" I replied, "Yes," whereupon he grunted, "Well, we want you." I asked, "Have you a warrant?" "Naw, we haven't," he rejoined, when the other officer stepped up and remarked, "There is one in the station."

I accompanied them to the station, where I was booked and
a warrant read for criminal conspiracy. I was then taken to the
chief's office, where Prosecuting Attorney Pugh put me through
the "third degree." Mr. Moore, attorney for the I.W.W., came
to the door and asked for the chief, demanding to see me, but
they unceremoniously slammed the door in his face. The chief
said: "Let him wait till we get through." At that time there
were present besides the chief and prosecuting attorney, Commissioner Tuerke, a stenographer and several other officials unknown to me. I refused to answer the prosecuting attorney
when he fired the first question, saying "I don't know who you
are." Indignantly the chief introduced us with the necessary
formality: "This is the prosecuting attorney, Mr. Pugh; Miss
Flynn, the I.W.W. organizer." They were all extremely courte-
ous, probably due to the information conveyed to them over
the phone that my physical condition was such that it would
be dangerous to be otherwise. But the ordeal of a rapid fire of
questioning is not as easy as it looks from the outside. Every
trick known to a shyster lawyer is resorted to. Every appeal
made to the honesty, sincerity and truthfulness of the average
citizen, that the questioners presumably had no respect for
themselves. Frankly, the only mistake I made was to talk at
all; but what I "forgot," "refused to answer," "didn't remember," and "couldn't recall" would fill a book. A man they
would have put in a sweat-box and broken his physique and
spirit, and eventually got him so faint and sick that he wouldn't
know what he was saying.

The idea of the third degree is evident—namely, to trap you
into attempting to prove yourself innocent, into forgetting
that it is up to them to prove you guilty. Some of the cross-
questions were entirely humorous. For instance, Mr. Pugh remarked: "You know it's useless denying what is an apparent
fact, easily proven by scores of witnesses." To which I retorted, "Well, why do you ask me so many questions about
an apparent fact?" The chief of police was anxious to know if
Katherine Flynn, who signed the Irish Socialist communica-
tion,[40] happened to be any relation of mine. Irish on both sides
of this fight annoys the chief in face of his assertion that we
are all foreigners.

With an assumption of innocence, Pugh asked: "Who are the executive committee, and who handles the finances?" The first I didn't know, the second I refused to answer. He asked, "Do you know?" And I answered, "Of course I know." And he asked, "You refuse to answer?" I said, "I certainly do." He asked, "Did you say so and so in your speeches?" to which I replied, "I talked so much I don't know what I said." They all gave me the laugh, and he asked if that statement wouldn't probably if published, injure my reputation as a speaker. Anxious he was for me to maintain my standing as an agitator, indeed! Finally he said, with a very smooth preliminary about not caring to prosecute a woman, that I might go if I would state that I had no connection with the free-speech fight, was not in sympathy with the tactics of the I.W.W., and had not induced men to go to jail. I refused to either deny or affirm, declined to be tried and found guilty or adjudged innocent, in the chief's office, and that settled me.

I was allowed to see Mr. Moore and Mr. Rogers in the chief's office after which I was taken to the county jail in the patrol wagon. The morning "Spokesman-Review" had a story that I had requested to be taken across the river in a hack. The idea never occurred to me, and if it had I would have known better than to lay myself open to be refused. The "Review" lied as usual.

I was placed in a cell with two other women, poor miserable specimens of the victims of society. One woman is being held on a charge that her husband put her in a disorderly house. The other is serving 90 days for robbing a man in a disorderly re-sort in Spokane. Never before had I come in contact with women of that type, and they were interesting. Also, I was glad to be with them, for in a jail one is always safer with others than alone. One of the worst features of being locked up is a terrible feeling of insecurity, of being at the mercy of men you do not trust a moment, day or night. These miserable out-casts of society did everything in their power to make me com-fortable. One gave me the spread and pillow cover from her own bed when she saw my disgust at the dirty gray blankets. I could not eat the heavy, soggy food, stews, etc., nor drink the terrible stuff called coffee; but the girls gave me fruit that had been sent into them. They moderate their language, apologize for their profanity and pathetically try to conform to some of the standards of decency when they see that you are "different." They have been so accustomed to being ill-used and brow-beaten they rather expect it, yet become indignant when it is done to another. In the morning they gave me soap and clean towels that I might not have to use common soap or dirty jail towels.

The jailers are on terms of disgusting familiarity with these women, probably because the latter cannot help themselves or don't care. Imprisonment does not seem to have any horrors for them. Content to sleep and eat, they seem to be as happy inside of jail as out. They are unconscious of their degradation and solicit no sympathy. Perhaps they shouldn't be conscious, for society is to blame and not they.

I was put in with them about 11 o'clock, yet the lights were burning bright and they showed no sign of retiring. Three little iron beds were the furnishings of our sleeping facilities, so I threw my cloak over me and tried to sleep. The younger girl still remained up, though she turned the light down that I might sleep. Several times she went to and fro, asking if she disturbed me. Finally the jailer came, opened the cell door and took her out. She remained a long time, and when she returned I gathered from the whispered conversation with the older one, the following: that he had taken her down to see a man on the floor below—a sweetheart she called him to me afterward. She went again and remained a long time, and whispering told the other woman that "Bert" (I judged to be the jailer) would have brought "Jack" up for this woman, indicating me. "They don't trust her," she said. Perhaps I am justifying her suspicion in writing this. But the whole performance bore the earmarks to me of a putrid state of morals inside the county jail of Spokane. Taking a woman prisoner out of her cell at the dead hours of night several times to visit sweethearts looked to me as if she were practicing her profession inside of jail as well as out! And what particular interest did that man "Bert," so intimately designated by his first name, have in the matter? It would bear investigation. Readers may well imagine the horrible night of restlessness I put in.

Early in the morning a man by the name of Bigelow, jailer, I presume, came into the cell with breakfast. Instead of leaving it in the ante-room of the cell and going about his business, he marched straight into the room where we were all still in bed. He laid his cold hand on my cheek and I awoke with a start. My anger blazed up and said, "Take your hand off me. I didn't come here to be insulted." He murmured some inarticulate excuse, "Of course not," or words to that effect, and got out.

It certainly is a shame and disgrace to this city that a woman can be arrested because of union difficulties, bonds placed so high that immediate release is impossible, thrown into a county jail, where sights and sounds, horrible, immoral and absolutely different from her ordinary, decent mode of life can be forced upon her. Her privacy invaded while trying to steal some sleep by a brute of a man in a jail that hasn't attained the ordinary standard of civilization that requires a matron for the care of women prisoners. This all for law and order! "O Liberty, what crimes are committed in thy name!"

The Workingman's Paper, Seattle, December 11, 1909

Miss Fair's Letter
By AGNES THECLA FAIR
Spokane, Wash., Nov. 11, '09

Dear Comrades and Friends: I am now labeled by police as a DANGEROUS CHARACTER. My offense was mixing in free speech fight and behaving so different from other women arrested.

I made four jumps, as the box filled with dry goods, standing at Howard and Riverside, in front of the White House was a high one. I talked for ten minutes and had a large crowd, when a detective came up and took me down from my high pedestal. He wanted me to walk to the station, but as I had never rode in a hurry-up wagon I asked to ride.

While waiting for a private automobile the crowd grew to thousands. Taking out a red handkerchief as I entered the wagon, I stood up and waved it at the crowd. Cheers went up for Free Speech.

Little did I dream of what was coming after in this en-
lightened age. You will pardon language used to get at facts,
as I never heard anything so vile. They put me in a cell with a
fallen woman and left. They were gone but a few minutes when
two officers returned and (although the other woman was not
to go until Monday, she told me), they told her to get ready in
two minutes and get out.

When she was gone they put me in a dark cell, and about ten,
big burley brutes came in and began to question me about our
union. I was so scared I could not talk. One said, "We'll make
her talk." Another said, "She'll talk before we get through with
her."

Another said, "F--k her and she'll talk." Just then one started
to unbutton my waist, and I went into spasms which I never recovered from until evening.

I was hardly over the first when they brought in a man dis-
guised as a woman and put him in a cot next to me. I thought
it was a drunken woman until the officers went out. Then I
felt a large hand creeping over me. It's too horrible to put on
paper. I jumped out into an enclosure, screaming frantically
and frothing at the mouth. Had not two of our girls been
arrested and brought in just then I do not think I would ever
come to.

Even then they showed no disposition to treat me as human.
I never slept or ate the three days I was in there. The third day
I was so weak when the doctor called and they would not have
let me out then only the doctor said (a "trusty" told me): "She
cannot stand it another hour, and her death will mean the end."
Then they hurried in and carried me out near a window.

When the matron, who is on the pay roll (a Salvation lassie),
but never around the women, was taking me into court, an
officer said, "Let her walk." The matron said, "She can't."
He said: "If she faints we'll throw a bucket of water in her face;
that will wake her up."

The court (through counsel) asked me: "Will you make any
disturbance if we release you on your own recognizance?"
I said: "I won't be able to for a few days. I don't know what
I'll do after that." "Counsel" worded it different to the court,

and the court ordered me to the receiving hospital. How kind
of the court! I only stayed there a few minutes when I saw a
fellow worker pass the door and I asked him to let me lean on
his arm to get to a hall a few doors away. As it cost money to
hire cabs and it would only keep from the public the brutality
of the bulls, and I looked dead, the fellow workers carried me
on a stretcher through the principal streets to my room.

While the bulls beat back a crowd of ten thousand twenty-
five more went in today.

AGNES THECLA FAIR
The Workingman's Paper, Seattle, November 20, 1909

47 Days in Spokane City Jail
By WILLIAM Z. FOSTER,[41]
Special Correspondent, *The Workingman's Paper*

On the afternoon of December 11th, when a contingent of
men left the I.W.W. headquarters for the purpose of speaking
on the street, I accompanied them, as usual, so as to witness
their arrest and be enabled to report any unusual features
attending it. On this particular afternoon Korthagen and
Holland, two I.W.W. members from Seattle among others,
were billed to speak, and having been closely associated with
them in Seattle, I was anxious to be in at the death.

I walked with them to the appointed street corner, and
while they spoke I stood some twenty feet away in the thick
of the crowd. They were duly arrested and a few moments later
the redoubtable Captain Burns came on the scene in answer to a
call sent in to the station, and although he knew nothing whatsoever as to what had taken place, and had no warrant for my
arrest, he immediately placed me under arrest when he happened
to see me standing in the crowd.

At the police station I had the honor of a half-hour talk
with Pugh, Sullivan and Burns, during the course of which conversation these worthies attempted to pump me. They adopted
a dozen different ruses by which they hoped to secure a
promise from me to desist from taking part in the street fight
in return for my liberty. One of these was ridiculous in the

extreme. Chief Sullivan (brainy man) said that he had just received a letter from the I.W.W., stating that I was a Pinkerton,[42]
his plan being to rouse my ire against the organization and to
get me to desert it, or at least promise to take no active part in
the fight. Failing in this he adjudged me guilty in his office of
some unknown offense, because I wouldn't answer for my
conduct for the future, and I was taken to the notorious
sweat-box, where I joined the balance of the street-speaking
"criminals."

Although we had not gone through the formality of a trial
in Judge Sham's (I mean Mann's) court, we were placed on
bread and water. The portion of bread was that customary in
I.W.W. cases, one-fifth of a five-cent loaf, twice daily. As a
punishment, criminals who refuse to work are sometimes confined in the sweat-box on a ration of a loaf of bread daily, but
we untried I.W.W. prisoners were so much worse than rebellious
convicted criminals that we got less than half the customary
amount of bread.

The next afternoon we were taken to Judge Mann's court
and were railroaded in the usual manner. In common with the
rest, I was charged with "Disorderly Conduct." Officer Mac-
Donald was the witness against me. He testified that I stood
in the crowd of prospective speakers and stimulated their ebb-
ing courage by urging them to go out and speak. MacDonald
has a good imagination, and in the pretty little picture he drew
of the affair I even went so far as to shove some of the weak-
kneed (?) speakers into the street.

Needless to say, this was a barefaced lie. These men needed
no urging, but if they had I fear someone else would have had
to do it, as I stood in the crowd at least twenty feet from them.
It was impossible for MacDonald to have even seen me in the
crowd, as during the whole affair he had his back turned toward
me. However, a little item like this is of no importance to the
Spokane police. MacDonald was made to "see" me in the
chief's office, and that was sufficient.

I put five witnesses on the stand who flatly contradicted
MacDonald, but it was no use and I got the same sentence as
the balance—thirty days, $100 and costs.

Judge Mann has recently expressed his determination to stop perjury in his court, and if he is sincere it would perhaps be good tactics if he would operate on a few of these imaginative policemen. My bond was set at $500, although the customary bond in all the I.W.W. disorderly conduct cases has usually been $200.

*   *   *

Although the I.W.W. had recently decided that the speakers arrested should go to work on the rock pile so as to avoid punishing themselves on the terrible bread-and-water diet, I refused to go to work, as I wished to be sent to the modern Libby prison,[43] the notorious Franklin school, where the authorities still held I.W.W. prisoners, who vainly demanded the privilege of going to work. (This was done because these men stubbornly refused to accept liberty on the condition that they leave town.)

My desire to get a little "local color" at Franklin school was frustrated, however, as next morning I was loaded with ball and chain (15-pound ball attached to ankle), and shackled by the leg to another man, and then marched to the rock pile, where I was told to work or freeze.

I felt quite flattered at so much attention, particularly so because the ball I wore had been previously carried by a notorious pimp who henceforth enjoyed the comparative freedom of simply being shackled by the leg to his partner.

*   *   *

The weather was intensely cold and I have no doubt the Rev. Jack Warner, the chain-gang boss, Bill Shannon et al., thought I would be stubborn enough to stand there and freeze rather than go to work.

The I.W.W. motto in Spokane is "Find out what the boss wants you to do, and then—do the opposite," so I went to work, and here began the most educational experience I ever had.

When talking to Pugh in Sullivan's office he jokingly remarked, "Why, Foster, you haven't got any kick coming; this
is money in your pocket." This is literally true, and though at
times the confinement was irksome in the extreme, I consider
my experience in the Spokane city jail as almost invaluable.
Through it I have learned a few of the possibilities of organization and direct action, and more especially of the marvelous
effectiveness of the passive resistance strike, in addition to
learning many new wrinkles about the law, police, etc.

At the time I arrived at the city jail the total number of
street speakers held by the police was forty (exclusive of "con-
spirators" in the county jail), and this bunch immediately after
getting settled at the jail proceeded to organize themselves.
So perfect did this organization become, both in the jail and
on the rock pile, that all the individualists were suppressed
and the collective wish was undisputed.

*   *   *

In the jail we held rousing meetings and in order to do it
systematically we elected a secretary and chairman and set
aside Sunday night for propaganda meetings and Wednesday
night for business meetings. It was surprising the amount of
business we had to transact, and we established rules and regulations of all kinds, from tactics to be pursued if our shackles
were put on too tight, to forbidding I.W.W. members from
shouting to the women prisoners who might be insulted by
some of the doubtful remarks continually bandied between
the men and women prisoners. Needless to say, these rules
and regulations were scrupulously obeyed by the I.W.W. members, and also by many of the ordinary prisoners, who fell
under the magic spirit of the well known I.W.W. discipline.

The Salvation Army annoyed us by raising a hideous clamor,
alleged to be religious adoration, but we settled them by completely ignoring them and their meetings were shortened 80
percent.

*   *   *

Our propaganda meetings were a howling success, and we made at least forty I.W.W. converts in the city jail. These were all workingmen who were arrested for the crime of being broke, and when they listened to our talks and saw how we handled ourselves they promised to read up on industrial unionism and to join the I.W.W. as soon as possible.

In the jail the cells are in a double row, opening from a corridor about six feet wide and it was in this corridor that we held our meetings.

Another good feature of our meetings was the spirit of democracy prevailing. We practically forced men to get up and speak who had never but once before attempted to speak before a crowd (said "Fellow-Workers" on Spokane streets), and a couple of these give promise of becoming excellent "soap-boxers."[44]

We were getting along swimmingly when someone decided that our meetings were too successful and that we must have some "leaders" amongst us. As a result of this, on Jan. 3rd, Fellow-Worker Jones of Los Angeles (commonly called "Voiende Sulpher Smoke") who was speaker of the evening, and myself, who had acted as chairman of the meeting the night previous, were "grabbed" and put into the "strong box" (a steel cage reserved for the more serious criminals). Our seizure simply stimulated the remainder to greater efforts, and from that time on the jail organization became a pronounced success. Once more the grabbing of men suspected of being "leaders" acted as [a] boomerang.

*   *   *

The effects of the organization upon the work done on the rock pile was remarkable, and the possibilities of the passive resistance strike, even as evidenced by us chained prisoners, was a revelation to me. We simply went through the motions of working. We accomplished almost nothing. For instance, two men chained together pounded for four days upon one rock, when it was accidentally broken. To break that small rock (about as large as a wash bucket) cost the city of Spokane

$4.00 for food alone, at the rate of 50 cents per day per man, besides the other expenses for guards, etc. This is only a sample of how we worked, and by no means an exceptional one.

The notorious Bill Shannon helped guard us and he became insanely angry scores of times at our studied awkwardness and deliberation, and on one occasion kicked a man so severely that he may be ruined for life (a suit for $20,000 damages against Shannon, and Warner, the other guard, for this assault is now pending), but he usually confined himself to calling us all the hard names in the calendar and putting us upon bread and water occasionally. He would shift us from shoveling to wheeling, carrying or breaking rock, but it was the same old story wherever we were put. Nothing doing. Passive resistance is an art, and many of the men have really become experts at it in this fight.

*   *   *

The organization spirit and tact of the men in our contest with our guards and the jail officials was good beyond praise. It has convinced me that it is possible to really organize the working class. Once in a while we had "labor difficulties," which were always precipitated by some wanton cruelty of the officers, such as tightening a man's shackles so as to stop the circulation of the blood in his leg, or chaining some victim to a telegraph pole, or as in one case, forcing a man who was boiling his shirt and underclothes, to go to work with nothing on above his waist but his coat. This man (Henry Rutter, an expert at passive resistance) was game, and tucking his coat back he took the lead in the chain gang, and marched through the crowded streets of Spokane, exposing his manly chest (and stomach) with a vengeance.

We had several hunger strikes in retaliation for these barbarities, and the police always caved [in] before we got really hungry.

*   *   *

On the whole, the worst hardship we suffered was from the arctic weather as we were poorly fed and naturally unable to resist the biting weather as well as we otherwise would. The I.W.W. came nobly to our aid and kept us fully supplied with socks, gloves, and tobacco, although on various occasions the police confiscated large consignments of tobacco "planted" for us by the organization.

*   *   *

Although Jones and I were allowed to go to work on the rock pile we were forced to make our jail headquarters in the "strong box." Here I had many experiences which I value highly. We were confined there for a month, and during that time there were several alleged murderers, a dozen forgers and numerous "hold-up" men, burglars, embezzlers, sneak thieves, pick-pockets, pimps and various other kinds of criminals, "dope" fiends and insanity cases.

We had the pleasure of spending a night in the same cell as Joe Vigue, the alleged wife-murderer, who was convicted recently in Sandpoint, Idaho, of having beaten his wife's brains out with the stock of his rifle. He was a mild-mannered, rather likable sort of fellow, and claimed that he was falsely accused, as his wife is not dead. He urged to support of this that the authorities refused to let him see her body and that he remembers nothing of having committed the crime. He was on his way to Boise, Idaho to do a term of fifty years.

His traveling companions in hardship were two burglars with 15-year sentences hanging over their heads. Another man was kept in jail a week while his victim hovered between life and death (he finally died). This man almost went insane from suspense. He is now to be tried for manslaughter.

Many of these "criminals" are very intelligent and some of them remarkably so. They are able to converse fluently on almost any subject of ordinary conversation. One man, Lindsay, since taken to Seattle for forgery, had the most remarkable memory of any man I ever met. It was simply uncanny in its thoroughness.

One ex-convict whom I became very well acquainted with gave me a clear glimpse into the doings of the underworld and initiated me into the mysteries of the "strong-arm"—a wrestling

hold used by highwaymen upon their victims. He also gave me
full instructions as to the proper method of cracking a safe. He
also gave me valuable information as to how to protect myself
from highwaymen.

Thus are criminals made in our jails. Put a man in jail with
a lot of experienced criminals for a few months and they will
soon teach him the intricacies of their various "trades."

*   *   *

Dope fiends, full of cocaine, and raving maniacs, their eyes
glittering with insanity, and their mouths spouting their delu-
sions, were allowed to roam freely amongst us, and sometimes
we were hardly in an enviable position.

Night after night the jail was made hideous by men in the
clutches of the terrible delirium tremens. One of these unfortunates actually died in his steel cell raving for whiskey,
which would have saved his life. He received no medical attention whatsoever, and died a terrible death. Nothing has been
done about this poor unfortunate's death, as he was only a
poor, old, broken-down workingman. His case is a matter of
record and can easily be dug up if anyone is interested in it.
Since his death the other unfortunates suffering from delirium
tremens are given a pretense of proper treatment.

The worst feature of my stay in the strong box was the un-
sanitary condition of the cell. The prisoners sleep in hammocks
without blankets. To keep them from freezing the windows
are closed, and as a result at times the air became almost stifling
from lack of ventilation.

I suffered from an ulcerated tooth while in jail, and the
pain was so intense that I was unable to sleep, and I walked
the floor for ten nights before I was allowed to have my teeth
filled. The doctor (?) refused to do anything for me, stating
that "we are not fixed to do any such work as that," and finally,
when I was almost frantic from pain and loss of sleep Chief
Sullivan accepted an exorbitant bond for me while I went to
the dentist.

At the end of forty-seven days, on Feb. 2nd, I was released
through the kind efforts of "The Workingman's Paper," its

Spokane representative, Mrs. Fiset, and Mr. O. Lund, a prominent Spokane Socialist.

In many respects the imprisonment was irksome, but after
all it was a most valuable experience, and aside from the
pleasure of being one of the free-speech jail-birds, the advan-
tages I gained from it are too numerous to mention.

The Workingman's Paper, Seattle, January 22, 1910.

The Spokane Free-Speech Fight
By ROBERT ROSS

Sept. 19th 1914.

To the Industrial Relations Commission.

Dear Sirs:-

I have been informed that a committee has sent out a call
for information as to treatment of members of the Free Speech
Fights and as to the arrests and trials. I happened to be working
in the city of Spokane, Wash. at the time of the trouble and
not being a member of the I.W.W. my sympathy was with
them. I have always been rebellious against the master class
from the treatment which I have received my share of and as
an American I thought it my duty to cast my lot with my
fellow workmen and hold what our forefathers granted us
years ago, which any American working man would do if he
was not kept ignorant of the truth. So I went out on the street
and all I got to say was fellow workers. There were twenty or
thirty men standing on the street. I was arrested by a man
standing by who happened to be a special police. I found out
after that he was a carpenter, a member of the A.F. of L.
I was taken down to the police station, searched and thrown
in what they call a sweat box. I did not measure the place but
I would guess it to be about 8 x 10 feet square. There were
27 men inside and I made 28. When the door was shut it was
air tight, with but one exception. There was a hole about four
inches in our side of the cell. There was a steam pipe about
four inches running through the cell with steam on in full

blast. We were kept in there 15 hours with the door shut.
We had to take our clothes off it was so hot. There were a lot
of men who could not stand the heat and had to be carried
out after 15 hours. We were then taken to cell No. 13, with
windows all open without any bedding at all. They then came
and took our shoes away from us, which made it all the worse
for us. It was very cold. The next day I was brought before
the would-be court for trial. The officer who made the arrest
swore on the stand that I had the streets blocked and that
traffic could not pass. Judge Mann asked me if I had anything
to say. I got upon the stand and told the court that I did go
out on the street, but I did not. That was all his honor would
let me say and I got 30 and 100. I have seen men brought in
with blood flowing from their face and head, some with
broken bones and some who had been kicked and beaten all
over. Although I was never struck by anyone all the time I was
in jail, they had what was called the club party. They worked
in the dark so as you could not see who they were. They first
gave each man 1/3 of a small five cent loaf of bread, then they
cut it down to 1/4 and finally they got it down to one loaf of
bread for five men two times a day. On one occasion they
marched us down from the school house where they had
moved us, when the city jail could not hold any more, with
the pretense of giving us a bath. They took us down to the
city jail and made us strip off our clothes and walk under a
cold shower bath but would not give us time to wash. This was
in November and it is very cold in Spokane at that time of the
year, so when we started back to the school house they marched
us in the center of the street and on the sidewalks people had
gathered with all kinds of tobacco, fruit, bread and everything
in the line of eatables, but the police held them back and would
not let them get near us so that the people began to throw
tobacco, fruit and everything they had brought. Those who
were lucky to get some of those things found themselves un-
lucky, for no sooner had they caught them when the police
knocked them out of their hands. In one case one man had just
caught an apple and had started to take a bite when the police
struck at the apple and hit the poor fellow on the nose and

broke it. This is only one instance of which there are many more. In the school house they would wake us up at all hours of the night and chase us from one room to another. There is no use of me trying to give a full detail of what I saw with my own eyes, for it would take a long time to write what I saw. This is the truth as I saw it, so help me God. There would be no use of me telling a lie because there are six or seven hundred men who could testify as to what I have written, which is only a part of what took place in Spokane.

Yours truly,

(Signed) ROBERT ROSS.

Letters, Etc., Addressed to Vincent St. John,
By Various Writers, Commission on Industrial Relations
File, National Archives, Washington, D.C.

The Spokane Free-Speech Fight—1909
By JOHN PANCNER[45]

Before telling you the story of the Spokane free speech fight, I must say a few words about the situation in the west at that time. West of the Mississippi River, there were about two million migratory workers, sometimes called hobos. They harvested the wheat, corn, hay and picked the fruit and even planted most of the crops. They built railroads, dams, power-houses. They did the logging in the woods.

The employers were ruthless. The conditions on the job were bad. You had to bring your own blankets, sleep in tents or bunk houses and many of them were full of lice and bed bugs. Cockroaches were in the cook houses and kitchens. Most of the men did not stay long on the job, and when the jobs were finished, thousands were laid off. So you see there always was a big unemployed army, floating from job to job or looking for a job, or waiting for a new job to open up. They had no families. Most of them did not belong to any church. They did not stay long enough in any town so that they could register and vote. They were considered outcasts in the com-

munity. Only when labor was badly needed were they welcomed.

The AFL trade unions were strong in the big cities like San
Francisco, but no attempts were made to organize these no-
mads. The only exceptions were the small mining camps where
the Western Federation of Miners were well organized. They
had higher wages, better living conditions, and more freedom
or civil rights because they had been organized long enough
and had the power. So the IWW tried to organize these migratory workers into industrial unions instead of trade unions.[46]
Because they had low wages, we had to charge low dues. The
human material was good, but the odds were against us. When
you slept and ate on the company property, you had no civil
rights.

In Spokane, Washington, we had a hall and four local unions.
There was a street full of employment offices where the employment shark would sell you a job for a dollar. The lumber-
jacks, construction workers and agricultural workers would
come to town and spend their money in the red light districts,
saloons, restaurants and lodging houses. When they got broke
or nearly broke, they would try to get another job.

It was hard and dangerous to go on company property to
get new members. The easiest way to get new members was
by holding street meetings. Some time in 1908, the city government stopped all street meetings. The case was taken to court
by the local unions, but the judge pigeon-holed the case, so in
the fall of 1909, the local unions planned to win free speech
by direct action.

The plan was to call for volunteers to speak on the streets
in violation of the city ordinance. If we were arrested, we
would go to jail until all of the jails were full. A joint meeting
of the four locals was held and a committee of ten was selected
from the floor of the meeting. These ten went into the office
of the secretary and picked a committee of five to be the
fighting committee. They in turn each picked one alternate to
take their place in case of arrest. The alternates were to appoint
other alternates. All names were to be kept secret. Every five
or ten volunteers would go on the streets and speak. When they

were arrested, they would go before the judge, plead guilty and go to prison.

It was about in November of 1909, that Walter T. Nef [47] and I jumped a freight train in Portland, Oregon, and we got there in time for the meeting. I was put on the fighting committee.

It must have been the month of November, 1909 when Nef and I arrived in Spokane, because the struggle went on all winter. At one time, we had the city jail, the county jail, the Franklin School House full, and a United States' fort had eighty-five prisoners in it. The rank and file who spoke on the streets got thirty days for violation of the city ordinance, the leaders got six months in the county jail under the state conspiracy law.

We made no effort to keep out of jail. Our aim was to fill the jails, so when the judge would ask us if we were on the committee, we would gladly admit it. The police closed our hall and confiscated our weekly newspaper, the *Industrial Worker.*

While awaiting for our trial in the city jail, the state prisoners were put in one row of cells on one side of the cell block, and the city prisoners, who were convicted for speaking on the streets, were across the hallway on the other side of the cell block. They were starting to serve their thirty day sentences, but they refused to go out and work on the rock pile, so they were put on "bread and water" and kept locked in their cells.

We, who were the leaders awaiting trial were being fed "steak and fried potatoes" and other such foods, so we the leaders went on a "hunger strike." It took a lot of will power, but when they brought our food, we threw it out through the bars on the floor of the hallway. There were steaks, potatoes, bread, coffee and tin plates and cups all over the floor.

After eight days of the hunger strike, the outside committee sent word that we must stop the hunger strike because some of us were getting sick. A few die-hards held out for thirteen days.

As soon as we were tried under the state conspiracy law, we were given six months each and sent to the county jail.

One of the characters in the free speech fight was a young
man who came there as a reporter for a Seattle weekly paper,
the official organ of the United Wage Workers Party of the
state of Washington.[48] This was a splinter group that had left
the Socialist Party. His name was William Z. Foster. He joined
the IWW, spoke on the street and was sentenced to thirty
days in jail. He served his term in the Franklin School House
on bread and water. A German society offered the IWW the
use of the German Turner Hall and defied the police to close
up the hall.

Our committee sent to Chicago to the general headquarters
for an out-state speaker for a meeting in the Turner Hall.
They sent a beautiful Irish girl. Her name was Elizabeth Gurley
Flynn. She had just married a guy by the name of Jones, the
head of the Dill Pickle Club in Chicago.

Private invitations were sent out for the meeting in the
Turner Hall, thus making it a private meeting and not public.
They did not raid the meeting, but arrested our speaker after
the meeting. The Women's Club of Spokane was aroused.
They raised $5,000 for bail and got her out. Her case never
came to trial. Public opinion began to turn. The newspapers
claimed that one of our members was clubbed to death in his
cell by the police. The powerful German Society and the
Women's Club were on our side.

After we had been in the county jail about four months,
the city government made an offer which was a big victory for
us. We were to be allowed four street corners for meetings.
All the police department asked was that we give them notice
when and where the meetings were to be held.

The mayor released all of the city prisoners at once, but we
were in the county jail and had to wait a few days until the
governor's pardon arrived. Everything seem peaceful in Spokane
after the free speech fight was over, but when I got back to
Portland, Oregon, the headlines in the papers said that the
Chief of Police Sullivan had been slain by someone with a shot-
gun on the porch of his home.

The papers tried to blame the IWW, but to our surprise,
Judge Mann who had sentenced us, defended the IWW and

said he knew they did not do it, that the chief had many
enemies. The murder was never solved. Thus ends the story of
one of the many free speech fights in the United States.

Writers' Group Journal, September 1959, published
by West Side YAW Retired Workers' Center, Detroit,
Michigan, copy in John Pancner Papers, Archives of
Labor History and Urban Affairs, Wayne State
University Library

3

Fresno Free-Speech Fight, 1910-1911

Introduction

Located in the heart of the San Joaquin Valley, the fruit belt of California, Fresno served as the key center for agricultural labor in the state. The city was also a center for construction workers who drifted into town in search of jobs. In November 1909, a small group of Wobblies set up headquarters for Local 66 at Fresno, held street meetings, and distributed literature to the migratory workers. When these activities were halted by the police, Frank Little and a few other veterans of the Spokane fight came to the aid of the local. Mexican laborers, imported to help construct a dam outside of Fresno, were organized, and the workers in the Santa Fe Railroad's electric power plant went on strike, led by Local 66. Anxious to stop I.W.W. agitation, the employers put pressure on Chief of Police Shaw to ban the Wobblies from the streets of Fresno.[1]

Police Chief Shaw revoked the I.W.W. permit to speak in the streets; the Salvation Army, however, was permitted to continue street meetings. This repressive measure temporarily curbed Local 66's growth. "If we had the streets so we could get to the workers we would build up a good fighting organization," Little informed the I.W.W. press, warning that a free-speech fight was brewing in Fresno.[2] The fight started on August 20, 1910, when Little was arrested while standing in the street. He immediately wired headquarters in Chicago for help. "F. E. Little sentenced before a perjured jury to 25 days in jail. A police conspiracy to get organizer Little out of town." These headlines in the *Industrial Worker* of September 10 put the members on notice that a real fight was imminent. The October 8 issue carried the news that the national organization officially supported the Fresno group in its fight for free speech, and called upon Wobblies "to go to Fresno and *break the law.* Break it, smash it into unrecognizable pulp." The I.W.W. journal did not hide the fact that those who went to Fresno would face brutal opposition. On October 26, it reprinted a threatening statement from the *Fresno Herald:* "For men to come here with the express purpose of creating trouble, a whipping post and a cat-o-nine tails well seasoned by being soaked in salt water is none too harsh a treatment for peace-breakers."[3]

By this time Wobblies were on the way to Fresno from the Middle West, Colorado, and the Pacific Northwest. On October 16, in defiance of local ordinances, the Wobblies announced an open-air meeting. Nine speakers were arrested as they in turn addressed the crowd. The following night, five more were arrested. However, not enough men had arrived in Fresno to continue the street meetings. The *Industrial Worker* announced on November 16 that the fight for free speech would be re-opened as soon as fifteen men were available to go to jail; in response to this announcement fifteen Wobblies arrived in Fresno. In less than a month, there were fifty men in jail for violating the ordinance against speaking on the streets, and more volunteers were on the way. "Industrial Workers Preach Discontent. Men Invite Arrest to Secure Sympathy," head-lines in the *San Francisco Call* screamed.[4]

On January 30, 1911, a "conference" was held in Portland to organize recruits for Fresno. "The way to win," the editor of the *Industrial Worker* wrote, "is to fill Fresno so full of men that the capitalists of Fresno will wish the I.W.W. were in hell and not Fresno."[5] On February 15, 1911, 112 men left

Portland for Fresno; they gained a few recruits on the way but
lost more. Besides harsh weather and a forced walk across the
Siskiyou Mountains, the Wobblies encountered hostility from
railroad officials and townspeople, although they also found
some helpful railroad laborers and some unexpected hospitality.
In the end they did not reach their destination. After twenty
days on the road they disbanded in Chico, after learning that
the Fresno fight had ended in an I.W.W. victory. With the jails
already filled and taxpayers lamenting the costs, the citizens
of Fresno decided that the fight must not be allowed to continue. Thus the impending arrival of these and other recruits
helped the Wobblies win their free-speech fight.

On February 22, 1911, a committee was elected to act as
mediator between city officials and the Wobblies in prison.
This group in turn met with a committee elected by the men
in jail to ascertain the I.W.W.'s terms of settlement. There were
two conditions presented by the spokesmen for the imprisoned
free-speech fighters: (1) the parole of all convicted and the release of all not yet tried; (2) the granting of a permit to the
I.W.W. to use specific streets for meetings. If these conditions
were met, the committee representing the men in jail would
notify the general headquarters and all locals of the I.W.W. to
stop sending men to Fresno and to intercept those on the way.

After the Wobblies had rejected a proposal that part of the
settlement be an agreement in writing by the I.W.W. to leave
the city, the citizens' committee reported the terms to a larger
body (at which the mayor and City Council were present) and
recommended granting them.

On March 2, the Fresno city officials rescinded the ban
against street meetings. Three days later, the men in prison were
released and immediately issued a statement announcing that
"at this writing, Sunday, March 5, 1911, the Fresno Free Speech
Fight has passed into history." A month later, Local 66 informed the I.W.W. press: "We are holding street meetings twice
a week, which are well attended."[6]

It had taken the I.W.W. six months to attain victory in
Fresno. The cost to the organization was less than $1,000.[7]
The publicity given the I.W.W. was enormous; the story was
featured in newspapers all over the country. The existence of

a labor organization dedicated to defend the constitutional
right of freedom of speech became known to all.

Two reports by participants offer invaluable firsthand accounts of different aspects of the Fresno free-speech fight. The
first was written by E. M. Clyde, a logger and farmer, who
started out on the aborted expedition from Portland to Fresno.[8]
Born in Wisconsin in 1874, Edward Mohammen Clyde came to
Washington in 1900. By 1911 he was a member of Seattle Local
432 and did organizational work for the I.W.W. His detailed
coverage reveals the many obstacles faced by the Fresno relief
brigade.[9]

Clyde's account of the men who did not reach Fresno is
followed by a detailed diary of the Fresno struggle written by
"one of the boys who went through the whole fight." At the
request of the I.W.W., he sent it to the Commission on Industrial
Relations. Nothing is known about the author, H. Minderman,
but his diary provides an important record of the Fresno free-
speech fight.

On the Wobbly Train to Fresno
By E. M. CLYDE

Seattle, Wash. March 24th, 1911

Fellow-Workers:—Having been selected by the final Committee
to write an account of the memorable march towards Fresno
I herewith present my report with the hopes that it will receive
the approval of the other members of the Committee.

. . . .

To no particular person can credit be given for organizing this
brigade as it seemed to be simultaneous with about 10 Fellow
Workers who happened to meet at 211 OX Ave., Seattle, on
Feb 12th, 1911.[10]

They immediately organized themselves and made a personal
canvass of the headquarters and by evening they had 31 names
on the list but as we were not to start until the next evening,
by that time we had 17 ready to start for Fresno.

As some of these were non-members they were initiated and
given cards.

Before leaving Seattle two business meetings were held at the first of which the following committee was elected as the duly authorized representatives of the body; Alfred Tucker, L.U. [Local Union] # 319; J. Train, L.U. # 322; E. M. Clyde, L.U. # 432. A. Snider was elected Sec'y.-Treas. and later was made ex-officio member of the Com. We opened donation lists and about $20.00 was subscribed for our use. We sent a letter to Spokane informing them of our departure and requesting that they also send out a bunch.

We also sent a letter to the S.P. [Socialist Party] of Portland asking them to arrange for a meeting in their hall for the 18th at which time we would be there and furnish the speakers.

At 5:00 p.m. Feb. 13th, we left Seattle, Some going to Tacoma by boat and others by train but we were all to meet in Tacoma and go from there to Portland together. Arriving in Tacoma those of us who went by boat held a street meeting at which we took a collection of $3.00, and then finding a train was billed out we decided to make it to Portland and let those who were coming by train to catch us at that place.

On leaving Tacoma we left $3.00 with Sec'y Foss to be given the other boys as they come through.

On arriving in the freight yards we found a train in waiting and upon first examination the only available place to ride seemed to be on some gondolas, loaded with coal and as some of our members were not experienced in catching trains while in motion they all got aboard these coal cars except Train and Clyde who proceeded to examine the train more thoroughly for an inside vacancy.

While on this mission they met a brakeman of the train and tried to square the boys for a ride and thought they had succeeded untill the conductor came along and told them to unload. By this time it began to look very much like rain would fall so it became quite imperative that we get inside so finally a refrigerator was found that proved susceptible to argument and the doors swinging open the boys all piled in except the two who rode outside to guard against the doors being closed on those in the car. They rode outside untill Roy was reached, 30 miles from Tacoma, at which place the doors on the other side of the car were opened and they also got inside. Upon investigation this car proved to be an empty meat car enroute home to the Union Meat Co, at Portland, and supplied with steel hooks on which meat is hung while en-transit, but now served us an entirely different and very useful purpose during the remainder of the trip to Portland.

Before leaving Roy the train crew discovered our presence and tried to get to us but in closing the doors we had left them slightly ajar to allow us air and some how some of those cursed meat hooks had swung into such position that they would allow the doors to be swung neither in nor out, and as we had all suddenly fallen asleep from which we could not be aroused to assist them in opening the door they did not gain an interview until the next town, Tenino, was reached.

At this place in response to their persistent request for admission we opened the door and a brakeman came in the car and asked: "Where are you going: What are you riding on?" and wound up by ordering us all out of the car. The committee explained to him who we were, where we were going, what was our mission, and took advantage of the occasion to explain to him the principles of Industrial Unionism.

The brakeman then spoke up: "I do not believe that what you say is true but if you can show me that you are all union men you may ride so far as I am concerned." We replied to that proposition by all producing our I.W.W. cards which seemed to be new to him and something of a curiosity.

After examining a few of our cards he left the car but returned in a few minutes with the conductor who was not open to argument but insisted that we "unload."

As no one made a start to get out he said, "Well hurry up, get out of there," but still no one moved. "Come, some one make a start there; say can't you hear what I am saying? I am speaking to you."

Up to this time none of us had spoken a word or made any move to get out; he became impatient at our delay and gave the door a slam with the evident intention of closing us in the car but again some of those meat hooks came into play in such a manner that the door would not close.

Seeing this he became wild with rage, he pulled from his pocket a 22 cal. revolver and with a flourish that would do justice to "Dead Wood Dick" he now gave the command: "Unload at once or some one will get hurt."

On being informed that it was some times the one behind the gun that got hurt he replaced it in his pocket and taking a lighted "Fusee" attempted to smoke us out, but one of the boys with a well aimed blow with a meat hook put the fusee out of commission. Now telling us that he would have us all arrested at the next stop he retired to the caboose and we seen no more of him until Centralia was reached, Arriving there he again endeavored to get us out but on being informed that we were not very particular as to where we went to jail, although our objective point was Fresno, he offered us no further molestation on the trip only to try at different times to close the doors on us, thinking perhaps we would all be asleep.

Arriving in Vancouver, Wash, at 9:00 A.M. we left the train there and took the street car into Portland, Or, reaching there at 11:00 A.M. Feb. 14.

The spirit of solidarity exibited on this trip of 145 miles from Tacoma to Portland will long be remembered by those of the party and will no doubt be of vast benefit in the future.

The only regretable feature of this trip was that D. Dearth, of L.U. # 132 came near creating friction by insisted upon smoking cigarettes which was prohibited while the doors of the car was closed as the smoke was very annoying to many from a lack of ventilation. At a meeting held later in Portland however, he made apology which was accepted.

On the 14th, a meeting was held in I.W.W. hall where a collection of $11.25 was taken and 20 names added to our list. On the 15th, the remainder of those coming from Seattle arrived and as each one came in they were given the price of a meal and told to be in readiness to start that night. We had also picked up a few in Tacoma who were now with us.

In the afternoon we held a business meeting at which our organization was perfected by the addition to the E.Com. of T.L.LaFord of L.U. # 92.

As there were many members of the S.P. who were not mem-
bers of the I.W.W. they wished to be represented on the Ex.
Com. and R. L. Brazzle was placed there to represent them.
At no time did he pretend to be traveling as a member of the
I.W.W. but rather as the representative of those members of the
S.P. who were in the party.

At this meeting also each one was given a number and a pass
word provided for which later proved of no value.

The S.P. members explained at this time through their spokesman, P. L. Brazzle, that their purpose was to go with us to
Fresno and later on to Mexico.

At 5:00 P.M. we went on the street and paraded the down
town district for 2½ hours with 7 banners and at least 500 men
in line but one peculiar feature is that neither the police or
press knew we were in town as no mention was ever made of
this parade which ended at the S.P. hall which was packed to
overflowing and addressed by S.P.&I.W.W. speakers.

A collection of $20.00 was taken and $7.00 more was
solicited by a Com. sent up town. A committee of two, Fred
Heyer & J. F. McGovern was now sent into the freight yards
to investigate the running of trains and be able to report to us
as we got there. After the meeting in S.P. hall we went to the
I.W.W. hall where a business meeting was held to complete the
final arrangements preparatory to our start.

This was to be a meeting only of those who were going to
Fresno so in order to exclude outsiders the chairman, after
calling meeting to order, began to call the numbers with the
request that as a number was called the owner would rise to
his feet and remain standing till the roll call was completed.
After all numbers had been called it was found there was two
men in the hall whose names we did not have and who were
unknown to us and as they made no satisfactory explanation
of their presence they were escorted from the hall.

Having concluded our business, meeting was adjourned and
we were ready to begin the trip.

As we filed out the door each one was searched for weapons
and on finding none they were given the pass word and on reach-

ing the street were lined up in double rank and marched across
the Burnside bridge where we were met by the train committee
who informed us that a train was billed out at 11:30 but would
probably be late so they escorted us to a place where we could
make ourselves comfortable until ready to leave.

On leaving the hall Jas. Gibbons, L.U. # 178 & Tom Hall,
L.U. # 432 left us and taking the boat to Frisco arrived in
Fresno in time to be there during the closing days of the fight.

While waiting for the train to pull out we were joined by a
man named Richardson (or Rochardon), member of the R.R.
telegraphers, and after making inquiries as to where we were
going expressed a desire to accompany us on the trip. We let
him remain with us but he was looked upon with suspicion
until at Ashland he proved to our satisfaction that he was
all right.

At last we were informed by the train Com. that all was ready
and on arriving in the yards found they had ready for our convenience two cars, one loaded nearly full of merchandise boxes,
the other loaded with kegs of beer/one sitting above the other.
We divided ourselves as near equally as possible in these two
cars but before leaving the yards the conductor came along
and taking us out of the merchandise car put us in an empty
box car on the head end of the train.

Our exact number is unknown as no count was made on
leaving the hall but it is believed to have been 112 at this time,
36 of whom were not members of the I.W.W.

At 1:30 all was ready and we pulled out of Portland with
every one happy and singing the "Red Flag." At Salem, 58
miles, our empty car was cut and we had to ride outside on a
car load of sand to Albany, 27 miles.[11]

It being 8:00 A.M. when Albany was reached the citizens
of the town congregated about to view the curiosities and ask
what it all meant.

The police chatted with us and bought us the morning papers,
assuring us that they had no use for us at that place.

Here the conductor picked up another empty car and bringing those out of the beer car put us all in this empty and billed
it directly through to Fresno at the same time informing us that

we would be bothered no more on the trip. Here the first
desertion occurred. T. D. Lauchlin got tired and quit.

The next stop was Junction City, 30 miles, and here what
was perhaps the most amusing stunt of the trip was pulled off.

I am informed by C. W. Meara, resident of Junction City,
that some one at Albany sent a message to Wm. Starr, Marshall
of Junction City, stating that a large body of heavily armed
men had passed through that place on the last train and no
doubt would attempt to rob and plunder the town of Junction
City.

Meara states that upon receipt of this message that Marshall
Wm. Starr ran through the streets imploring every one to arm
themselves for the protection of their property and honor of
their wives. He also states that before our arrival all was confu-
sion and excitement, that men quit work, business houses were
closed and placed under guard, women took to the cellars
and children were crying.

Whether by accident or design is not known but as we pulled
into town the car in which we were riding was stopped directly
in front of the depot where many of the citizens had assembled
armed with all manner of weapons. We all remained quietly in
the car with both doors wide open and when it was seen that
we were making no effort to get out some of the more venture-
some among them came close enough that we could engage
them in conversation and after peddling them the "bull" about
their beautiful city, their thrift, prosperity, business sagacity
and evident contentment they became convinced that they had
been humbugged and expressed a desire to learn more about us.
We were now pulled to the outskirts of the city and placed on
a siding while the switching was done and as a crowd soon congregated we gave them a talk on the object of our trip.

There was no attempt at harm or violence on either side
and no cause for alarm by any one.

Our next stop was Roseburg, which we reached at 5:00
Feb 16th, 197 miles from Portland. We had been on the train
16 hours with out food.

Here we purchased bread, bologna, cakes and cookies which
was brought to the depot where we lined up in single file and

as each passed he was given his portion. After supper we held
a well attended street meeting at which we got $3.00. The
Com. also solicited $5.00 in other places.

At 10:30 P.M. we were again aboard of the same empty car
and on our way to Ashland.

We all now began to feel sleepy and as this was a small car
(only 30 ft, long) it was filled to capacity and the Com. became quite expert in the art of packing human beings as it was
necessary for one to lie partially on another in order to find
room for all of us to sit down. But sleep was wholly out of the
question.

We were all glad when Ashland, 347 miles from Portland,
was reached at 5:00 A.M. Feb 17th. Here we bought sandwiches,
bread, bologna, and made coffee which was enjoyed by all but
not supplied in sufficient quantity to be entirely satisfactory.
A meal such as this cost $9.50 besides many who had money
was paying their own way.

As we were eating breakfast we were visited by the police
who assured us we would receive their assistance in getting out
of town as they did not want us there.

After breakfast we returned to the R.R. yards where we
found a train ready to pull out but on finding they had cut
out our empty we concluded to ride a string of flats which they
had on the head end.

We all climbed aboard these flats which stood in full view of
the depot and division officials but we were no sooner loaded
than we were informed from the Superintendants office that
no trains would be moved as long as we were on. It now become evident that we would have difficulty in riding out of
this place.

The officials told us that if we would walk a short way out
of town the train would stop and pick us up as it came along.
We all knew that this was simply an attempt to get a train past
us and that they had no intention of slowing down for us to get
on but at this point R.L. Brazzle took it upon himself to interview the city and R.R. officials and agree to walk a short distance out of town. When learning this agreement had been made

the Ex. Com. decided that we would walk 1 mile up the track
but having no confidence in their promise to stop for us, and
being assured by R.L. Brazzle that he could stop the train at
will, we left Brazzle, J.M. Bennett and C.B. Emery behind to
ride out the train and to cut the air at the proper time and
bring the train to a stop providing they made an attempt to run
past us. The rest of us walked out the track 1 mile and when
the train came by it was under a full head of steam and no one
could get aboard although A. Snider made the attempt and
narrowly escaped serious injury. By mis-judging the distance
those on the train did not cut the air soon enough and before
they got the train to a stop it was 1 mile past us and before we
could get up to it they had cut in the air again and gone on.
This was the first train we had missed on the trip and naturally
every one was disappointed.

A meeting was called on the track to determine what we
should do and at this meeting all the Ex. Com. except Brazzle
presented their resignation but it was not accepted.

After considerable discussion it was agreed to walk 10 miles
up the track to where all trains were supposed to stop.

At this meeting the Com. came in for considerable censure
but it only justice to them to say that they agreed to the plan
only on the positive assurance that the train could be stopped
as desired. It was now evident however, that they had acted on
the advice of those who could not make good but as their resignation was not accepted they now called forward the operator
who joined us in Portland and put him through a most searching examination. Showing himself O.K. he was voted in as one
of our party and given a regular number.

We also at this time found 4 strangers among us whom we
proceeded to investigate as we allowed no one with us unless
he was voted in by the body. One of this 4 was accepted on
the strength of showing a card from Butte No 1, W.F.M. We
later had to discard him.

The other three could give no account of themselves so
after giving them some sandwiches from our stock we told them
to come among us no more.

We now picked out 4 volunteers to remain behind and ride
out the next train and stop it where ever we chanced to be.
We now dismissed the meeting and after dividing our sandwiches we began to hike to Steinman, 10 miles up the hill. It
was raining all the way and the snow kept getting deeper and
when we finally arrived at Steinman at 4:30 P.M. we found
ourselves wet, cold and hungry, with 18" snow on the ground
and no chance to get food or shelter for the night.

We borrowed shovels and axes and after clearing away the
snow started camp fires and tried to dry our clothes. The wife
of the section boss, which was the only family at the place,
gave out some apples and crackers but as there was only enough
for a few considerable friction arose as some seemed to think
that partiality was being shown. The Com. had nothing whatever to do with the distribution of this stuff and did not know
of its presence until it had been disposed of.

At 9:00 P.M. a train came through but to our surprise only
one of the boys left behind had made it out and before he
could get the air cut the brakemen had kicked him off the train.

Here we gave out the first press interview of the trip as we
were visited by a representative of the United Press.

Here Brazzle informed him of their intended trip to Mexico
but the Ex. Com. ordered it stricken from the report which he
promised to do but on getting the papers we found us reported
as on the way to Mexico.

He promised to give us a square write up but on getting the
papers we found that he had mis-represented nearly everything—
even the trip to Mexico. Perhaps he was biased from the fact
that after the interview we called his attention to our donation
list to which he contributed $2.00.[12]

As the boys were now suffering terribly from the exposure,
wet, hunger, cold and loss of sleep, and knowing there would
be no more trains that night, and knowing also there was no
food to be had at this place for breakfast should we remain
here, it looked for a time like dissolution was sure to take place.

The Ex. Com, called a meeting by the camp fire at 11:00 P.M.
where all but Brazzle again presented their resignation which
was again refused.

In the Treas. now was $41.25. During the remainder of the
night some hunted a box car, others a vacant shack, but most
of them remained by the outside fire where some of the dis-
turbers who now began to show themselves worked faithfully
all night trying to create friction among us.

At 3:00 A.M. a call was made for a business meeting, notwithstanding the fact that one had been held 4 hours previously.

72 came onto the track to see what was doing: Joe Risik of
L.U. # 92, in calling the meeting to order stated it was for the
purpose of changing the personnel of the Ex. Com, and had
been called by the rank and file.

16 had signed the call some of whom later repudiated it after
learning the real purport. The motion was made that Clyde of
L.U. # 432 be discharged from the Com. Those speaking in
favor of the motion were Snider, Moore & Clyde of # 432,
Risik of # 92, Ward of # 178 & Chandler non-member,
Dearth [sic].

The vote carried the motion by 35 to 33. 4 not voting.

Snider, Laford & Train now presented their resignations and
insisted upon their acceptance which was done. The following
were elected to fill the vacancy: Ward of # 178, Dearth of
132, Michaell of # 92, Smye of # 92.

Snider resigned simply from the Ex. Com, and not as Sec,y
Treas.

The meeting adjourned to allow the Com. to confer on what
should be done and they soon decided that we were to walk 4
miles over the hill to Siskiyou where all trains had to stop.

We began this hike at 4:00 A.M. Feb 18th, and had proceeded but a short way when J. Train became exhausted. Being near a hay barn we gave him $1.00 on which to catch us
and left him there while we continued on up the hill through
the snow. We had just got started again when we learned that
Brazzle was "all in." We left him in company of Train and proceeded on to Siskiyou where we found about 3ft. of snow.

They both recuperated with a few hours rest and caught up
with [us] again at Siskiyou. Here we found the operator kept
a small store at which we bought potatoes, onions, cabbage
etc, and borrowing shovels, axes, wash boilers and water

buckets we here had the first mulligan[13] of the trip.

It was purely a vegetable "combination" as no meat was to be had.

The one wash boiler which answered the purpose of a stew pot proved to be too small so we had to take dinner on the installment plan as we kept the good work up till all were satisfied.

The Section Boss here assisted us in many ways and donated $1.00 to our fund. He allowed us to cook our coffee on his kitchen stove and loaned us axes, shovels etc.

A passenger train came in from the north and two R.R. guards dropped and immediately began to interview our Com. We gave them all desired information and impressed upon them that we were unarmed and meant no destruction of property. We requested that they search each one of us which they did after lining us up on the track where they could count us.

The count showed 110 in line. Here is the first and only time the operator with us proved of value. After searching us and getting such information as they could the guards went to the depot to send a message to their chief and the writer seeing the opportunity requested the operator to go there and see what he could learn.

The guards sent away a message embodying the results of their investigation and also stating that we were unarmed and harmless. In reply they got a message telling them to come to Ashland on the first train where they would be joined by 4 others who would return with them to keep us off the trains.

While the operator was up the track giving this information another message went over the wire and some of our boys in the depot becoming excited cried out: "Where is our operator? Why is he not here to take this message?" The guards cast knowing glances at each other and after that when sending messages would make us get out of hearing of the instruments. The operator on shift gave us the purport of all messages sent and received as well as what had been sent the previous night by the reporter who interviewed us. He was also called up by phone from Ashland and advised to look out for us but he

replied that we were now in the depot, that two of us was at
that time in his private office, that each of them were members of the Masonic order, and that all reports going over the
wires concerning us were untrue. He was a Revolutionist.

So instead of our operator receiving many messages as may
be reported he received but one and that of slight value to us
although we all appreciated his willingness and desire to be of
assistance to us.

When a train did finally come along at about 2:00 P.M. the
6 guards were on as reported. They were under the leadership
of Ed Oconnor who came over to us and had a long conversation with the Ex. Com. but persistently refused to let us ride.
The train laid over for some time to meet one from the south
and in the mean time the chief called aside one of our number, J.M. Bennett member of Portland S.P., and by working
upon his vanity and pride tried to get inside information but
fortunately all he could learn was that we had a general Treas,
and that Snider carried the money. The chief then called
Snider aside and informed him that unless he got away from
us he would be arrested as soon as he crossed the California line,
but that if he would leave us and take Bennet along he would
put them on a light engine going south and arrange so they
could make the first train out of Hornbrook and get away
from us.

To this Snider readily consented and working his way back
among us and unnoticed to but a few he slipped the money
over to Alfred Tucker who in turn passed it to Stoehr. From
then on it was unknown to many who held the funds.

Many conferences took place between the Com. and the
chief and at last he told us we would not be permitted to even
walk the track.

When the train was ready to pull out about 2/3rds of our
number made a run to get on. The guards were now on the
train and ordering us to keep off although they attempted no
violence or force.

When it was seen that many of us made no attempt to get
on civil war nearly broke out in our own ranks. Those who
wished to stay off made no effort to dissuade the others but

those who wanted to get on were inclined to force the others aboard. After heaping abuse upon each other as well as upon the police and the S.P.R.R. [Southern Pacific RailRoad] it was plain to be seen that some were determined not to make an attempt to ride that train.

When it became so evident that we were not a unit, and that greater organization was absolutely necessary they all withdrew and allowed the train to pull out unmolested.

The guards all remained behind after seeing none of us got on.

A meeting was held at which it was decided to send Train and Brazzle ahead into Hornbrook, as they were sick, and they would be able to let us know if the militia was in Hornbrook as reported.

It was decided that we walk to Hornbrook, 19 miles, and then a discussion arose if we should try to walk the track but it was finally settled that we would go by the trail over the hill.

Snider and Bennet as per agreement had been sent out on a light engine.

At seeing the walk through the snow staring them in the face the courage of about 10 failed them and they returned down the hill towards Ashland. 3 of that number later caught up with us at Montague and proved O.K. for the rest of the trip. The other 7 have not been seen since; their names are uncertain.

As the main body went over the hill Clyde, LaFord, Emery and Parson remained behind to see just what would take place.

The chief came over to us and began to "guy" us on losing our treasury, asking us what we would do now that we were broke and in three feet of snow with more ahead of us, that the militia was in waiting for us, and wound up by offering us a ride back to Portland if we would turn back.

You could see his face color though when he was told that Snider carried no money.

While waiting at Siskiyou S. Dixon and E.M. Clyde were called aside at different times and given some R.R. torpedoes with instructions how to use them to stop a train. They were refused with thanks.

Here Fred Parsons left us and took the train over the hill although he had been pretending broke. I seen no weeping of tears at his departure as he had been a disturber and a nuisance all the way. He later on down the line represented himself as our advance agent but the turn was called on him at Sacramento by E.J. Corbett of L.U. # 174. At no time during the trip did F. Parsons of L.U. # 322 have authority or permission to speak or act for the body.

Clyde, LaFord and Emery left by way of the track at about 3:00 P.M.

No one not present can possibly have any idea of the extent of hardship and suffering encountered over this hill.

Many were thinly dressed, some were nearly bare-foot, others were most sick but to their credit it should be said there was but little complaint or murmurings of dissatisfaction during the trip to Hornbrook.

At Hilt they stopped and buying some crackers etc, they made a light supper then most of them continued on in to Hornbrook, 10 miles further.

Some of us remained over night at Hilt, others stopped in barns along the way, but most of them made Hornbrook where they found a good "mulligan" in readiness and after making a feed they spent the night as best they could, some in the round house, some in box cars, others by the camp fire. We all arrived in Hornbrook next morning, Feb 18th, in time for breakfast which was served at 11:00 A.M.

On reaching there the previous night our boys found that instead of the citizens being up in arms against us they were disposed to lend us assistance and had got together provisions enough for two meals.

Sheriff Dudley was there to meet us and gave assurance that we would not be molested by his force while passing through Siskiyou Co.

There were many of the R.R. police force in town, which consists of 120 men, and the remainder were scattered along in the towns through which we passed. They kept alternating them so the same ones were with us only a day or so at a time.

There will [be] no attempt made to describe the misery, exposure and hardship endured on this trip of 19 miles through the
snow, slush and water but the suffering will long be remembered
by us and stands out as a shining example of what men will pass
through in defense of a principle.

Coming over trail from Siskiyou there was deep snow for a
considerable distance and as many were thinly clad and had
poor shoes; their condition at the end of the first walk is more
easily imagined than told.

Here is where one of our number (the operator) had his feet
frozen and was sent to the hospital.

At Hornbrook we organized our police force and hospital
corps.

S. Mortimar of # 350 has had extensive hospital practice,
and he was made medical director, and no doubt the success
of the trip was due in great measure to the able and efficient
manner that he cared for the sick and disabled. On sending the
operator to the hospital Brazzle and Train pledged the Gen.
Office to pay the bill. Where they got their authority I do not
know and I have heard nothing of it since.

From Hornbrook the same two were sent ahead to
Montague to arrange for our coming. The citizens here supplied us with provisions enough for two days so we laid over
and took a rest. Before leaving here J. Train was discharged
from the advance guard and Fred Heyer elected to fill the
vacancy. On leaving here Train still insisted upon riding which
he continued to do nearly all the way. Here we stayed in the
ball park and while we had our own guards continually on
duty we found before leaving 10 lbs of dynamite in a toilet
on the grounds. We turned it over to the police who after an
investigation came to the conclusion that it had been left there
two years previously by a gardener who set some trees in the
park.

This may be true but it looks rather odd that it should not
be discovered until our arrival.

Leaving Montague Feb 21st we made Weed that night which
is at the foot of the Shasta range. We built camp fires and remained on the side hill in the snow and after a sleepless night

started for Sisson early next morning. All the way from Siskiyou to Chico we had a Com. preceding the main body. Arriving
in Sisson we prepared a mulligan feed and as we were finishing
our meal we were visited by the manager of the May Roberts
Theatrical Co. who volunteered to pay our fares into Dunsmuir,
14 miles, we readily accepted and on arriving there attended
show in a body and were supplied with coffee and sandwiches
at the expense of Miss Roberts.

Here also J.M. LaDue, saloon keeper, R.A. Waschan and A.H.
Sharvey, members of the S.P. gave us valuable assistance. The
former gave us the use of a lunch counter in his saloon, bought
us food etc: the other two took some of the boys home with
them to sleep, gave them meals and donated to our fund. Our
pictures were taken twice at Sisson and twice here but the
picture of R.L. Brazzle and J. Train (which appeared in the
papers over the caption "leaders of the I.W.W.") was taken and
published unknown to the body. The same two also, from
money donated for our use, bought a picture album which was
presented to Miss Roberts. This album was bought over the
protest of Fred Heyer, and in justification of its purchase,
Brazzle later stated that it was agreed to by all the members of
the Ex. Com but investigation proved that none of them knew
of the purchase until some time later. Brazzle and Train completely ignoring Heyer took the train at 7:06 P.M. Feb 23rd
for Kennet 46 miles ahead. They left word with some of the
boys that we should make Kennet as best we could.

For breakfast on the 24th was served to us the lightest meal
of the trip on which to start this 46 miles walk. At this time
less than $3.00 was in the treasury and things were looking
rather dark for our future.

During this hike we were strung along the track for a distance
of 20 miles or more. The first day some made LaMoine, some
Delta and others Antlers. E.J. Corbett, who as a committee
from L.U. # 174 arrived in Kennet, there meeting Brazzle and
Train who informed him that the body was making their way
as best they could; he took the train and come up to Delta.

Those staying over night at LaMoine had a little money as
well as most of those who had made Antlers, but those at

Delta were nearly all broke. The store keeper gave them a sack of potatoes and some bread for supper but they were in bad shape when Corbett appeared.

He fitted them out for breakfast then returned to Kennet.

The last one, Clyde, arrived in Kennet at 9:30 P.M. Feb. 24th. The boys there had got busy, especially Karl Scheidt of # 432, and Henry Evans Sec'y W.F.M. local. Lawyer Brainard also donated $10.00 making a total of about $50.00 collected there.

During the 24th, and before all were in, a meeting was held at which a motion was passed discharging Sec'y Treas Snider, not with-standing the fact that he had carried no money since leaving Siskiyou.

R. M. Blake of L. U. # 432 was elected Treas and the money turned over to him. There was also passed a motion calling for a report of the advance Com but as they could give none at that time they were granted till the next day to report. When meeting was called next day it was found that they could give no straight report as they turned over to the Treas $10.05 and no matter how it was figured they always brought it out the same $10.05. Their report was finally accepted and Corbett was elected as a member of the advance Com. thereby making it Brazzle, Heyer and Corbett. We left Kennet on the 27th, A.M. A few having gone the previous night to Coram, 6 miles below, where a street meeting was held and $17.00 solicited besides considerable provisions.

We all came together at Coram and went into Redding where we found that Mrs. Clineschmidt of the Temple Hotel had volunteered to care for us as long as we remained in the city.

As an attempt to justify the purchase of the picture album for Miss Roberts it was secured in Kennet and perhaps 1/3 of the boys inscribed their names therein. Also while at Kennet the man with the card from Butte No. 1, went to Coram and on the strength of representing himself as our advance agent he got considerable donations. He later came to us at Chico but we turned him away.

The reason we rested so long here was that Brazzle represented that he had an agreement with May Roberts that she

would furnish us with transportation from Redding if we
would be there to attend the show as an advertising feature
on this particular date, but it developed that the receipts did
not justify the expenditure as they played to a $60.00 house
of which they gave us $15.00.

At the Temple Hotel we were supplied with 5 meals and
beds for a considerable number. Leaving Redding we made
Cottonwood that night where we were joined by Geo. Reese
of Portland who remained with us one day and then went
ahead to Sacramento.

Before leaving Redding a business meeting was held at which
Brazzle was discharged from the advance Com. and Corbett and
A. Tucker went ahead.

Red Bluff was the only city to show us hospitality but they
furnished us with an empty building and some provisions—we
remained there one night.

The next stop was Vina where Pape Bryan a 72 year old
Socialist donated $5.00 and his son $5.00, and Dan Potter,
saloon keeper, gave us the use of his yard supplied with wood
to do our cooking.

E.J. Hatch, Socialist Sec'y, went good at the store for some
of our supplies and we fared well here. Fred Heyer was the advance here and his worth began to be shown.

After supper which was served in the rain and eaten with
relish by those who had traveled all day through the rain we
went inside the saloon and tried to dry our clothes by the stove.

A meeting had been held in the hall and after it was over the
saloon keeper suddenly became generous and began to pass out
the booze quite freely. No less than 12 large bottles was distributed among the boys.

After some of them had got "keyed" to the right pitch
speeches was called for. It did not require much effort to get
Brazzle to climb on the bar, from which all speeches were
delivered, and his talk was about as follows: The proprietor
of this place is the most generous and benevolent fellow I have
ever met (drink); all working men should spend their money
with him—he is their friend, (drink); the I.W.W. should organize this town, make this saloon the union headquarters and

decorate the walls with charters of the I.W.W. (drink); the
bartender here (who was the city Marshall) should be made
Sec'y of the union as he is a working man and would make a
most efficient officer; J. Train from the rear of the saloon
echoes up "Correct, brother Brazzle, correct" (DRINKS). Con-
tinuing Brazzle said, "We will return to this place and organize
all the men of the neighborhood and when they come to town
with a stake they will have to come here to pay their union
dues and so long as they will spend their money some place
they might better spend it with this man who is their friend."

At this time the drinks were coming so fast that it was
necessary to give up either the talking or drinking, so choosing
to give up the former Brazzle was succeeded by Train who
spoke in practically the same manner.

When Train was done E.J. Hatch, Socialist, took the floor
to show how and why both the I.W.W. and the S.P. were necessary. How and why they were a complement to each other and
made a harmonious whole, and eventually after gaining political control we would assert our economic powers and establish
the cooperative society.

A slight review by way of explanation is here in order. D.
Dearth of L.U. # 132 was cook from Ashland to Kennet but
there so much dissatisfaction was manifest that he was succeeded by Sam Dixon who remained cook to Cottonwood
where he was succeeded by E.M. Clyde who served for rest of
trip. At Red Bluff we were joined by two members from
Spokane who continued with us. At Kennet, we were joined
by—Robinson, of Portland, who had been in Fresno, but as his
record was none the best we discarded him before entering
Redding.

At Kennet the whole Ex. Com. was discharged and a new
one consisting of D. Dearth L.U. # 132, Tom Pearson L.U.
434 and J. Kerley L.U. # 93, elected.

D. Dearth followed Hatch as speaker and he in turn was
followed by others of our number.

There has developed considerable discussion as to who was
drunk that night but all seem agreed that Brazzle and Dearth

was drunk as well as a few more who become affected towards morning.

Kerley of the Ex. Com. took a few drinks and while some try to make it appear that he was drunk that assertion is far fetched indeed as he was at no time under the influence of liquor to any great extent.

Tom Pearson, 3rd member of the Com, may it be said to his credit took so far as is known only one drink.

Some time after mid-night the drinks began to lessen and at this time D. Dearth, member of Ex. Com. began an agitation to take the money from the Treasury (about $15.00) and spend it over the bar. His argument was: The fight is now off in Fresno and we need go no further, and as we will disband any how in a day or so we may just as well do so now and spend this money as a mark of appreciation for the assistance rendered by this saloon-keeper. We have breakfast now on hand so do not need this money to eat on and, as the object of our trip is now accomplished we should spend this money and disband right here. (We had not at this time received official notification that the Fresno fight was off, it was three days later that we received this notice.)

When Sec'y-Treas Blake heard this discussion he began to provide for the safety of the money in his possession. There was also some few who had been for some time harboring a grudge against ex-Sec'y Snider and now an attempt was also made to organize their force to beat him up.

At this stage of the proceedings A. Snider, Alfred Tucker, J. Train and Sec'y-Treas Blake left the saloon and walked out of town towards Chico and when morning came they took a train and paid their fare as well as that of a couple more who had joined them on into Chico.

The remainder left Vina in the morning and on arrival in Chico found that Heyer and Corbett, who had preceded them the night before, had secured a hall, well equipped, for our convenience. This hall and our provisions were supposed to be paid by the Socialist Party but it proved that they paid but little of the expense. We reached Chico on March 5th and on the 7th received a telegram from Corbett who had went ahead to Sacramento, that the fight was off and our presence not needed in Fresno.

We held a meeting where it was decided that we disband unless those in Sacramento had collected enough money to take us there, so we telephoned there and were informed that no money to speak of was on hand.

The committees and the Sec'y-Treas now all resigned and a Com. composed as follows, Fred Heyer, Tom Pearson, C. F. Miller, C. W. Mison and E. M. Clyde was elected to take charge of the matters incident to our disbanding, cleaning the hall, etc. The Treasury ($14.50) was now turned over to them and after all joining in singing the "Eight Hour Day"[14] a motion was passed that we disband. 96 men were in attendance at this time all of whom were quite willing to continue on to Fresno.

It should be mentioned that on entering this hall it was found there was considerable fruit, both dried and canned, which was stored by the owner of the building. It was soon discovered by members of our party and before being discovered by the committee they had made quite a hole in this fruit. Also as soon as it began to appear in the papers that the fight had been won we were joined by many who expressed a desire to go to Fresno but we refused to accept them. As most of the boys were to stay over the night it was necessary to provide supper and breakfast which cost $12.50 leaving on hand $2.00, and after cleaning the hall and were ready to make final settlement we discovered that the Socialist Party had agreed to pay but one night's rent of the hall and that we were short $6.00 of having enough to settle all bills held against us.

We received a $1.00 donation towards the deficit and committee man Heyer remained behind to pay in labor the remainder of these bills.

At the last meeting held before disbanding there was considerable animosity shown as a result of the Vina Fiasco. Many members came in for censure but the meeting ended with practical harmony prevailing. During the course of this meeting it became quite evident that the reasons for the discharge of A. Snider as Sec'y-Treas was simply to satisfy a

grudge some held against him; a motion was now passed that
the matter be stricken from the minutes of our meetings.
Finally all of our minutes were burned.

Beginning at Hornbrook we held meetings in all towns and
took up collections the largest of which was at Weed $9.00.
The citizens also contributed clothing and tobacco all along
the way.

It should be noted that J. Train was discharged from all committees at Montague and Brazzle at Redding. That after being
off the Com. they rode the greater part of the way on money
donated for our use.

Also that they never gave us an understandable report of receipts and expenses. That all disbursements should have been
made through the Treas which was not done. That they made
all possible attempts to ignore committeemen Heyer and
Corbett, and that on leaving Dunsmuir they did not even inform Heyer that they were going. And it remains as yet un-
explained why and upon whose permission did Train ride from
Montague to Sisson and from Dunamuir [sic] to Kennet, and
with whose permission did they spend money without first
passing it through the hands of the Treas. Why did they ride
from Dunsmuir to Kennet while Fred Heyer walked.

True, they did nearly all the speaking during the trip for the
reason that they always forced themselves in and no attempt
was made at any time to utilize other talent except at Montague
and Coram and in each of those instances it was well known
and so stated that those called upon to speak had never made
the attempt before.

The first meeting in Montague was a good one but at the
2nd one the "Red Flag" was sung and it was plain to be seen
that it was entirely out of place. Certain discretion must in the
future be used in singing that song as it is evident that it does
not take well in all places and at all times.

We were continually discussing the matter of going down the
river on a barge or raft from Red Bluff or Chico and that was
the chief mission of E. J. Corbett while on the advance Com,
but he was unable to make a connection for this transportation.

Some few members of the party were impossible to submit

themselves to discipline, James Howe and A. Brasher of L.U.
432, A. Mack of the S. P. require special mention in this
connection. Many others would at various times become un-
governable but it was only temporarily so and as a result of the
misery, exposures and hard ships they were enduring.

In the main harmony prevailed through-out the trip.

On starting in [it] was decided to permit of no individual
begging but it was absolutely impossible to enforce this regu-
lation.

Those requiring especial mention for assistance rendered us
along the way are: Sheriff Dudley of Siskiyou, Co, Proprietress
of the Opera Restaurant of Montague, May Roberts Theatrical
Co, J. M. LaDue, saloon keeper of Dunsmuir, R. A. Waschan,
A. H. Shervey, members of Socialist party Dunsmuir, Karl
Scheidt member of # 432 working at Kennet, Henry Evans
Sec'y W. F. M. Kennet, Attorney Braynard, Kennet. Mrs
Clineschmidt of Temple Hotel, Redding, Pape Bryan, E. J.
Hatch and Dan Potter of Vina, and Swift and Ely, members
of the Socialist Party of Chico.

We found many places that looked quite favorable as fields
for organization work, we were all well received by the working
class along the way and greatly regret that greater attention
can not be given that district by our organizers. Many R.R.
employees expressed sympathy for us and evidenced their
intention of investigating the matter further.

If we should have had a supply of literature, especially
papers, we could have done good business with them.

At Weed no doubt a good live local could be easily built up
as great interest was shown at our street meeting. This is a
Lumbering and mill town. Sisson is also a Lumbering center
and should be looked after at the earliest opportunity.

This is our report of the Fresno Relief Brigade.

The trip is over; The Fresno fight is won,[15] We are disbanded; Now let us all get busy on the fight for the eight hour
day May 1st, 1911.[16]

Committee: Fred Heyer, Tom Pearson, C. F. Miller, C. W.
Mison, E. M. Clyde.
Per E. M. Clyde

("Addenda")

As it remains to this day a debatable and unsettled question as to whether or not it was good tactics on our part that we walked out of Ashland and again at Siskiyou, and, as I am one of those who defended the idea of walking, in defense of that position I feel disposed to argue thusly: Leaving out all consideration of the later advertising we received, and taking into consideration nothing but the actual conditions as they existed at that time we find, that, at Ashland and the Superintendant positively refused to move any trains while we were on.

True we could have remained there indefinitely providing we could get food. We must also bear in mind that there was but two freight trains each day and one of them was a local and carried but few cars.

We had in the Treasury on leaving Ashland $39.25 and each meal cost no less that $9.00. We also received information (whether correct or not is unknown) that an agreement had been affected whereby no one in Ashland would sell us more grub.

Also it was generally admitted by all of our number that we stood a good chance of being able to catch a train some where on the hill and after all being taken into consideration I believe it to have been the better judgment that we walked out of Ashland.

At Siskiyou there was a string of flats which we could have ridden.

This train was under guard of 6 men besides the regular train crew, and while at no time was there fear of violence from this 6 men as it is well known that 6 guards cannot handle 110 organized and determined men even though they be unarmed. So the question of fear does not come within the realm of discussion, even though there have been attempts made to inject it in.

It was 2:00 P.M. and we had just eaten dinner. The nearest place where we could secure another meal was Ashland, 17 miles north, or Hilt, 11 miles, south. There was about 3 ft. of snow on the ground.

Should we have all gotten on this train no doubt but the guards would have made a great bluff but I am also satisfied that no attempt to use force to eject us would have been made, for at close range 6 men would stand but little show against us.

But, unfortunately for us all elements of warfare were against us, elemental, legal, and otherwise.

All that would have been necessary on their part would have been to abandon the train until such time as they could get reinforcements, or to use an other alternative i.e. let the train stand a few hours and we would be frozen and starved off and eventually be compelled to walk to some place where we could secure food.

I feel satisfied that should we have made a persistent show of strength at Siskiyou that in the end we would have been beaten, or perhaps shot to pieces, all our efforts nullified, our progress blocked everywhere, and in the end we would have segregated and the object of our trip remained unrealized.

Again, it had been reported to us that the militia were waiting for us at the California line, so granting that we could have ridden this train we could not expect to be able to cope with the state militia.

It must at all times be admitted that the Southern Pacific Rail Road can muster a greater fighting strength in the state of California than we could at that time. So much for our position.

Later developments I believe have justified the correctness of this position and prove beyond all question that we pursued the better tactics in consenting to walk and thereby emphasizing our determination to go to Fresno.

We later gained the support and sympathy of the citizens and press, we succeeded in advertising the Industrial Workers of the World as never before had been done, we were a great factor in winning the fight in Fresno, the trip was a school to us and the lessons learned there will be no doubt reflected and mirrored in the future work of organization.

It brought out the true character of men, there was a constant shifting of opinions, it was the means of drawing more closely together members of the organization between whom differences had been existing, and, while we suffered misery, hardship, exposure, and was a test of endurance, all readily recuperated and experience no ill effects of the trip, and, 'tis hoped we made REVOLUTIONISTS.

This report will be submitted to the remainder of the Com, for their approval so soon as their addresses are learned as we each pledged the other to allow of no false or mis-leading reports or statements of this trip to stand unchallenged and unrefuted, we wish but the truth to be circulated.

E. M. Clyde.

"On the Wobbly Train to Fresno," *Labor History* 14
(Spring 1973): 264-90.

The Fresno Free-Speech Fight
By H. MINDERMAN

One of the boys who went through the whole fight.

1910

October 16th	Arrest thirteen men. They have to sleep on the stone floor without blankets.
October 17th	Brought up for hearing; trial set for the 15th of November, 1910 and bonds are $250.00. Put in the cells four men in one cell and cell is like a steel cage. Cells are 7 feet 2 inches by 6 feet 9 inches and 8 feet 4 inches high.
October 19th	We are not allowed to wash ourselves or to use the toilet and we decided in the future not to eat if we didn't get a chance to wash ourselves. We got the watercure for demanding a wash.
October 20th	Hunger strike don't go through and we got the watercure again for demanding a wash. In our cell was an old miner eighty years old and he was game through the fight. Got bread diet,—two fifths of a five cent loaf of bread and two cups of brown beverage was all that we got.

October 21st   Got one minute to wash ourselves and we
                        got bread diet again.

October 22nd   Only bread and at 8:00 o'clock our clothes
                        were dry. 10:00 o'clock A.M. move to the
                        bull-pen. Bull-pen is eight feet high and 40
                        feet by 20 feet six inches and had eight little
                        windows, bath tub, closet and watersink. We
                        have a view of the street and the park. Seven-
                        teen beds for thirty-four men. At four
                        o'clock P.M. we got for meal, beans and punk
                        [rotten meat]. In the evening we have a
                        propaganda meeting and everyone is per-
                        mitted to speak five minutes. Majority de-
                        cided to obey the jail rules and to be good
                        prisoners in order that we get the good will
                        of the sheriff. The reason that our hunger
                        strike did not go through in the beginning
                        was that we were in jail not to eat, but to
                        win free speech.

October 23rd   Salvation Army in jail.

October 25th   Propaganda meetings cause trouble. Cause
                        the few to cry out and the men are hungry;
                        that makes them cranky. Kicking against the
                        jailor or sheriff is against the rules and so we
                        kick one another.
                            Decided to cut our propaganda meetings
                        and we find that we get twice a week, raisins
                        in place of meat.

October 26th   Kicking one against another. Decided to
                        make two crews to sleep.

October 27th   Nineteen beds for forty-seven men. Last
                        night some of the men got back their fight-
                        ing spirit and kicked against the jailor. In the
                        day time we sent a committee to the sheriff

to ask him that we shall be treated the same
as the other prisoners. Answer was because
we did not obey the rules of the jail. (We
had obeyed them all the time we were in the
bull-pen) — he can't do this. A little later on
he promised us a bed for everyone, provided
we were good boys. We decided to be good
and about every one was a jailor over the
other. I count my beans today, — (146)
beans, two little potatoes, two fifths of a
five-cent loaf of bread, one half cubic inch
of meat, sometimes bone and two cups of
brown beverage, and twice in the week some
raisins instead of meat. In the evening we
got thirty mattresses, thus a bed for everyone. We send Little out on bonds to com-
municate with the outside. Bull-pen in-
spected and repaired.

October 28th   They put three lamps on the outside of
the bull-pen and they put a guard there to
watch us. Three of the men who did not
come to jail to eat but to fight for free speech,
plead guilty and left us.

October 29th   Three more of the fighters leave us and we
remain with forty-four.

October 30th   Chew the rag over the Salvation Army.

October 31st   Three men plead guilty and eight more
come in making forty-nine.

November 1st   Motion for hunger strike lost, eleven for
with twenty against. Doree organized four-
teen men to plead guilty at once and refuse
to stay in jail one day longer. We got them
as far so they would stay if we sent a committee to the sheriff that we shall all be

liberated if we quit this fight and if the sheriff or chief refuse this they will stay until Hell freezes over. We elect a committee.

November 2nd   All brought to police court and have to plead guilty. Committee had told us nothing about this. Three men refuse to plead guilty and were put into jail again. The rest get three month floaters and had to leave town and county within three hours. We all got to our camp and postponed the fight and intended to come back if the rank and file of the I.W.W. is willing to fight.

November 27th   Little made a speech and told what the master-class has done in the Goldfield and Cripple Creek Country.[17] Pointed out the necessity of organization and as example took the police. He told them that the law in California is that every State, County or City officials shall work not more than eight hours a day, but that the police in Fresno work ten hours a day. If the police obeyed this law, they lose their job because they are not organized and the best that the police could do in Fresno was to organize, in order to enforce the law in their own behalf. This was called by the authorities, abusing the police and dangerous for Fresno, and for this reason the permit was revoked. One man who got a floater was arrested.

November 28th   We send three men out to get arrested in order to make a test case.

November 29th   Everybody except committee goes out to speak on the street, twenty-three men altogether. We did this to prevent the men being isolated in the cells and their spirit being broken in the start of the fight. Two men clubbed in jail.

November 30th   Five men got a hearing and trial set for some time in the other month; all men put in the bull-pen except Roe, LeBlank and Lefferts because they had floated. Our feed is three times more than in the first round. We had exposed what feed they had given us. The Socialists promise us a lawyer for one man in the test case, — bonds are $500.00.

December 1st   The others get hearing, — get the same dope, — Two arrested.

December 2nd   Seven men arrested. We are permitted to use tobacco and bought $1.00 worth and got tobacco and towels which were sent from camp.

December 3rd   Thirteen came in.

December 4th   Five came in and we got a small piece of bread for our breakfast. Some think they are shortening our rations and others think that they were short on bread this morning and that it is better to wait until we know if they are shortening our food before taking action.

December 5th   We are fifty-six men strong and get notice that three of our men are on a hunger strike in the black-hole.

December 6th   Battleships,[18] are made in the black-hole and got the watercure. This is the first time the night jailor has given someone the water-cure in eight years and the men in the black-hole are raising hell, too. At 11:00 o'clock A.M. Lefferts is taken out of the cell and brought into the bull-pen. He had not eaten or drank anything for four days and was soaking wet.

December 8th   Little brought to trial without jury and gets free. Roe and LeBlank are permitted to visit us. Roe had not eaten in five days and LeBlank in three days.

December 9th   One in and told us that ten men more are coming but nobody came. Murdock got a jury trial and found guilty. Jury out three quarters of an hour. We got notice that we had a splendid meeting in the street last night and that nobody was arrested except the man that came into the bull-pen this morning.

December 10th   We got notice that the police had organized a mob with the help of the fire department, Pinkertons, and thugs and had mobbed our speaker, — after this the mob had gone to our camp and burned down the tent and took away everything they could carry. The mob was about five hundred strong. After this the mob came to the jail and wanted to mob us. The jailor and a trustee, in for murder, and who had helped the thugs in clubbing two men in jail, thought the mob was an I.W.W. mob and they closed the safety doors and hid themselves in a safe place in jail. Murdock got six months.

December 13th   We get underwear and shoes every day for two or three men. Filigno brought for trial and found guilty.

December 14th   Filigno got six months.

December 15th   Got a telegram from headquarters if we
                       wanted a lawyer (Moore). We meet and thirty-
                       two noes to thirty-nine yeas.

December 17th   Twelve men came in.

December 18th   Lawyer Moore, visits us and stated that
                       he had an understanding with the prosecuting
                       attorney, — that all prisoners be liberated
                       and that the men who had a sentence, paroled
                       if the chief agree to this and that the city
                       shall make an ordinance and the legality of
                       this ordinance shall be fought out in the
                       courts. He advised us to accept this. In re-
                       gard to the mobbing of our members and
                       burning of our camp he could not do any-
                       thing, because headquarters did not have the
                       money to meet the expense. We called a
                       meeting but there was so much misunderstand-
                       ing that we decided to take no action in this
                       matter until we got some better information.

December 19th   White of the free speech committee visited
                       us and wanted our vote on the following
                       proposition, — All prisoners shall be liberated
                       and leave town. We notify headquarters that
                       the fight is over and that they send no more
                       men to Fresno. That the City Council shall
                       make an ordinance against street speaking
                       and we obey this and test the ordinance in
                       the courts. We refuse this by a unanimous
                       vote. Roe, LeBlank, Murdock and Filigno
                       were brought from the six months tank.
                       The sheriff bluffed them with the black-hole,
                       etc. They were breaking the discipline and
                       were a bad example for the other prisoners.
                       The sheriff told them they were permitted to
                       sing but that they had to keep quiet when the

telephone rang or was in operation. If we had
a kick coming to send a committee to him
and he promised to make it all right if he
could.

December 21st   Five men came in and bull-pen is overful.
Andrews brought to trial and found guilty.

December 22nd   Andrews got six months and White arrested.
In the evening a drunk in handcuffs got
clubbed by four thugs. We protested against
this and raise hell and called the sluggers all
kinds of names. We nominate a committee
as editor of the work. Stirton got the most
votes and was nominated.

December 23rd   We got water and bread diet. The big
majority refuse to take the bread. We de-
cided to go on a hunger strike because no
food at all was better and healthier than
water and bread. The experience in Spokane
had shown that the boys who had not eaten
at all, got back their health and of the boys
who took and ate the bread, two died and
some became invalids. For supper we sing
the red flag and other songs and that brought
some spectators to the jail. Five speeches
were made through the windows, explaining
what was going on in the jail. Every time the
spectators leave, we start to raise hell again
until there were some others and then the
speakers started to explain. The sheriff orders
the speakers to stop this, but we ordered him
to go ahead. Then we got the watercure. With
our mattresses we prevent the jailor from
driving our speaker from the window. There
are two sewerholes in the bull-pen and the
water flows into them as fast as they put it

in. This lasts for two hours, — then the fire
department came. They started with twenty
pounds pressure and the pressure is getting
stronger until it is one hundred and fifty
pounds. The stream bored a hole through
our mattresses in one minute. It knocked
the men down on the floor and they had to
stand against the wall in order not to get
drowned. Every time the stream struck a man
his body was paralyzed where the stream
struck. Schulz got the stream on his head and
he was lifted from the floor and then dropped
down. The top of his hat was torn off and
his eye badly hurt.

It is a wonder that nobody was killed. Another man got a sore ear and many got black
eyes. The fire engine was in operation for
one hour. After they quit, the water was one
foot deep but soon the sewer got stopped up
and we were refused a wire to fix this. After
this the sheriff told us that he was sorry
that he had done this, but that he was ready
to do it again and that we were to get our
full rations again in the morning. We get fifteen dry blankets for eighty-one men.

December 24th   One hour before breakfast time we got
breakfast and it was the biggest portion we
ever got. After breakfast we get underwear
for fifteen men and the sheriff told us the
same dope of four days ago about good treatment. We get eighty new mattresses and the
blankets were dried in the laundry. The
spirit of the men is the best they have ever
had in jail before.

December 25th   Sheriff puts guard on the outside of the
bull-pen. In the evening we had songs to kill

our victims in harmony. The mayor brought
a letter from Lefferts' mother and had a talk
with him. He said that he would never get
free speech and called him an intelligent
young man. Lefferts got no chance to talk
to him and said it was unnecessary waste of
time to talk any longer and he goes back to
the bull-pen and waited until the jailor came
and let him in.

December 27th   Five men came in. We learn that the papers
had printed that we had insulted women in
the jail and that was the cause the fire department gave us the watercure.

December 30th   White out on bonds. We don't get any
underwear or overalls till the new administration takes charge of the office.

1911

January 1st   Some of the boys lose their courage; there
is talk of giving up the fight, because the fight
is lost. The same cowardly arguments are
used in the first round, hiding their real
thought behind a lot of nonsense. Got news
that last night again a mob was before the
jail.

January 2nd   Nobody comes in and the future of the
fight looks dark. Murdock puts up a good
bluff in the way of a speech and that brought
back the spirit of the discouraged ones. After
he finished his speech, he got a slime cough
for an hour and a half and it was necessary
to call a doctor. The doctor got him in good
shape in ten minutes.
       At 10:00 o'clock P.M. the night jailor
came in the bull-pen and said that this was
his last night and he wished us good luck.

January 3rd   Only the men who are sentenced can get
                   clothing from the sheriff. Four men were
                   arrested for giving out leaflets. In the evening
                   the new jailor forbade us to sing, but the boys
                   did as they liked and sang a little bit louder.
                   The conservatives try to prevent this, — they
                   are afraid of the fire department set and a
                   big strong fellow strikes a little one because
                   he was singing. The boys stop singing to
                   prevent rag chewing and disorganization.

January 4th   They searched our beds and us, but they
                   find nothing. We were warned. One of the
                   searchers was very polite and he promised
                   us a dollar in the tobacco fund. Five men
                   came in.

January 5th   Three men plead guilty and that strong
                   fellow who strikes the little fellow for sing-
                   ing pled guilty also.

January 6th   The prosecutor came into the bull-pen and
                   had a talk with the men who had a sentence
                   and asked if they were willing to work in
                   the park. They said yes because that was
                   healthier than being inside of the jail all of
                   the time. He asked the men who had a float-
                   er why they came back and they told him
                   the treatment they had received in the first
                   round had forced them to accept the floater.

January 7th   Twelve men can go to work but only six
                   go out to work in the park. The health in-
                   spectors inspect the jail and the bull-pen.
                   They declare there is room for fifteen men
                   in the bull-pen but there are eighty-five.
                   Five men came in. Got telegram that Chief
                   Sullivan of Spokane is killed which made
                   some of the boys happy, —too bad.

January 8th   We are permitted to use Copenhagen [a
                               tobacco that gave a bitter, smokey aroma].
                               The old administration had refused us this,
                               because they were afraid of their eyes.

January 10th   Lefferts leaves the park gang and made a
                               speech in the city and got arrested. The
                               sheriff told him that he was fighting the city
                               himself and that it made it harder for him if
                               the boys made trouble with him. He prom-
                               ised not to punish him for this if he promised
                               not to do it again and the matter was settled.

January 11th   Little had a conversation with the health
                               inspector and he told Little that he was on
                               our side in the fight.

January 12th   Got the papers and there was a fine re-
                               port from the inspector in it about jail con-
                               ditions. Four men came in.

January 14th   We are allowed in the backyard for two
                               hours.

January 15th   Jealousy and chew the rag because some
                               men who had money got something out of
                               the store.

January 16th   The jailor cut the store business out. Two
                               volunteers who came in on the 9th and 16th
                               of December, plead guilty. Trouble over our
                               sour bread. After supper we get a letter from
                               Haslewood, and he stated that the locals are
                               against this fight and the locals are right to
                               do so and that the best for us to do was to
                               make a compromise. (It looks as though
                               everything is lost.) In the evening at our
                               propaganda meeting Filigno and others made

good speeches and statements about the way
of fighting and cause and effect in fighting
and that drove the clouds away.

January 17th   Four men plead guilty.

January 18th   One case dismissed and the man set at
                    liberty.

January 20th   One case dismissed.

January 21st   One case dismissed and two sent to the
                    hospital.

January 22nd   Two cases dismissed.

January 23rd   We get notice that we have a house from
                    Mr. Story free of rent as headquarters and
                    are prepared for an attack.

January 24th   Five men came in.

January 26th   Health inspector is a half day in the bull-
                    pen and everyone whose health is abnormal
                    write in his notice what ails him and sign his
                    name. We boycott the coffee store because
                    the Inter-Californian, a Socialist paper, whose
                    treasurer is the owner of the Coffee store,
                    knocked our fight in Spokane.

January 29th   Six men plead guilty.

January 31st   Three cases are dismissed and the men
                    liberated one minute before supper. The
                    Socialist Party condemns the actions of the
                    authorities in Fresno against the I.W.W. and
                    the health inspector is again for a long time
                    in the bull-pen speaking with us.

February 1st   Two cases are dismissed and two men
                      have rheumatism and can't leave their beds.
                      The first stone for the rock pile is delivered
                      Little got a trial in Selma and got free. Jury
                      was out four minutes.

February 2nd   The guards in the park gang made trouble
                      and the park gang went back to the bull-pen.
                      The sheriff had a talk with them and told
                      them they could work as they liked, but that
                      they must not divide themselves over the
                      whole park because then the guards could
                      not know where they were. After the trouble
                      was settled the sheriff said that the rock was
                      not there for the I.W.W. to crush. Fifteen
                      cases are dismissed and two men taken to
                      the hospital. Sixty-seven men are now in
                      jail.

February 3rd   Five cases are dismissed. Some of them
                      come under the new City Ordinance. Thirteen
                      men arrested.

February 4th   Eight cases are dismissed.

February 5th   Seven men arrested and six of them liber-
                      ated before they arrive at jail. They spoke
                      again and got rearrested. Five men liberated
                      and ten came in.

February 6th   Eleven came in and two out.

February 7th   The Health Inspector interviewed us
                      through the bars. He is out of his job and
                      gave us tobacco, and stated that we would
                      win this fight if we stuck to it. Six came in
                      and one case dismissed because the man had
                      sold out papers and had not spoken on the

street. The sheriff complains that we have
a chance to smuggle something into the jail
from the store. He said that we must give
the money to him with our order for tobacco
etc. and that he will buy the things we want
himself. We instruct our committee to tell
him that he can appoint a store where we
shall buy and that our committee on the outside will pay the store and not the sheriff.
In case the sheriff refuses this they shall tell
him that we do not believe in discrimination
and that we will not behave as we are doing
at present. This motion was carried by a vote
of 33 to 23.

February 8th

The city demanded that the sheriff starve
us out of jail. The Mayor offered Murdock
his liberty, if we went back to Seattle. (Murdock had been sentenced to six months.)
He refuses this. Three came in.

February 9th

Three came in.

February 10th

Roe's time is out.

February 11th

Lefferts' time is out; he was very cranky
the last few days and some more of the old
timers had the same sickness.

February 12th

Two came in.

February 14th

One half hour we get in the backyard.
One pled guilty and got forty days. Three
men before the jury trial and they got forty
days. Telegram from Whitehead Seattle
that help is coming and that we must stick
to it.

February 15th   We get ten mattresses. Five men came in
                       and two got fired from the park gang. Ten
                       were up for trial and got forty days.

February 17th   Work on the rock pile starts. Nine men
                       came in.

February 18th   Ten men got fired from the rock pile. One
                       man went to the hospital. This makes three
                       men in the hospital who are very sick.

February 19th   The prosecuting attorney had a conference
                       with our committee and offered that if we
                       plead guilty that we would not get more than
                       forty days; that he would do all he could to
                       liberate the men who are sentenced and that
                       we can speak on the county ground in the
                       park. At our meeting we instructed our com-
                       mittee to ignore the proposition. Ten men
                       taken out of the bull-pen and put in another
                       part of the jail.

February 20th   Six men to jury trial at 7:30 P.M. and get
                       forty days.

February 21st   Two men came in and eight were for trial.
                       We are now one hundred and fifteen men
                       strong in jail.

February 22nd   We had a meeting in regard to the Portland
                       Conference and we protested against the ac-
                       tions this Conference has taken in establish-
                       ing a district organization and decided to
                       send this protest to our papers and our locals
                       on the coast[19] by a vote of seventy-nine to
                       four in the bull-pen. The sheriff notified the
                       police that the jail is over-full and that he
                       would refuse to take men in the jail for
                       breaking the city ordinance. The chief said

that in that case he would arrest our men on another charge.

February 23rd   Man came in for disturbing the peace.

February 24th   We decided that we would advise our fellow worker to take a change of venue to the county judge.

February 25th   The chief visited the rock pile and got an ovation from the boys and they told him such fine things that he leaves us very quick. A committee from the Chamber of Commerce interviewed our committee about the fight and what our demands were.

February 27th   The sheriff offered us a compromise that he says he can make stick.[20] This compromise is all that we are demanding, with the exception of one street of minor value to us. We notified him that we are in favor for this if we got it in more definite form. We got all of the men in the jail and bull-pen to decide on this proposition. We got news that the public is mobbing our speaker again. The time for three of the men is out.

February 28th   Ten men taken out to clean the streets by the courthouse, but they refuse to do this. They were brought back to the bull-pen and in order that the city could not put us on bread and water, the sheriff put all sentenced men on the rock pile. The amount of rock crushed per day and per man is one fourth cubic foot. The citizens committee gave us the statement that we can get what the sheriff had just put before us if we promised to leave the city and to make no more inflammatory speeches. We refused this and instructed our committee to strike out the clause referring to leaving town and inflammatory speeches and to bring this before the citizens committee. The committee accept this and bring it before the citizens committee at 10:00 o'clock tomorrow morning.

They declared they have no power to accept or refuse this and that at 10:00 o'clock tomorrow morning they will be discharged. One man came out of the hospital. There are now one hundred and twelve men in the jail and one man is very sick in the hospital.

March 1st   The sheriff notifies us this afternoon that our terms had been accepted by the city.

March 2nd   The men who need shoes or underwear or overalls can get them if they go to work on the rock pile. Thirty-five men are liberated.

March 3rd   This is the last of the diary. There is only to be added that within three days all of the I.W.W. men in Fresno jail were released and that when they left the jail they took most of the rock pile with them. They had made it up into souvenirs of the Free Speech Fight. These souvenirs they distributed among their different locals and their friends. We might also add that from this time on the police did not intercept their meetings, neither did they molest members of the organization. They even quit arresting men for petty offenses such as vagrancy, disturbing the peace, etc.

United States Commission on Industrial Relations,
National Archives, Washington, D.C., C.M.E., 12-7-14,
Serial No. 819.

Aberdeen Free-Speech Fight, 1911-1912

Introduction

For several months after the Fresno victory, the I.W.W. in California and other Pacific states had only to threaten to use "Fresno tactics" to win the right of free speech. Wobblies who had been arrested for speaking on the streets and arraigned before a judge were quickly released because of fear of an I.W.W. invasion similar to the one that had taken place in Fresno. Thus the Wobblies could hold their street meetings unmolested.[1]

Employers frightened by these I.W.W. successes decided that new tactics were needed to prevent the Wobblies from achieving victory after victory. The M. & M. (Merchants' and Manufacturers' Association) in various West Coast cities and towns organized a counter-free-speech movement to smash the I.W.W.'s right to free speech as the first step in their drive to destroy the I.W.W. The M. & M. strategy was to organize small armies of vigilantes or deputies to invade the jails, drive the Wobblies out of town, and, by the most brutal terror, keep them out. Harrison Gray Otis, whose *Los Angeles Times* was an official spokesman for the M. & M., summed up the brutal strategy: "During the visit of the Industrial Workers of

the World they will be accorded a night and day guard of
honor, composed of citizens armed with rifles. The Coroner
will be in attendance at his office every day."[2]

The tactic of deputizing citizen police and deporting I.W.W.
members was first unfolded in Aberdeen, Washington, chief
center of Grays Harbor, heart of the lumber kingdom belong-
ing to Frederick Weyerhaeuser. Anticipating an organizing
drive by the I.W.W. among the lumber workers who came into
Aberdeen, the City Council issued an ordinance in the summer
of 1911 forbidding speaking and assembling on all the principal streets. This was later amended to permit all organizations
except the I.W.W. to hold meetings in the streets. Although
the Socialist Party, which had not been banned from the
streets, declared itself satisfied with the action of the City
Council, Wobblies and liberals in Aberdeen demanded the ban
be rescinded. They were supported by the national office of
the I.W.W. Chicago headquarters warned the mayor of
Aberdeen in November 1911 that the I.W.W. would not accept
the ordinance, and intended to force its repeal or "make the
grass grow in the street."[3]

When this warning was ignored, the Wobblies violated the
law. Police arrested five speakers on the evening of November
22, 1911, and marched them through the streets to jail. Late
that same night, a mob of vigilantes, including many of the
leading businessmen of the city, attempted to break into the
jail and lynch the prisoners. They were held back by the police,
but let the Wobblies in jail know that they would return.
The next day, the vigilantes organized themselves more effi-
ciently. Five hundred of the city's "most prominent business
and professional" men formed a battalion of special police.
The Mayor deputized them immediately and, armed with clubs,
the deputized vigilantes took command of the city. When
Wobblies and liberal sympathizers attempted to hold a mass
protest meeting in the Empire Theatre, the deputies roped off
the street and assisted the police in arresting all persons approaching the theatre. The *Aberdeen Daily World* proudly announced that "W. J. Patterson, president of the Hayes and
Hayes bank, and Dudley G. Allen, secretary of the Chamber

of Commerce, cooperated in making the first arrest in front of the theatre."[4]

In spite of the "armed terror," the Wobblies persisted in speaking on the streets. They were arrested and turned over to the citizen police to escort them to jail. The *Portland Oregonian* gleefully reported that few of the prisoners arrived in jail without broken heads and limbs. "The citizen police have been armed with wagon spokes and axe handles for use as clubs, and these weapons have proved most effective." The *Industrial Worker* condemned the conspiracy of "the gang of sluggers in Aberdeen to club our members to death," but advised against meeting terror with terror: "We must be prepared to meet these new tactics and we must not meet them with axe handles because we have the queer faculty of knowing that there is no such thing as *equality before the law.*" The Wobblies met the "new tactics" with the usual pattern of free-speech fighting. Wobbly after Wobbly spoke, was arrested, and jailed. And the usual appeal went out to Wobblies throughout the West: "On to Aberdeen. Free Speech fight on. . . . Help is needed at once. On to Aberdeen."[5]

In December the citizen deputies decided to end the practice of keeping the Wobblies in jail, "allowing them to feed off the taxpayers." They collected the prisoners at the jail, beat them viciously, escorted them out of town, and warned them not to return. "God bless you if you go, God help you if you return" were the usual parting words to the workers, some of whom had lived in Aberdeen for many years and left families behind who depended on their support. The armies of vigilantes patrolled the streets, ready to attack and deport any Wobblies on sight, and even broke into outlying jungles where Wobblies congregated while preparing to invade Aberdeen, and drove them out.[6]

Terrorist tactics did not stop the Wobblies. With the aid of new arrivals, I.W.W. headquarters, previously closed down in raids by the citizen police, were reopened, and the speaking at street corners resumed. "Not one sentence was finished by any of the speakers," the *Portland Oregonian* reported from Aberdeen on January 12, 1912. That night fifteen men were

arrested, blindfolded and taken in automobiles beyond the
city limits by the citizen police, who beat them and warned
them never to return. But there were enough Wobblies on
hand to put ten men on the street every night for two weeks.
Speakers continued to be arrested, but the mayor, at the suggestion of the "pick-handle brigade," began to negotiate with
a committee of the I.W.W. elected by the men in jail. (A boycott of Aberdeen merchants by workers in the Grays Harbor
area, outraged by the reign of terror, helped bring about the
move to negotiate a settlement.) The negotiations resulted in
"a clean-cut unqualified victory for the Industrial Workers of
the World."[7] On January 7, 1912, the City Council passed a
new ordinance setting aside five of the most populated streets
in the city for street meetings. No permit would be required
by any organization wishing to hold meetings on these corners.
In addition, the City Council agreed to indemnify the I.W.W.
local for damages to its headquarters (to the sum of $40) dur-
ing the fight.[8]

"Aberdeen recently made famous as the city ruled by wagon
spoke and axe handle, has again restored the right of free
speech to its citizens," a New York paper reported. A huge
victory street meeting was held on the evening of January 18,
at which it was announced that a new campaign to organize
the lumber workers would be launched. A month later, the
I.W.W. local reported the formation of the Marine Workers'
Industrial Union in Aberdeen, with 31 charter members, and
noted gleefully: "This is a pretty pill for the pick-handle experts to swallow."[9]

The account of the Aberdeen free-speech fight was published
seven years later in the I.W.W. journal *One Big Union Monthly*.
C. E. Payne, the author, had been secretary of the Aberdeen
Free-Speech Committee, and his account discloses the I.W.W.'s
determination to uphold free speech despite police brutality.

The Mainspring of Action
By C. E. PAYNE

In the fall of 1911 occurred the Aberdeen, Washington,
Free Speech fight. Altho shorter than many of the contests of

this character that took place thruout the West shortly before and after that time, it was, while it lasted, one of the most bitterly contested struggles in which the organization took part. Also, it was by all odds the most clean-cut victory that was won by the organization in struggles of this character.

One phase of the fight that has not to my knowledge been touched upon was the psychology of the men who took part in it at the time the final and winning attack was made to regain the use of the streets for purposes of agitation. I had an exceptional opportunity to observe this state of mind, which for a better term may perhaps be properly called a religious fervor.

I had been for some time the secretary for the Free Speech Committee, and had been in the town for about six weeks before the evening of January 10, 1912, when the grand rush was made to use the streets for "free speech." As I had the correspondence of the Committee in hand at the time, I was ordered not to take any part in the demonstration for that night. However, some one had been making it his business to find out my business, and this, together with my interest in the proceedings, made a change in the program, and this change gave me the opportunity to observe this psychological phenomenon.

The demonstration was timed for 6:00 P.M., when it was figured the members of the Citizens' Club would be at supper, and it was thought this would give some of the men a chance to make a few minutes' talk before they could be arrested. Fifteen men had been selected to make the first attack. The manner of selecting them was by refusing to permit any one to speak unless he plainly stated that he would speak anyhow, permit or none. The Committee had decided that fifteen should be the number, but seventeen was the number that actually took part in the "speaking."

Wishing to be able to make a first-hand report of what took place on the streets, I went among the crowd, which in a few minutes after six o'clock had grown to some 3,000 persons, all eager to see the demonstration. These were gathered around the principal street corner, but there was no one in the center of the street. By common consent this was left entirely to the participants in the battle.

The first speaker would have been able to hold a crowd with a speech of half an hour or more had he been allowed the time, but he was arrested and hustled off to jail within less than two minutes after he had shouted "Fellow Workers." No sooner had he been taken thru the crowd toward the jail by two members of the Citizens' Club, than another man stepped out from the crowd and began, "Fellow Workers!" This man's voice had the twang of the Down East Yankee, and his bearing was that of a descendant of the Pilgrims of the Mayflower.

Following him came a short, swarthy German, evidently from the Schwartzwald. "Mein Fellow Vorkers! Schust you listen by me vhile I tells you sometings!" But what that "something" was he could not tell before he was seized and hustled in the wake of the other two. After the German came a large, raw-boned Irishman with the brogue of the ould sod thick on his tongue. "Fellow Workers! Oi'm not much of a spaker, but Oi don't suppose Oi'll be allowed to talk long, anyhow." That was all the speech he was allowed to make before he too was led away.

Next in line was an Italian who shouted the regular greeting of "Fellow Workers," spoke a few rapid fire words and was taken towards the jail. From another part of the crowd a five-foot man with the unmistakable rolling gait of a sailor sprang to center of the cleared street, shouted "Fellow Workers," and had time enough to make perhaps the longest "speech" of the evening. "I have been run out of this town five times by the Citizens' Club, and every time I have found my way back. This proves conclusively that the world is round." But when he had gone thus far with his remarks he was seized and half carried toward the jail. Behind the sailor came a lumber jack, no talker, but a power in the woods where men hold their place by strength and nerve. "Fellow Workers! There is one of the Citizens' Club fellows over there. He is going to arrest some one." The man pointed out at once made a run for the lumber worker, and he too was taken to jail.

Thus came one after another, made the common salutation of "Fellow Workers," started to talk and generally managed to say but a few words, when he too was hustled to the jail. The entire demonstration was over in less than half an hour and the crowd began to disperse. It was while leaving the scene of the demonstration that I was approached from behind by two men who came one on either side of me, and with the re- mark, "Oh, say! The chief wants to see you," they led me to the jail.

My arrest was the last one of the night. After being searched and questioned by the police, I was put in the "tank" with the rest of the "free speech fighters." My reception was the hearti- est demonstration of welcome I have ever received. Their joy seemed to be combined with an appreciation of the joke on me, but it was none the less hearty.

After the greetings had been made, and things became com- paratively quiet, I was able to look about me and see at close range the manner of men they were. Outwardly, they were of the careless, happy-go-lucky sort to whom dolce far niente appeared to be a more appropriate motto than any other that could be selected. Not one had any ties of kindred, job or financial interest in the town. Most of them had never been in the place before. Perhaps a majority never would have been there had not some member of the I.W.W. flashed the word over the country that he and others were denied the rights they claimed. Many of them would never be there again.

Here they were, eighteen men in the vigor of life, most of whom came long distances thru snow and hostile towns by beating their way, penniless and hungry, into a place where a jail sentence was the gentlest treatment that could be expected, and where many had already been driven into the swamps and beaten nearly to death by members of the Citizens' Club for the same offense that they had committed so joyously to- night. All had walked the three miles from Hoquiam in a rain to take part in the demonstration that all confidently felt would mean that they would be sent to jail until midnight, and then be driven into the swamps with clubs and guns, and that perhaps some of them would be killed, as had nearly been the case with others before them. Yet here they were, laugh- ing in boyish glee at tragic things that to them were jokes.

One man said, "This is cold after the orange groves of California." The man he spoke to replied, "It is not as cold as the Canadian railways." One man remarked, "The snow in the Rockies is a fright," to which another replied, "It don't be worse than the Siskyouss."

A ponderous German recited the Marxian battle cry.[10] Two men compared notes on their arrests, and laughed gleefully at some joke on a policeman. One boy who had taken a "vacation" from college to attend the Free Speech fight had composed a "yell," and this was frequently shouted with all their power. "Who are we? I.W.W., don't you see! First in war, first in peace, first in the hands of the Aberdeen police. Rah! Rah!! Rah!!! I.W.W." As the city council had been called into extra session to consider the situation, and their meeting hall was just above the tank where we were locked in, there was always extra emphasis put on the "I.W.W." for their benefit.

But what was the motive behind the actions of these men? Clearly, they would take no part in the social, political or economic life of the town, after the fight was over. No place in the country could treat them worse than Aberdeen was trying to treat them. Why were they here? Is the call of Brotherhood in the human race greater than any fear or discomfort, despite the efforts of the masters of life for six thousand years to root out that call of Brotherhood from our minds? Is there a joy in martyrdom that the human race must sense at times to make its life complete? Must humanity ever depend on the most despised of its members for its most spiritual gifts? Is it among the working class that we may see the fulfillment of the prediction that there shall be no Greek or Barbarian, no Scythian or Parthian, no circumcision or uncircumcision, but all one? These things have I often pondered as the result of the twenty-two hours in the Aberdeen jail.

One Big Union Monthly, March 1919.

San Diego Free-Speech Fight, 1912

Introduction

Brutal as the struggle in Aberdeen was, it was surpassed by
the free-speech fight in San Diego, California, which began
early in 1912 and continued for more than a year and a half. On
January 8, 1912, the San Diego City Council passed an ordinance creating a "restricted" district of forty-nine blocks in
the center of town on which no street-corner meetings could
be held. Unlike ordinances in other cities banning street-speaking, the one in San Diego made no exception for religious
speeches. All street-speaking was banned in the so-called con-
gested district. The reason given was that the meetings blocked
traffic, but it was clear that the real purpose was to suppress
the I.W.W.'s effort "to educate the floating and out-of-work
population to a true understanding of the interests of labor
as a whole," as well as the organization's determination to
organize the workers in San Diego who had been neglected by
the A.F. of L. Among these neglected workers were the mill,
lumber, and laundry workers and streetcar conductors and
motormen. The I.W.W.'s actions had infuriated John D.
Spreckels, the millionaire sugar capitalist and owner of the

streetcar franchise; he and other employers had applied pressure on the council to pass the ordinance. Certainly, San
Diego's traffic flow was not the problem; no one believed that
this southern California town would suffer a transportation
crisis if street-corner meetings continued.[1]

On February 8, 1912, the day on which the ordinance went
into effect, 38 men and three women were arrested for violating
the ban against speaking on the streets. During the next few
days more street-speakers were arrested, and on February 12,
I.W.W. Local 13 informed I.W.W. headquarters of what was
happening and affirmed: "Will fight to a finish." The word
spread in the hobo jungles that

> Out there in San Diego
> Where the western breakers beat,
> They're jailing men and women
> For speaking on the street.[2]

Wobblies began to arrive in San Diego. On February 13,
Superintendent of Police John C. Sehon issued orders for a
general roundup of all vagrants. That same evening the police
arrested several men as they rose to speak to an audience of
a thousand people. On foot and by rail, Wobblies continued
to pour into town, and within a few days the police filled the
four jails with 280 men and women. Still they came, and the
I.W.W. assured San Diego authorities that the fight would be
fought to a finish "if it takes 20,000 members and twenty
years to do so."[3]

The response of the authorities was to follow the advice of
the *San Diego Union.* Beatings, deportations, and other tactics
of terror should be invoked if necessary, it declared, "and this
is what these agitators (all of them) may expect from now on,
that the outside world may know that they have been to San
Diego." "If this action be lawlessness, make the most of it,"
the *Union* challenged.[4]

Following this advice, the police did not merely arrest the
free-speech advocates; they beat them en route to prison;
shoved them into a jail built to accommodate not more than

sixty inmates but which already had over 150 prisoners
in it; fingerprinted and photographed them for the rogues'
gallery; provided the prisoners with meager foods twice
a day, which frequently caused them to suffer from diarrhea.
Vigilantes began to work hand in hand with police soon after
the first arrests. Prisoners were turned over to squads of
vigilantes at midnight, night after night, and were rushed in
autos to the county line or twenty miles into the desert. There
they were beaten with clubs, threatened with death if they returned, and left in the desert. Not content with these tactics,
vigilantes met the freight cars at the San Onofre county line
(where there was a large camp of heavily armed cohorts),
ordered the Wobblies off the cars, beat them unmercifully,
forced them to kiss the American flag and to run a gauntlet
of 106 men armed with clubs, whips, and guns, and put them
on trains going north.[5]

Michael Hoey, a sixty-five-year-old member of the I.W.W.
and a veteran of three free-speech fights, was arrested and
jailed by the police, who kicked him repeatedly in the groin.
Seriously injured and insensible, he was thrown into an over-
crowded cell where he lay on a cement floor for several days.
The prison physician who finally visited him let him remain
in jail. After forty days in jail, Hoey was removed to the hospital, where he died several days later. The coroner's jury
rendered a verdict that death was caused by tuberculosis of the
lung and valvular disease of the heart. Not a word was said
about the rupture caused by the police beating, nor about with-
holding proper medical treatment from an old man in jail.[6]

Responding finally to widespread protests over events in
"Barbarous San Diego," Governor Hiram Johnson sent State
Commissioner Harris Weinstock "to investigate charges of
cruelty in all matters pertaining to the recent disturbances
in the City of San Diego, California." Commissioner Weinstock
held open hearings on April 18-20, in the grand jury room of
the San Diego Courthouse, at which he heard testimony from
many free-speech witnesses and some city and county officials.
In addition, he conducted his own extensive investigation of
the free-speech battle. Then he submitted a long and closely

documented report to the governor which was officially published by the state of California in 1912.

Although he was critical of the I.W.W.'s general principles
and specific practices and attacked their free-speech tactics,
Weinstock vigorously condemned San Diego's police and other
officials, its press, and its leading citizens, who comprised the
bulk of the vigilantes:

> Your commissioner has visited Russia and while there has
> heard many horrible tales of high-handed proceedings
> and outrageous treatment of innocent people at the hands
> of despotic and tyrannic Russian authorities. Your com-
> missioner is frank to confess that when he became satis-
> fied of the truth of the stories, as related by these un-
> fortunate men (victims of police and vigilante brutality
> in San Diego), it was hard for him to believe that he still
> was not sojourning in Russia, conducting his investigation
> there, instead of in this alleged "land of the free and
> home of the brave." Surely, these American men, who as
> the overwhelming evidence shows, in large numbers
> assaulted with weapons in a most cowardly and brutal
> manner their helpless and defenseless fellows, were cer-
> tainly far from "brave" and their victims far from "free."[7]

Despite repeated appeals to Governor Johnson to follow up
Weinstock's report with an indictment of the vigilantes, no
such action was taken. So the free-speech fight continued during the summer and early fall of 1912, with new replacements
arriving each week. At various times there were 500-1,000
Wobblies in San Diego. The original strength of the I.W.W.
when the campaign started was not more than fifty men![8]

Some free-speech fighters in San Diego were released from
jail; others, however, were tried, fined, and sentenced to prison
terms. Still the battle continued. In January 1914, the I.W.W.
pledged that "the fight in San Diego shall be carried to a finish
for absolute and unrestricted free speech with no compromise."
It took until the summer of 1914, but the right of the I.W.W.
to hold street meetings was established. San Diego had been

restored to civilization, and George Edwards, one of the decent elements in the city who supported the free-speech fight, noted that "out of the fire (of the free-speech fight) has come the intellectual salvation not only of the martyrs, but of all the inhabitants of the city."[9]

The two personal accounts of the San Diego free-speech fight that follow are by Wobblies who suffered the travail of police and vigilante brutality and reported their experiences to the Commission on Industrial Relations. Charles Hanson was also a veteran of the Fresno free-speech fight. Alfred R. Tucker is mentioned frequently in E. M. Clyde's "On the Wobbly Train to Fresno."

The last piece is the eulogy delivered at the funeral of Michael Hoey by Laura Payne Emerson, an active I.W.W. speaker, organizer, and songwriter, who was a leading figure in the San Diego free-speech fight.

My Experience During the San Diego Free-Speech Fight
By CHARLES HANSON

Twenty members went from Los Angeles to San Diego on the boat from San Pedro. We arrived in San Diego and immediately asserted our right of Free Speech. We were arrested, locked up in the courthouse, kept all day, were taken out at eleven o'clock at night in automobiles, hand-cuffed together in three's, taken out 25 miles from San Diego and beaten up and what little money we had taken away and were told that if we returned they would kill us. We started on our way back to Los Angeles and were arrested at Ocean Side and were locked up for the night, turned out in the morning and told to keep on a moving with the law and order gang in the rear taking a drink now and then, all the while looking for trouble but we gave them no chance.

They left us at Cafestrana. We were in an exhausted condition by this time, as we had not had anything to eat since the time we landed in San Diego. We proceed to Los Angeles the next morning to organize again. This happened the latter part of March.

My second trip to San Diego, I left Los Angeles the second of April with 65 other fellow workers. We started to walk but soon a freight came along. We jumped in and got to Santa Ana, camped there for the night and next day held a street meeting. Miss T. Smith talked at the meeting which was a success. We left that night on a freight. This was April 3rd. We were all on a box car, the crowd cheered us as we left Santa Ana. The boys were in good humor and singing. I told them to be on the alert for something was sure to happen, because she was not making a stop at Cafestrana, but was going right on. My suspicions were soon to be realized, for all at once she came to a stop and a drunken mob of vigilantes came up both sides of the car with a gun in one hand and a club in the other, and on both sides of the track gunmen with rifles. They proceeded to club us off the car. There was no use resisting as we had nothing to defend ourselves with, although I felt like taking my chance. After we got on the ground we were made to hold up our hands while they were going through us. I was lucky to have the committee money, something like $38.00 besides $2.00 of my own money, wrapped around my leg. We were kept holding our hands up for an hour if not more. I was clubbed several times for letting my hands down, being tired. Clubbing became general when we were too exhaused to hold our hands up any longer. They then herded us in a cattle pen, made us lay down on the ground or rather manure pile. We were all bruised by this time. One fellow laying next to me had a couple of ribs broken, some were so bruised as to be uncomfortable to lay down, seeking relief by sitting up. Were punished by further clubbing and the usual expression "You son of a B— kill em." The whisky was arousing their spirits wonderfully. In the morning we were told to get up. We were wondering what was in store for us, but we were soon to find out. We were taken out in groups of five to be made to run the gauntlet as we were taken out in fives, another bunch were coming in from San Diego. Their looks told us of clubbing. Some could hardly walk, but their faces were determined. As the bunches of five were taken out and up the track to run the gauntlet, my experience, and as I saw them run the gauntlet the first thing on the program was

to kiss the flag. "You son of a B—, Come on Kiss it G— dam
you." As he said it I was hit with a wagon spoke all over; when
you had kissed the flag you were told to run the gauntlet. 50
men being on each side each man being armed with a gun and
a club and some had long whips. When I started to run the
gauntlet the men were ready for action, they were in high
spirits from booze. I got about 30 feet when I was suddenly
struck across the knee. I felt the wagon spoke sink in splitting
my knee. I reeled over. As I did I felt the club being withdrawn
with some effort. I fell on the side of the track. Two of the
vigilantes came up to me pointing their guns at me saying
"Get up you Son of a B—". The pain was intense. "You broke
my knee, you might as well kill me" I said. He lifted the club
and was about to strike when an onlooker grabbed him and
said "You let him alone, you coward or I will kill you." I told
him my knee was broken. He felt it and buried his hand in between my kneecap. As I was lying there I saw other fellow
workers running the gauntlet. Some were bleeding freely from
cracked heads, others were knocked down to be made to get
up and run again. Some tried to break the line only to be
beaten back. It was the most cowardly and inhuman cracking
of heads I ever witnessed. This happened at San Onofre April
4th. I was taken from there to Ocean Side in an automobile
and put in a lodging house there and kept up until April the
12th. Dr. Reed and partner, do not remember his name, has a
drug store in Ocean Side, tended to me while there. I was
watched day and night, a gunman sitting opposite my room
with a gun on the table. Two other fellow workers were
brought in there, Marcus and Hope. Hope had 9 or 10 stitches
in his head. He stayed with me for 7 days. Marcus was kept
one day. My knee all the time was swelling up and nobody was
allowed to see me. I was in constant fever, fever being as high
as 100. I was constantly asking the doctor when they would
send me to the hospital, but got no satisfactory answer. They
were trying to bring the bones together, which I told them
they could not do without an operation. At last came the day,
the 12th of April, when they took me on the train to San
Diego and put me in the County Hospital. Was in the County

Hospital two days before they operated on me. I will give Dr. Norten credit for doing a good job. He told me the knee cap was broken in three places. I laid in the hospital eight months, was treated bad on account of ignorant nurses with the exception of two that were radicals. The doctor told me that my good constitution was all that kept me from losing my leg, as it was it was a wonder. My lesson is passive resistance no more.

Yours for Industrial Freedom,

(Signed) CHAS. HANSON.

Letters, Etc., Addressed to Vincent St. John, by Various Writers, Commission on Industrial Relations File, National Archives, Washington, D.C.

San Diego Free-Speech Fight
By ALFRED R. TUCKER

In March, 1912, I was living at Victorville, Calif. The I.W.W. then was engaged in a Free-Speech Fight in San Diego for the right to speak on the streets. About the 10th of March I went to Los Angeles to see how the fight was coming out. I found it was lagging and no one willing to go. I met several of the free speech committee from San Diego. They were holding meetings and raising money but did not seem to be able to get any men to go to the fight. I talked with all the members around the hall and I found about a dozen men who said they would go if I would. Fellow Worker Reisick was then local secretary. He had been in the long march to Fresno and expressed the belief that we could get a bunch to go to San Diego if we could pay their fare on some boat. So the San Diego committee told us to get the men and they would furnish the money. So we went to work and soon had 27 men ready to go but the committee failed to come through with the money, so fellow worker Reisick went to work to raise the money by collection. As I had enough money to take myself I was sent two days ahead of the bunch to see how things were. I took passage on the steamer Governor from San Pedro to San Diego. When I arrived there I found the jails of both city and county

were full of free speech fighters; also a large bunch had been
sent to Riverside and Orange County jails. A committee of
some 2,000 small business men, mostly real estate dealers, had
been organized for the purpose of running the fighters out of
town. As they had no more room for them in jail, the city
authorities had prohibited speaking or selling papers any where
in the city. They would grab men and drag them into an automobile, take them outside of the town, give them a clubbing
and threaten their lives if they ever came back. This was about
the 18th of March, 1912. Two days later fellow worker Reisick
and the 27 men arrived by boat from Los Angeles, and after
resting a day we started to sell papers on the streets. We divided
up in threes, two going ahead selling papers, while one stayed
behind to watch the action of the police and vigilantes. We
had sold quite a few papers before they bothered us. Then they
commenced taking the papers away from the boys, arresting
some and turning them loose, so we soon ran out of papers.
They then confiscated the *San Diego Herald* and the *San Francisco Bulletins,* and would not allow us to sell any papers that
gave a fair report of the fight. The next day, being the 22nd of
March, at 2 o'clock P.M. 13 of us went out on the corner of
6th and E. Streets to hold a meeting. We started singing a song
entitled Casey Jones, the Scab Engineer.[10] We were immediately surrounded by plain clothes men, some of them police
and some vigilantes. They arrested the 13 of us and marched
us to the police station. We were placed in the court room and
our names taken. We asked what charge was placed against us
and they told us we would find out. Then they began picking
out men from among us and taking them in to another room
where, surrounded by police, they were put through the third
degree. In the meantime they brought in the rest of the 27
men. None of us had eaten for 24 hours, but they kept us
without food until about midnight. Then they divided us and
gave us a very severe lecture, telling us if we ever came back
they would bury us on some of their beautiful real estate. Then
we were ordered to march and they, I suppose returned to their
homes feeling they had done a good job. Hanson, Ross and I
walked on for a little way and overtook 3 more fellow workers
who had been brought out ahead of us. We then laid down on

the side of the track to rest and wait for the rest of the boys and before daylight there were 13 of us and some of them badly beat up. We walked to the next town and bought some food and then decided to go back to Los Angeles and get a bigger bunch of men and go back to San Diego. Just before we reached Ocean Side that evening we were arrested by a bunch of mounted constables and locked up in the Ocean Side jail over night. 13 of us in a cell 6 x 8 feet. The next day we were driven 30 miles without food or water by mounted constables. We had now reached the county line which is 70 miles from San Diego. Here our mounted escorts left us. We then waited till late in the night and caught a freight train and some rode clear into Los Angeles. However, a part of us were put off at Fullerton, 26 miles from Los Angeles and walked into town the next day.

After resting a day we went to work to get a large bunch of men to go back to San Diego. About this time 50 men from Fresno joined us and we recruited the bunch up to 93 men. About half of the bunch were boys under 21 years of age full of courage and enthusiasm, so we started again for San Diego. We walked out of town to a little station and caught a freight train and rode to Fullerton, when we decided to hold meeting and wait until the next night, which we did. Then we caught a train and rode to Santa Ana, where we stopped over another day and held meetings and tried to visit the 30 men we had in jail there from San Diego, but were unable to do so. That night April the 5th at 11:30 P.M. we boarded another train for the south. Train never stopped for 50 miles. It was then about 1 o'clock A.M. The train slowed down and we were between two lines of something like 400 men armed to the teeth with rifles, pistols and clubs of all kinds. The moon was shining dimly through the clouds and I could see pick handles, axe handles, wagon spokes and every kind of a club imaginable swinging from the wrists of all of them while they also had their rifles leveled at us. The train had stopped on a side track in the foot hills, where the only sign of civilization was a cattle corral, where they loaded cattle for shipment. We were ordered to unload and we refused. Then they closed in

around the flat car which we were on and began clubbing and
knocking and pulling men off by their heels, so inside of a half
hour they had us all off the train and then bruised and bleeding we were lined up and marched into the cattle corral, where
they made us hold our hands up and march around in the
crowd for more than an hour. They searched us for weapons
and not even a pocket knife was found. They searched us several
times, now and then picking out a man they thought was a
leader and giving him an extra beating. Several men were carried out unconscious and I believe there were some killed, for
afterwards there were a lot of our men unaccounted for and
never have been heard from since. The vigilantes all wore con-
stable badges and a white handkerchief around their left arms.
They were all drunk and hollering and cursing the rest of the
night. In the morning they took us out four or five at a time
and marched us up the track to the county line, which is about
a mile from the rest, where we were forced to kiss the flag and
then run a gauntlet of 106 men, every one of which was striking at us as hard as they could with their pick axe handles.
They broke one man's leg, and every one was beaten black and
blue, and was bleeding from a dozen wounds. We walked north
a few miles for the rest of the bunch. Some managed to ride
back to Los Angeles, but the most of us walked all the way
back to the city. My feet were swollen so I could hardly walk
for two or three weeks. Several other big bunches of men
went to the fight after this, but I was unable to go so this ends
my experience in Free-Speech Fights up to date. If I ever take
part in another it will be with machine guns or aerial bombs.

Yours for a better way of fighting and better results as well
as our final emancipation from all slavery and tyranny and
the building of the world-wide industrial commonwealth.

(Signed) ALFRED R. TUCKER,
Box 163,
Victorville, Calif.

Letters, Etc., Addressed to Vincent St. John, By Various Writers, Commission on Industrial Relations,
National Archives, Washington, D.C.

Eulogy to a Free-Speech Martyr
Delivered over the Remains of Michael Hoey
By LAURA PAYNE EMERSON

Fellow Workers:

I count it an honor to be accorded the privilege of paying a tribute on this occasion, to our martyred dead fellow worker, Michael Hoey. He was a soldier in the war for industrial freedom. Early in life he joined the forces that were making for better conditions for his class, the working class and to the day when he fell mortally wounded, and was carried from the field of battle never did he falter. It was in San Diego, California. A fight for free speech was on. An infamous ordinance had been passed by the common council denying the natural and constitutional right of free speech and public assembly to certain citizens. Many brave souls had undertaken to test the odious law by attempting to speak on the streets, and had met the policeman's club and the jail. Among those on the firing line in that contest was Michael Hoey at mid-sixty three years of age. When told by a friend he was too old to enlist in such a fight, and that he should leave it to younger and more vigorous men, he replied, "I have nothing to give but myself and life is not worth living when all liberty is gone." That night, amid a cheering crowd, his fine face appeared for a moment, while his voice was raised in a last appeal to his class to stand firm for human rights. Then burly guardians of the law snatched him down, and with kicks and clubs, jail and starvation silenced his voice forever. Shall we say forever? Can it be that such souls die? If it be true that the sea of oblivion engulfs those who leave this shore, and their voices are hushed in everlasting night, then Michael Hoey is dead: but from his ashes will spring ten thousand soldiers of freedom more powerful than he and the message upon his dying lips will be carried by millions of voices, shouted from the housetops and mountains of the world.

But if, as many teach, there is no death, and what seems so is but transition: if, within the infinitude of nature there is room and possibility for all creatures, and beyond the sunset

gates of earth the countless so-called dead survive, then
Michael Hoey is not dead, but with the hosts and martyrs to
the cause of progress he stands today transfigured, perhaps,
in form and face, wearing a garb and mien to suit the time and
place, yet the same in mind. If so, then the victims of the
snow-covered plains of Siberia, the dripping loathsome vaults
of San Juan Abua, the Hay Market riot,[11] and the thousands
from gallows, stake, bull pen and bastile are with him today,
and with us in spirit in our struggle for the abolition of this
capitalistic hell.

Our fellow worker was a hero in the strife. The army with
which he marched was not mounted, booted, not spurred,
neither do they carry arms, but from Maine to California their
camp-fires are burning, and from ocean to ocean the world
over their banner floats. What army is this? The grand army of
organized labor. They hope to win, not by taking up arms, but
by laying down tools. England at this moment is engaged in a
desperate conflict, where by these tactics the power of the
army is shown as never before in the history of the world.[12]
Michael Hoey belonged to that army, though on this side of
the sea, and freedom of speech is necessary to its existence.
That army is entrenched and its recruits fast being mustered
wherever wage slaves bend beneath their burdens, wherever
capitalism has laid its withering hand. They hope to win peacefully, but if that be not possible, they will win. They must.

And today standing beside the bier of this our fellow worker,
martyr in the world's greatest revolution, we solemnly swear to
carry on the battle with renewed energy, and to never stop
until we avenge his death, and achieve victory in the cause for
which he died.

And now, friend, fellow worker, we leave you to rest. Far
from friends and relatives of other days, we are your friends.
Today, after your long, labourious life, you repose beneath a
coverlet of flowers. Your weary body oft neglected in life,
is tenderly cared for in death. Such is the irony of fate. You
who, no doubt as others of your class, oft driven from place
to place with no shelter, nowhere to lay your head now find
a place of abode where hunger shall not overtake you, and

where no policeman's club, will bruise you, nor gruff voice
bid you "move on." You have fought your fight, you have
finished your work. Although a private in the ranks you wear
a laurel wreath upon your brow. You have given your all.
A Christ could do no better. "An injury to one is an injury
to all." We shall not forget.

San Diego *Labor Leader*, April 5, 1912.

6

Denver Free-Speech Fight, 1913

Introduction

The year 1913 found the I.W.W. engaged in free-speech fights in points as far separated as Cleveland, Denver, Detroit, Peoria, Philadelphia, Omaha, Hilo (Hawaii), Juneau (Alaska), and Minot (North Dakota). All but the one in Peoria, Illinois, were victorious.[1] The free speech fight in Denver, Colorado, was the longest of these battles. It began on December 26, 1912, when three I.W.W. speakers were arrested and jailed. The customary call was sent out for volunteers, and within the next few weeks, over forty Wobblies were arrested for speaking to crowds in the streets. Although the I.W.W. in Denver expressed disappointment at the "apathy of the rebels throughout the country in not responding more readily to the call," the Wobblies in Denver kept up the fight and were rearrested shortly after being released from jail.

Then, in March 1913, the battle began in earnest. Early in the month, Frank Little and a group of California Wobblies, most of them veteran free-speech fighters, left from Taft, California, to take part in the Denver battle. They traveled on freight cars through Bakersfield, Fresno, Stockton, San Francisco, and Sacramento, gaining recruits on the way. By the time they reached Denver, several hundred free-speech fighters were ready to do battle with the police.[2]

Scores of Wobblies were arrested early in April, and on April 12, 75 men entering the city were arrested and thrown into the "bull pen" when they told the judge that they had come to Denver to speak on the streets. Fed only on bread and water, the prisoners decided to go on a hunger strike. They informed the authorities that if they were kept in jail for the duration of the 61 days of their sentence, the city would have the additional expense of burying them since "61 days is ample time for all of us to starve." The authorities held a hurried council and decided to release the prisoners. The men promptly took up positions at various street corners, were arrested, and gained release when they announced their determination to renew their hunger strike.[3]

On April 28, the fight ended after the I.W.W. won the right to speak in the streets unmolested. "Since the settlement of the free-speech fight," Local 26 of Denver wrote to headquarters in June 1913, "extensive agitation has been carried on with splendid results."[4]

The first account of the Denver free-speech fight covers the Wobblies' trip from California to Denver to aid in the free-speech fight. Prepared mainly by Ed Nolan, a member of the group's Press Committee, it originally appeared in the *Industrial Worker* and is followed by a report of the Denver free-speech struggle by Dave Ingler and Joe Parry, two Wobblies who recounted their experiences for the Commission on Industrial Relations.

From Frisco to Denver
By ED NOLAN

The start was attended by the usual argument with those aristocrats of labor, the trainmen, but they reckoned without their host as the personnel of this free speech crew are all young men, seasoned to the long trip they have undertaken, many of them veterans of the battles of San Diego, Spokane and other points.

We have twenty leaving Frisco, while as many more await us at Stockton, Sacramento and various other points an route. Despite the differences in climate we are travelling light, no blankets hinder us, overcoats are in evidence and good warm clothes are worn by the crew. Speed by all means.

Upon leaving Oakland a painful sprain of the ankle was sustained by fellow worker Frank Little but he will follow shortly with another crew. A sprain is nothing to that indomitable spirit of his.

Organization is the soul of this contingent. Three committees are in force: scout, to attend to ways and means of transportation; financial and the press committee.

We are often confused with Carl Browne's army,[5] a movement to establish free soup houses and municipal lodging houses for California's unemployed. Brown's venture proved a failure and its founder says its demise was due to the antagonism of the I.W.W. It is to laugh, Soup House Brown, you are in the category of the A.F. of L. The One Big Union has no ideal of crummy lodging houses; its ideal is happiness of the workers, laughter in the eyes of little ones, instead of blanched faces, floods of tears and heart-rending cries of hunger.

There is no danger of mistaking the two signs we carry: "On To Denver. Free Speech Denied the Right to Organize One Big Union" and "We are in your town and must eat."

Leaving Sacramento was uneventful, but the arrival at Oroville was our first real test of solidarity. Our spokesman and a fellow worker were arrested and handcuffed together, while the balance of us were locked in the car where we remained until daylight. Being released from the car we were marched in double file to the county bastile, fifty strong. We at once cleared for action. Court commenced but bedlam was started and the court had to adjourn. The parasites sued for peace, a twenty minute armistice was allowed them and at the end of the truce we were declared at liberty. Our stay in the Oro-

ville jail was timely as it afforded us some much needed rest.
One of our fellow workers was sent to the hospital with a bad
case of the piles.

Our next stop, one hundred sixteen miles to our goal, was
not quite so pleasant or exciting. We had to camp in the
jungles, were actually refused the comfort of a jail. Our literature was eagerly taken, men and women coming to our line
of formation to get leaflets as we marched past the Western
Pacific depot. This is a great propaganda trip.

> March on! March on! All hearts resolved
> On Liberty or Death!
> —By Ed Nolan, Press Committee.

Later.

If we continue on with our present good fortune this expedition will be a marked success. Our goal is Denver. This crew is
doing fine in the way of travelling, but it regrets it can't spend
a week or ten days on the rock pile (the judges won't let us)
in order to make souvenirs, being sadly short on that valuable
aid to our finances, but it seems at this writing the powers are
heartily sick of having their courts (?) adjourned by this bunch
of noisemakers. No lungers here. Evidence shows there is no
way to arouse the exuberance of these rebels except by putting
them in durance vile, the viler the better.

Remember, we on this trip are doing good propaganda work
and advertising One Big Union so what is the matter with you
fellow workers putting the motion to send leaflets and pamphlets to Denver for the use of the fighters. Don't stutter
about it.

Pyramids of Capitalism have a great pulling power, to be obtained from the Worker, Box 2125, Spokane. Do this and
Denver will wish the I.W.W. were in the infernal regions.

The neat appearance and good behavior of this crew having
much to do with getting easily over a long, hard stretch of
desert and mountain ranges. A unique pastime was held at
Elko, Nev. Sham free speech fights were staged between the
fifty-five members of this crew. Our two cops, decorated with

gigantic stars, had their troubles clubbing and man-handling
the persistent soap boxers while the starvation army preyed
peacefully a few feet away. It was a lesson in strife to those
of us who have never felt the gentle touch of a grafter's club.

Fifty-five miles from Salt Lake we were sabotaged by a
worthy (?) engineer on the Western Pacific. He, or it rather, reported his engine in bad shape, consequently the train crew
were ordered to Salt Lake with two cars only, leaving us
heavily ditched in the dismal desert. No blankets, very little to
eat or drink, but amidst it all, Mr. Block, The White Slave,[6]
The Red Flag and other songs were rendered by the quartet in
tuneful melody. Obstacles are only stepping stones to this
bunch of rebels,—success comes only by striving, by bending
every effort to the accomplishment of the end desired.

Salt Lake City welcomed us with open arms (of the cops).
No sooner had we arrived at the hall, the cops came in and invited us to see hizzoner, the chief. It was too much work to
search fifty-five huskies. After a short conference with the
chief we marched back to the hall, a feast, and, to bed. The
would-be cops who lined us up were sharply balled out by the
chief for bringing us in.

Much credit is due to Secretary Sam Scarlet of Local 69 for
the admirable manner of handling the Frisco crew on very
short notice. This is the third bunch to pass through Salt Lake.
The Socialists also helped materially. All fighters passing
through Salt Lake to Denver will be welcomed by Local 69,
Salt Lake.

Frisco to Salt Lake: 921 miles, in less than nine days!

Fellow worker McAvoy and ten rebels will wait for us at
Grand Junction, Colo. and together proceed to Denver.

The departure from Salt Lake will linger long in our memor-
ies. We found a special express car attached to the train, pulled
by a special engine, and a special policeman piloted us to the
car. It was providential that none of us are troubled with heart
failure, as that shock would have proven fatal. The car had
electric lights, to be turned off and on at will.

Provo, Utah, was waiting patiently for us to arrive. Veni.
Vidi. Vici! We came. We saw. We conquered! Provo didn't
want us. Too many. The real test of strength came at Green

River, two hundred miles from Salt Lake. A Thing, resembling a gorilla, but far below that animal in intelligence, ordered sixty-five human workers, at the point of two massive forty some odd, from the car. Its demands not being gratified, it became panic stricken, fear replacing bravado—Cowardice crowning all—although backed by four nondescript business men, less brainy by far than the Thing. It wanted to stop us at Helper, Utah, but Helper wouldn't help.

How did we do it? Solidarity, gentle reader, Solidarity. Near Denver we may be stopped temporarily, but in the meantime, Denver unrelenting.

The arrival at Grand Junction, Colo., a socialist town, was marked by a rousing demonstration when we were met on the street by fellow worker McAvoy of the Stockton, Cal. contingent. The sheriffs of Mesa county were waiting for us at the depot, but this body of workers are continually doing the unexpected.

Shame on you! gun bound parasites, to let an organized body of producers outwit you. The city council appropriated twenty-five dollars for sustenance the day we would lay over in their town. The most composed of the entire city were the I.W.W. fighters and the Socialists. The pinheads of the town were wrought to a high tension over a fancied menace. This crew voted their thanks to the Mayor and Chief of Police, for which the Chief expressed his gratitude. He said it was a political frame-up on the part of bankers, lawyers, and other grafters to oust the S.P. from office, which he fears will be successful, but manhood before job is his slogan. The Chief said he doubted whether the plutocrats of the city would have acted in the same orderly manner as the I.W.W. if conditions were reversed. Lack of space forbids dwelling on Grand Junction at length.

A mass meeting called at the behest of the editor of the Sentinel was one of great disorder. Resolutions were drawn up to tar and feather the entire crew and drive them into Grand River, but when a banker was chosen to lead the miserable cowards, he declined with emphasis. To repay the loan of twenty-five dollars advanced by the Socialists of Grand Junction, fifteen fellow workers volunteered their services to the Chief of Police for street work. Their labor was refused; no tools.

The workers along the Western Pacific and the D. & R. G. are waking to industrial unionism.

Pueblo, Colo. was the next to show its hospitality. Upon our arrival an imposing array of brass bound police, plain clothes men and deputies with shifting eyes and toboggan slide heads, fifty in number, surrounded fifty of the Denver fighters. They went to jail. But fifty was not all; forty more were anxiously looking for their fellow workers, not being aware of the reception given the other fellow workers, and upon learning the truth there were expressions of jealousy at being snubbed by the Pueblo police. They promptly formed in line and searched for the jail. It being four a.m. it was some time before they found a guide—one lone cop—he led them to jail, forty huskies. Five hours later we were turned out, the city blowing itself for bread and tobacco. A switch engine with four cars hove in sight; we were escorted six miles to a nice mountain stream, where all freight trains go slow.

Fellow worker Engel has been detailed to press committee with the writer.

Later.

Colorado Springs was another port in a storm; a hospitable port. That jail is sure a nice one (on the outside); it is fitted with a good cement floor, hot water and disappearing cots. The hamburger was fine, we appreciated it; the bread also, it was adamant. The first hike in sixteen hundred miles was pulled off at this point, to Pike View, four miles, where we found our special.

There are now plots and counterplots, and both thickening. We intended to get off at Littleton, 10 miles from Denver, but that train fanned through there like a bat out of the devil's boarding house. It is now a battle of wits. Brakes were set, she stops, we unload and scatter to the four winds. Sixty are captured by as many cops. City police far from city limits. The battle of plenty against that of want. But all are not caught. Twenty or more reach Denver. Their sole wish is to be taken from a soap box, not from a box car.

This is a critical time to have advocates of One Big Union in Denver, as the entire state is strike ridden; slaves fighting for more bread, but, like misguided men, taking the wrong path. Scatter out, live ones of the Coast! Get posted yourselves, then come to the middle west and post others. The field is broad and fertile. Happiness must replace misery; the right to earn plenty must replace want and suffering. The time honored Colorado way—deportation—will be followed in our case, but it will have no terrors for the California fighters. They have braved the desert and snow capped mountains, day and night, and will do it again. In sixteen hundred miles we have had two cases of sickness, two deserters and one expulsion—the latter not a member. We left Oakland, Cal. with twenty; arrived at Military Post, seven miles south of Denver, with ninety men, eighty of whom are members. Much credit is due to Fellow Worker Jack Law for his fidelity to the men of his expedition. Fellow Workers Sherman and McKenzie handled the finances with marked ability and without question. Eighty-two per-cent of this crew are American born. Denver sheets tell the opposite.[7] A strict censorship has been maintained by this body upon all press matter along the entire route, all articles being freely sabotaged, much to the discomfort of the press com-mittee, but said committee has a wholesome regard for all con-cerned.

Our goal at last! Sixteen hundred and sixty-six miles in four-teen days! —Nolan and Engel, Press Committee.

Industrial Worker, April 17, 24, 1913.

Denver Free-Speech Fight
February 2nd, 1913, to May 1st, 1913
By DAVE INGLER and JOE PARRY

On February 2nd, 1913, a group of members of the Industrial Workers of the World, called a meeting to order on the corner of 17th and Market Streets of Denver, Colo. about 12 o'clock noon.

After addressing an audience for a short while, a uniformed police officer appeared and asked the speaker if he had a permit for the "Fire and Police Board." The answer was "yes." The officer then told him to appear before the "Fire and Police Board."

The meeting was adjourned, and a committee from the I.W.W. appeared before the Board, the Board informed them that the permits of the I.W.W. had been revoked. The committee reported back to the I.W.W. headquarters and a special meeting was called, where it was decided that in view of the fact that the "Fire and Police Board" granted permits to other organizations to use the streets for meeting, the I.W.W. would continue to hold meetings without permits.

Accordingly, at noon next day a group went out as usual and opened a meeting at 17th and Market. The speaker upon the box was arrested by a uniformed officer, which followed by others mounting the box and being arrested. Eight (8) members of the I.W.W. were arrested in this manner that afternoon.

The next morning in the Police Court (Judge Stapleton presiding) they were charged with Vagrancy. They plead "not guilty" and demanded a separate jury trial. This was refused and they were fined $80.00 and costs. They refused to pay the fine and were placed in jail.

This same procedure was followed by both sides up until April 24th, during this time 65 more arrests were made. On Sunday April 24th, 14 members of the I.W.W., mostly residents of Denver, opened a meeting at 17th and Market. All of them were arrested and the next day were brought before Judge Bock of the County Court for trial. All pleaded "Not Guilty" to a charge of Vagrancy and demanded a separate Jury Trial. They were placed in the County Jail with the exception of one who was granted a Jury Trial. He was tried in Judge Bock's Court the same day and was found "Not Guilty." Judge Bock discharged the man and he was re-arrested during a raid on the I.W.W. headquarters the same day. The other

thirteen were kept in the County Jail awaiting trial and were
released with those in the City Jail at the conclusion of the
fight without going to trial.

The same day April 24th, a party of men numbering about
one hundred and twenty-five (125), mostly members of the
I.W.W. got off a train at Petersburg. They had come all the way
from California. They were met by a number of Denver Police
and about 80 of them were arrested, this took place outside
the city limits of Denver, the rest of them escaped from the
police and got into the city. Those arrested were placed in some
waiting passenger coaches and brought into Denver and placed
in the City Jail. One man was badly beaten by the police. The
next day the local I.W.W. Headquarters were raided by the
Police and about twenty (20) arrested.

The prisoners numbering now about One Hundred (100)
were all crowded in one room in the City Jail. This room was
about twenty-five (25) by thirty (30) feet.

On April the 25th, about thirty of them were brought before
Judge Stapleton for trial, they were charged with Vagrancy.
Some pleaded "Guilty" and promised to leave town and were
released, but the majority pleaded "Not Guilty" and demanded
a separate jury trial. This was refused and each was questioned
by one Deleany acting as prosecutor. To each, he asked the
following questions:

1. What is your occupation?
2. Where did you work last?
3. Are you a member of the I.W.W.?
4. What was your reason for coming to Denver?
5. Did you come to Denver to violate the City Ordinance
   regarding street meetings?
6. Will you leave town if you are discharged?
7. Will you speak on the streets of Denver without a
   Permit if you are discharged?

These questions varied a slight degree according to the
answers made. Those who answered "yes" to questions 3, 5
and 7 and "no" to Number 6 were given sentences ranging

from $40.00 and costs to $160.00 and costs. The men refused
to pay the fines and were placed in a cage 25 by 40 feet on a
bread and water diet.

This procedure followed for three days until there were 58
men confined in the same cage with the others.

On Wednesday evening April 27th, the 58 voted to go on a
Hunger Strike to secure full jail ration, which lasted until the
evening of April 29th, when the officials gave them the full
jail ration.

Saturday, April 30th, Mayor Arnold requested the men in
jail to appoint a committee to appear before him and settle
the fight. A committee of 6 was elected without power to act.
The Mayor informed the Committee that he would agree to
grant permits to speak in the streets to the Members of the
I.W.W. providing the men that had no business in Denver would
leave. The committee reported back and were instructed to re-
appear before the Mayor and accept the agreement providing
the Mayor would grant a few day's work for the men that they
could get some money to travel on. This was accepted by the
Mayor and the fight brought to a close. All men being released
that were so connected with the fight.

At the time of the fight the following city officials were
directly connected with it.

Mayor Arnold.

Fire and Police Board members, Conway, Blakely and Thum.

Chief of Police Felix O'Neil.

Captain of Detectives Leyden.

These men were under instructions of the Chamber of Commerce and the Knights of Columbus.

A contractor by the name of Dooley, representing some
construction firms of Denver and some Employment Offices
appeared before the Fire and Police Board and demanded that
the I.W.W. be stopped from speaking on the streets just before
the first arrest was made.

The Chamber of Commerce forced all the daily papers of
Denver to stop publishing any news regarding the fight with
the exception of the Denver Express.

The police opened mail addressed to members of the organization and to the organization, the Secretary of the I.W.W. of
Denver receiving many letters that had been opened, also the
telegrams were opened.

This has been submitted by

DAVE INGLER AND JOE PARRY.

Letters, Etc., Addressed to Vincent St. John by Various
Writers, Commission on Industrial Relations File,
National Archives, Washington, D.C.

Two Free-Speech Fights in the Dakotas— Minot, North Dakota, 1913, and Aberdeen, South Dakota, 1914

7

Introduction

The Minot, North Dakota, free-speech fight was the bloodiest of the 1913 battles for free speech.[1] City officials and vigilantes violated every constitutional right of the men involved in the struggle, and so outrageous was the deprivation of civil liberties that Grant S. Youmans, a local banker, publicly objected, allied himself with the free-speech fighters, and suffered disastrous economic consequences as a result. Although the I.W.W. won the free-speech fight in Minot, it was a costly victory; the brutality took a serious toll on the physical well-being of many Wobblies.

The two accounts of the Minot free-speech fight published below were submitted to the Commission on Industrial Relations. The first is by Jack Allen, a Wobbly and victim of the brutality of police and vigilantes. The second is a selection from *Legalized Bank Robbery* by Grant S. Youmans, who upheld the right of free speech despite the animosity of former associates and friends. His account of his role in the free-speech fight was sent to the Commission on Industrial Relations by William D. Haywood.

The free-speech fight in Aberdeen, South Dakota, was part
of an organized I.W.W. drive to unionize the agricultural
workers and gain for them higher wages, shorter hours, and
better working conditions. It lasted from July to September,
1914, and is described below by a contributor to the Commission on Industrial Relations. Although the contribution was
not signed, it may have been, according to evidence in
Solidarity of August 8, 1914, by "Fellow Worker George Carey."

A Review of the Facts Relating to the Free-Speech
Fight at Minot, N. Dak. From Aug. 1st to Aug. 17th 1913
By JACK ALLEN

Being one of the vast number of unemployed and having
poor prospects of obtaining work in the section of the country
in which I happened to be at the time, I determined to risk it
and go west in search of some one who would, perhaps require
my services.

I arrived in Minneapolis, Minn. on or about the 12th of July
1913 and looked around in search of employment for some
two weeks, without securing any, and being a member of the
Industrial Workers of the World I offered my assistance in
organizing the workers into the One Big Union in that city.
After working at that until about the 20th of the current
month, I had about decided to leave the city and search for
employment in some other section of the state. Before I could
do so, However, I was required to accompany Fellow Worker
Jack Law on a trip to the town of Minot, N. Dak. for the purpose of organizing a number of construction workers who were
employed at that place. I consented to do so when I was given
to understand that some one had requested an organizer from
the joint locals of this city and we left a day or so after the request was received.

Arriving at Minot we immediately hunted up the Editor of
the Socialist weekly publication called "The Iconoclast" and
making known our purpose to him we received an explanation
as to what could be accomplished so far as he thought. The
Editor having arranged for an outing for himself and family,

in company with Mr. Arthur Lesner and his family left for a
trip into the Mountains, and to some lake — Upsillion, I think
it was called. He left Fellow Worker Law and myself to size up
the local situation and to see what could be done toward
establishing a concrete form of local union that would best
suit the needs of the workers in the branch of industry represented there.

Law and I repaired to the street on the following evening at
about 8 o'clock and sang a few songs, after which we spoke on
the Necessity of Organization, and were accorded a warm welcome from the workers who surrounded us and after holding
forth for some two hours the meeting closed, some seven or
eight men joining as a result of the first attempt at explaining
the relative merits of the I.W.W. as compared to those of the
A.F. of L.

On the following evening we repeated the dose and were
indeed gratified to see so much interest manifested by the
workers on behalf of the ideal of One Big Union. These meetings continued for about two weeks and were conducted in an
orderly manner at all times. Nothing was said of an inflammatory nature by either of the speakers. We prevailed upon
the workers to consider at all times the fact that any one who
had no desire to stop and hear what we had to say were at
liberty to move along in either direction, and the Industrial
Workers of the World had no desire to curtail the liberties or
to infringe upon the rights of any industrial. We told them that
any person had and should be permitted to enjoy the privileges
of disbelieving any or all the statements made by us—just as
much right in fact as we had to express our views.

I wish to say that from the start I as an individual anticipated
no trouble. I had been given to understand that the Knights of
Columbus were quite numerous in Minot, but never thought
for a moment that any trouble would spring from that source.
It did, however, all statements to the contrary notwithstanding,
for after we had held meetings for about two weeks and taking
in a great many new members, the storm burst upon us. All the
fury of an Orthodox Hell seemed to be unchained for that
especial occasion and our evening, just after finishing what I

had to say and a few minutes after Law had mounted the "box" there appeared upon the roof of the Ireland Hotel, situated on the opposite corner from the one we were using, several young fellows whom I had seen around the town and who commenced to hurl what had the appearance and the odor of rotten eggs. They were thrown into the crowd striking the bystanders and completely ruining their clothes. This bombardment kept up for several minutes, and stopped only after the supply of eggs was exhausted.

The Chief of Police Smith was standing on the corner nearest the Ireland Hotel and was in plain view of any who happened to be looking in that direction. He offered no word of protest against this outrage nor did he make any attempt at finding out who the guilty parties were. Whether he did or not later, I am not in a position to state. This was the commencement of hostilities and on the following evening several members of the Socialist Party attempted to speak upon the corner that had been occupied by us. The first speaker was the Business Manager of the Socialist Weekly, "The Iconoclast", and was arrested for his pains. Immediately following him came the ex-mayor of the town, Arthur Lesner, by name, a prominent banker of that section, and a well known lawyer who was supposed to control the most stock in the socialist paper. He met with the same treatment as that accorded Mr. Thompson, the Business Manager, and while they were being hustled off to jail, another man, who wished to make an individual protest against the curbing of constitutional rights, climbed upon the box and this time I am told it was Dewey Donnan, who was then holding the office of commissioner of streets. He too was arrested and all three spent the night in jail.

On the following evening Law and myself, after notifying the Joint Locals of the I.W.W. located in Minneapolis, Minn., decided to call into conference the members of the I.W.W. and ascertain if possible the position they intended to take and were not surprised to learn that the sentiment was unanimous in favor of a fight. Not for the sake of fighting but for the sake of retaining that to which every man or woman in this nation is entitled, to wit: the constitutional right of free speech and peaceable assemblage. We realized that more or less bloodshed would result and told the recruits in the movement the truth of the matter and gave them to understand that more than our broken head would undoubtedly be their portion. They were determined however to go through with it, and decided that the fight would be fought without compromise and that the I.W.W. must stand upon its dignity in this, as in all other occasions and on the following evening several of them made their appearance on the street in front of the post office and attempted to speak. They were clubbed by the police and arrested for their pains and as fast as one was pulled off the box another took his place until some seven or eight were within the toils. All were placed behind the bars and were maltreated within the confines of the prison to the extent of being struck several times with clubs in the hands of the police.

Not being satisfied with arresting men on the streets and abusing them, the officers of the law proceeded to the "jungle"[2] to the west of the town and arrested some twenty four or five men whom they chanced to find there. These were placed in the county jail while the first lot were put behind the bars of the city prison and after arresting as many as the county and city jails would accommodate, they caused a stockade to be erected and confined a number of prisoners there, while around this they placed a number of special deputies with high powered rifles in their hands. Some seventy-five or a hundred of these fellows being necessary to keep the peace, these in due time were mistreated also, as I will show further on in this article.

One of those sworn in as special deputy was a Swede who had been attending the meetings of The Salvation Army and testifying of the great love he had for the balance of the human race. This by virtue of the fact that Christ, Jesus had first manifested a very great love for him, and whom he considered as one worthy of worship, and while the Salvation Army was a "sample of Goodness" that could well be emulated in example. He, the Swede failed to remember any occasion where the Salvation Army had been treated in the same manner as the I.W.W. were on this occasion. This Swede, while walking up main street with his head turned in the opposite direction failed to

notice a very frail looking young lady approaching who had
as an escort her own child tucked away comfortably in a Go-
cart. The Swede collided with the baby carriage and whether
from the excitement brought on by the recruit conflict with
the "Obnoxious Element" or whether it was because he
supposed he had been attacked by the Sympathizers of the
Working Men, is still a matter of conjecture, these things either
one or both had the effect of making him mad clear through.
At any rate, he, *THE Man Who Loved His Jesus*, proceeded to
kick the baby carriage, baby and all into the street, but woe
was he. The mother pounced upon him and administered a
thrushing that would make Jack Johnson[3] a novice. She had
been an instructor in the womanly art of self defense in some
one of the larger institutions of an eastern city, before coming
west as the wife of a painter by the name of Jours. He was
licked in fine shape and while the baby was not seriously injured the case aroused public feeling against the authorities to
a high pitch for permitting a man like that to have police
powers and when the case was reported to the state's attorney,
it was squashed with the Swede being relieved from duty as a
special deputy, a day or so later.

Night after night the police kept up their brutal attacks
upon the fellows who had the courage of their convictions to
the extent of making a protest in public against curtailing of
personal liberties and during two weeks of this kind of thing
there were some seventy-five or eighty men arrested, brutally
beaten and thrown into jail. They were fed on the poorest
kind of food and thrown in what was called the "Bull Pen"
were compelled to sleep on the bare ground with nothing over
them except the North Dakota sky. Blankets there were none.
The men not even permitted to remove their outer clothing
or their shoes owing to the chilly weather. They were compelled
to remain there in the rain on more than one occasion and
when asked why they were treated like wild animals were told
to shut up under penalty of having the fire hose turned upon
them.

Finally after the county jail and city prison and Bull Pen
were filled no more arrests were made and those who dared get
out on the street with the purpose of speaking were clubbed

into the Great Northern Yards and left to shift for themselves.
If they were seen in town again they were treated to the same
thing again.

On one occasion, which I would call special attention to,
there was a fellow who had never been a member of the I.W.W.
or any other organization that seemed to be man enough to
have taken Caesar's job made an attempt to speak five nights
in succession, and was nearly killed as a result. He like the
others was dragged into the Gt. Northern Yards and left to
perish and would undoubtedly have done so were it not for
the women of the town, such as the wife of the State Secretary
of the Socialist Party and the wife of another prominent Socialist Business Man. These noble hearted friends of labor
brought the man back into town and tried to obtain medical
attention for him and the doctors who attended him made the
remark that if the officer responsible for the condition of the
fellow could not do a better job he deserved to lose his position on the force. Some consolation. From last accounts this
man was still protesting against such nefarious schemes to rid
the world of its only useful element, The Laboring Class.

Many of the town's most respected citizens openly deplored
the state of affairs that existed and were in favor of calling the
State Militia but for some reason unknown to the writer, they
refrained from doing so. Offers came from many people in and
around the town to assist us in any way possible, but the only
case where it was accepted at least to my personal knowledge
was that of a banker, Mr. Grant S. Youmans by name, who
contributed something like one hundred dollars to be used for
the purpose of buying food for the fellow workers who were
without funds. He was responsible for a wagon load of good
things to eat being sent to them and helped in various other
ways. He was ostracized from society as a result of that friend-
liness and lost everything he had merely because his principle
held full sway in everything he did. He tells his own story of
his losses and the reason is given very plainly in a small book
published by himself entitled "Legalized Bank Robbery" and
for fear that I may not be able to do him justice in this account
would refer those interested to him.

In his account of the affair Mr. Youmans tells of the settlement and says: In the first seven days of the trouble, the bank clearing dropped to the tune of "53,000" and that is only about one-fifth of the total loss. The guardians of the town inflicted upon the tax payers in the city and surrounding districts, there being some twenty-one farmers who banded themselves together for the purpose of sending to Sears, Roebuck and Co. for their groceries and refused to spend a dollar in the town until the officials granted the requests or demands of those men who had been arrested. They also refused to haul a grain of wheat to the elevators of the town and in that manner ably assisted us in settling our differences with the city fathers. The railroad employes, such as switchmen, brakemen, firemen and engineers as well as the shopmen would have their groceries sent them from surrounding towns and in all the affair cost the city of Minot approximately $280,000 for the sixteen days conflict.

On the morning of about the 27th of August the writer was seated in the office of the State Secretary of the Socialist Party when one of the members of the S. P. entered and informed me that Judge Davis, the president of The Commission, was seeking to arrange a meeting between himself, City Attorney McGhee and Police Commissioner Shaw on behalf of the city, Mr. Lesner, Fellow Worker Law and myself on the part of the I.W.W. and Socialists. I told above mentioned member that trying to arrange a conference with Law and myself was simply a waste of time, for while we had both been arrested again the following day on the same charge, we were in no position to settle anything for those men in jail. They themselves were the ones to deal with and that if the city officials wanted peace to reign in their little city a committee of men must interview them, allow the prisoners to take a vote on it and in case the majority was in favor of settling the fight, their word would be their bond. But if they voted to continue the struggle those who started the unpleasant affair would have to abide by the consequences and as I had been told that afternoon we were asked to go to the office of the district attorney and see what could be done. We were asked what could be done on our part toward a peaceful ending of the affair and they were told to go to the members in jail and ask them, that we were forbidden by the I.W.W. membership to make any agreements or contracts in their behalf. We were not abused in any manner while in that office but were treated in a way that would suggest a strong desire on the part of the officials to settle the dispute, with the result that that afternoon a number of men were released from the city "Bull Pen" and the next day all those in the county and city jails were restored to their liberty, so far as the town was concerned. The men in the county jail first having been tried on a trumped up charge of vagrancy and sentenced to pay a fine of twenty-five dollars or so many days in jail, among those tried for disturbing the peace were the ex-mayor, Mr. Lesner, the Business Manager of The Iconoclast and Mr. Donnan Commissioner of Streets. They had their fines of twenty-five dollars remitted, I believe, for I know it was never paid.

I have attempted to give a detailed account of the brutality connected with the affair and have adhered to facts at all times. I shall endeavor to make known the cause in as brief a manner as possible. In the first place a contractor by the name of Dinnie, who was building the State Normal School, knew that if the I.W.W. gained a foothold in the minds of the slaves of that job his cake would be dough, so far as further contracts were concerned, for he knew they would expose him to the public and warn them that very poor material had been used in the construction of the school, and that the tax payers were being swindled out of their money in an indirect way, consequently it was to Dinnie's interest to prevent the propagating of industrial unionism. He posted notices to the effect that no I.W.W.'s were allowed on the premises and what caused him to become all the more angry was the fact that some fourteen members were in his employ at the time and he had so far failed to discover their idenity, and he caused a man by the name of Olander, a Cigar Manufacturer of the town, to stop his automobile in the crowd with muffler wide open with the intention of disturbing the meetings. When the speakers requested that he close the muffler he ignored them completely and several fellows in the crowd would have closed it for him

and did him bodily harm if it had not been for the man on the
box, who reminded them that the I.W.W. had no desire to start
any trouble.

The bitterness of the fight became so intense and the sentiment of the populace aroused to such a pitch that it became
necessary to act quickly if they were going to prevent a Factional Fight between the Catholic element on the one hand
and the anti-Catholic on the other. It could be called a fight
between those in favor of Free Speech and those who were
opposed to it, for the Mayor, Judge Davis informed the writer
that the city officials had lost control of the situation and that
he could not be held responsible for the happenings of the next
attempt at holding a street meeting and it was a self evident
fact that he told the truth, consequently the I.W.W. members
agreed with about 77 per cent majority that they would allow
the tension to relax to normal, and they attempted to finish
their work and it was agreed that on the first day of October,
1913 would be an appropriate time for recommencing the
work they were sent there to do.

The whole affair terminated satisfactory for all concerned,
and the I.W.W. has since established a local union in the town
and peace with the authorities and everyone else seems to pre-
vail, so far as the writer has been able to learn. Many have
suffered as a result of the struggle and more suffering may be
the outcome of it, but the writer would make bold to say that
the working class suffered to the greatest extent.

(Signed) JACK ALLEN.

Letters, Etc., Addressed to Vincent St. John by
Various Writers, Commission on Industrial
Relations File, National Archives, Washington, D.C.

Extract from *LEGALIZED BANK ROBBERY*
By GRANT S. YOUMANS

The Labor Troubles.

This then was the beginning of a struggle into which I was
thrown; a struggle which transformed our city into a snarling,

plotting mob. It was only a small side battle in that eternal conflict, having wealth and power on the one side against labor and poverty on the other. In this case it was merely a question as to the right of labor to organize. The leaders were trying only to accomplish this one thing. Were they wrong in doing this? Most certainly not, provided the laborers themselves desired it. They wished to use the street corner as their forum. Were they wrong in this? Again, most certainly not. This is the country boasting freedom of speech. These were but the simple requests on the part of labor. As to organization, this is a city of organizations. The firemen are organized; the engineers are organized, the pressmen are organized; the merchants, bankers, doctors, machinists, even the blacksmiths are in some form of organization. No one molested them but it brought a crying protest when it became noised abroad that unorganized workers of the city were about to form a union. These men were dependent upon the street corners for their meeting places, for public speaking in spreading their truth. Others had marble palaces, some had club rooms, skilled labor had its halls where all this work could be done, but these men had no place of meeting. The street corner was their only hall and if denied the right to agitate there then they must be silent. The question of the place of meeting, of the truth spoken, of free speech, were not paramount issues, but the fear of organization and consequent loss of profits through higher wages made the officers and business element wild with rage and these furnished the pretext through which their brutality found expression.

One day while walking to the bank, I met Mr. R. E. Barron, Cashier of the Second National Bank. This is the bank that finances contractor Dinnie. "They tell me, Grant, you gave those fellows $5.00 to feed them," he said. "Why yes," I replied, "Why not? Many of these men at the meetings are harvest hands who came here on account of the alluring advertisements of the Railroad Companies and Employment agencies offering from $3. to $5. per day, and these workers are the salvation of the country at harvest time. We can't get along without them."

"Well, I don't mean the harvest hands, but those fellows who are stirring up trouble down town, with their meetings they are holding," he answered.

"Those are the men I mean too, because most of them are harvest hands. They are simply trying to organize a union for themselves. What possible objection can any of us have to their doing that?"

"Well, they won't work. They aren't looking for work. They wouldn't work if you offered it to them. Then, too, they are liable to interfere with the work on the Normal School, but if they do, Dinnie is the boy who will drive them off with bricks and clubs."

I looked at him in amazement, to hear such remarks from him. He further added, "There ain't any use in treating those fellows with kindness. The only thing to do is to club them down. Beat them up. Drive them out of the city. That is what the police do in other places when they start agitating trouble, and I'm going to see Shaw about it," he said and left me.

Mr. W. S. Shaw was the city police commissioner; a former gambler. His chief pride lies in his connection with big business and his unjust discrimination against a square deal for the common people. Every city has his type.

That same night when the street speaking commenced the police as one man carried out the orders from the authorities. Judge Davis, President of the City Commission had said, "Pull them off the box," He might as well have said, "To hell with the constitution, to hell with everybody and everything except myself and the business interests which keep me in office."

That night a horrible scene was enacted. Many harvest hands who had been lured into the city by promises which would never be fulfilled, after their long dangerous ride in coming here, for many of them had to beat their way, found they had not only been deceived and duped but were greeted upon their arrival in the city, with threats of death; many of them clubbed and jailed, others driven from the city. Terrible brutalities prevailed. Men, for no other reason than trying to form a worker's union, were clubbed and beaten into unconsciousness. Some such were dragged to jail, while others were thrown into auto-

mobiles and taken into the country, and left along the roads
to crawl to shelter in the dark or lie beside the way to die. In
their loyalty for their husbands even wives of local sympathizers
were knocked down, roughly handled, then thrown into jail.
Even little children of the poor were kicked from the sidewalk.

It was that evening that I met Judge Davis; he was the Honor-
able President of the City's commission. He came storming
down the street, shouting out one foul oath after another. He
was wild with anger, barking, swearing, frothing at the mouth
like some mad beast. He condemned the laboring men as a
damned, ungrateful, dangerous class.

I stopped him. "Judge, Can't you do something to prevent
the beating down of innocent men?" I asked.

"Prevent Hell. We'll drive the G-- D--- Sons of B-----s into
the river and drown them. We'll starve them. We'll kill every
damned man of them or drive them together with the Socialists
from the city," he thundered back.

I avoided his honor after that, for I knew we have nothing
in common.

The vindictive treatment on the part of the officials brought
forth a mighty protest. The question involved now was the right
of any group of men to use the streets as a forum to present
their arguments. Defeated for a moment, the workers carried
the protest in a new form. Cards were printed bearing these
words, "We believe in Free Speech." This was one of my firm
beliefs and when they asked permission to place one of these
cards in my bank window, I gladly gave consent. This then was
the second great sin I committed, namely, standing loyal to my
convictions. The first sin consisted in giving money to help
feed hungry men.

The consequence of my actions came quickly. About 2:30
the next day while hard at work at the bank three representative business men called upon me, They were J. A. Roell, a
hardware merchant; F. W. Youngman, a real estate broker, and
F. L. Householder, a dentist. They stated their mission briefly.
They had been appointed as a committee, chosen by the Commercial Club Members then in session, to invite me to the meeting as there was something to be brought up in which I would

be interested. My suspicions were at once aroused, for I expected the experience would not be pleasant so in a kindly way I declined the invitation. They pressed me to go. So I stated my objections, namely, that I wished to have no words whatever with my former business associates. So earnest were they that they convincingly assured me that there would be nothing unpleasant at all. They stated the Club simply wished to ask my advice regarding the Labor Troubles. That at moment seventy-five of the members were seeking some means of compromise, through this session and they wanted me to help in securing a settlement of our Labor Troubles. After this explanation, I gladly went with them to the meeting.

As we entered the room, I was surprised to see that the presiding officer was D. C. Greenleaf, a local Attorney, who a few nights before in a drunken condition, had done all in his power to interfere with the street meetings. We all went quickly to some vacant chairs near and when seated, Greenleaf arose and in his haughtiest manner addressed me. "Mr. Youmans, we understand you are in favor of Free Speech. We have invited you up to make a speech." He then sat down; the room became instantly tense and quiet. I looked carelessly around and found the entire body glaring at me with unfriendly eyes. So this was their game, and broken were all the promises of the three men who so kindly invited me to this friendly session. I accepted the challenge.

"I think that request somewhat unfair. I don't fully understand the purpose of this meeting, and until it is explained to me I do not see that I have anything in particular to talk about." No answer from the presiding officer. The silence of the room became oppressive. Finally, J. M. Devine, former Governor of the state, arose and began to mumble an explanation. He told them what a good citizen I had been, what a fine neighbor and understanding me as he did it seemed incredible to him that I should so far forget my social standing, my duty towards the business interests, as to help feed a bunch of bums who had come to the city—here he was interrupted by angry growls and hisses directed against me. The uproar became so violent, Mr. Devine could not be heard. The cry was raised, "Let Youmans

speak, Let Youmans speak, speech, speech," demanded angry
voices; "Let him speak, he believes in free speech," snarled
others. I arose and waited for silence, then addressed them in
this manner:

"Mr. Chairman, Gentlemen. This having to make a speech
without any wanting or preparation and especially upon a subject about which I fear you all have the same opinion, is anything but pleasant. I will, however, do the best I can. I understand that you have called this meeting for the purpose of discussing the unfortunate labor condition in this city. I feel
perfectly safe in saying that all this trouble could easily have
been averted if the men had been left alone and not treated to
showers of rotten eggs and other insults." (Groans, growls,
hisses and jeers.) "Instead of certain business men plotting to
prevent, disrupt and abolish these meetings, they should have
displayed the same energy and interest in showing the workers
some little consideration. These toilers were entitled to fair
play, which they did not get. They were entitled to police protection which was denied them. Had you men been only human
and allowed them to have in Minot that liberty guaranteed
them under the Constitution, a labor union might have been
perfected, the leaders have gone quietly to other cities, and
all this unpleasantness and bitterness been avoided. I have only
done what I firmly believe to be right. These men are mostly
harvest hands, who have come for the harvest and threshing.
They came here seeking work." (Cries of "No, no they don't
want work, they only want trouble.") "I admit I gave $5. one
day and later gave larger sums because men were hungry and
needed help. I did for them what I have done for almost every
man here. Nearly all of you have come to me at some time or
other with a subscription paper or request for money; I have
always been generous with you. Never have any of you been
turned down." (Voices of "That's true, we admit that.") I continued: "If even now a little tact and kindness be used in dealing with this question, further conflict can be avoided." (Cries
of "What would you do?") "Why bless you, that's easy. I'd
negotiate with those fellows for a friendly settlement. They
are after all very human. I would arrange for a conference be-

tween the labor leaders and the ----." I got no further, for I
was here silenced by roars of "Never, never, not by a damn
sight." "Not with those damned bums. We'll hang them first,
we'll drive them from the city." Though still standing waiting
to continue, I was deprived of the floor by L. D. McGahan, one
of our leading citizens. He is the editor of the weekly *Demo-
crat*, a politician by nature, former Police Commissioner, who
found it very convenient to resign over night. It is said his decision was hurried because of a polite request from the State's
Attorney. When he arose he was in a highly excited state. He
worked himself into a furious passion, swinging his arms as
though guarding off demons. After comparing the present
situation to the days of the French Revolution, he made the
following threat: "There are just two sides to this question,
either a man is on the side of the business man or on the side
of the anarchy. Any man who is not on the side of the business
man is a TRAITOR to his country, and should be driven out
at the head of the vags, bums and scum who call themselves
Working Men." (Spirited applause, cries of "That's right.
That's the dope. Give 'em hell. Show no quarter.") An uproar
was created and when quiet came again, I thanked the committee for their kindness in inviting me there to be insulted.
Then quietly left the room. No good could be accomplished
by remaining longer, as anything I could do or say would
simply fan their bitter passion of class hatred into hotter
flames. The situation was plain. I stood alone among my former
friends. I was with the workers and firmly believed in their
right to organize, and fully intended to give my best judgment
in bringing about a satisfactory termination of the trouble but
not at the sacrifice of principle. Being called a traitor did not
exactly apply to my case. During the year 1898, I had resigned
my position as clerk in the First National Bank, of Winona,
Minnesota, to enlist as a recruit in the Spanish-American War.
As a soldier, I served creditably but without distinction. I
thought of my sacrifice in army life when McGahan called me
a "Traitor."

The confidence I formerly held among my business associates
and friends can best be established by the letters which follow.
They were given only a few weeks before that session at the

Commercial Club rooms. I came from that meeting bearing this
one impression "That I was a marked man." Later developments justify that impression.

Typed copy of extract in Letters from William D.
Haywood Relating to Free-Speech Fights, U.S. Com-
mission on Industrial Relations, National Archives,
Washington, D.C., F.A.C. 11-9-14, Serial No. 735.

Free-Speech Fight in Aberdeen, S.D.
ANONYMOUS

In response to a call issued in *Solidarity* of June 27th for all
members of the I.W.W. who intended to work in the north-
western harvest fields, and in pursuance to an agreement made
in Kansas by the fellow workers then present to congregate in
Aberdeen the latter part of July;[4] the writer, in company with
W. C. King and several other members from Omaha, arrived in
Aberdeen July 17th and found that although the I.W.W. was
much in evidence, not only in Aberdeen but in surrounding
towns, yet not much had been done to line up the slaves to
agitate for better conditions.

There were perhaps two thousand unemployed men in
Aberdeen at this time, and while the newspapers everywhere
were advertising the great harvest, the Commercial Club of
Aberdeen was advertising to the farmers, telling them that
plenty of help could be secured through them. (The C.C.)

They were also telling the farmers to refuse to pay more
than $2.50 per day. After holding a meeting in the east-side
"jungle" on the night of July 17th, we were besieged on every
side with applications for membership, for literature, etc.

Although we had literature on the way, none was then
available. During the meeting that first night it was unanimously decided by those present to hold out for $3.00 per day for
ten hours work. Everyone present insisted that the agitation
be carried to the slaves up-town despite the fact that a permit
for street speaking had been refused the I.W.W. some days
previous, some decided to test the ordinance prohibiting street
speaking. A meeting was arranged to take place uptown at
2 P.M. Saturday, July 18th. Gamblers were at this time plying

their vocation in open defiance of all law and were not molested.[5]

About two hours previous to the meeting scheduled I was approached by a man, who, hearing that I was to speak, asked me to inform the workers of the inhuman treatment accorded his wife, who, at that time was in the C. M. & St. P. depot, sick and about to give birth to a child. The city had refused them shelter, the hospitals has refused her admittance, and even the physicians had refused to attend her without payment in advance. Although he appealed to me to take up a collection for him, I, scenting a frame-up of some kind, assented, but privately decided to inform the public of their condition, and through public sentiment, force the authorities to act.

At the time scheduled for the meeting about 1500 persons were assembled at the designated place. After mounting the platform of the Aberdeen Fruit Commission Company's building and before I had started to speak, I was approached by a policeman who asked for a permit. Upon being informed that we had none save the First Amendment to the Constitution of the U.S. I was requested to accompany him to the police station, which I did.

There the chief of police informed me that I would not only be refused permission, but would be immediately arrested if I attempted to speak. My reply was that it made no difference as I was accustomed to that sort of thing. I returned to the meeting and had uttered about a dozen words when I was seized and placed under arrest. Other speakers followed until about 17 were incarcerated. Those whom I remember by name were W. C. King, Omaha, Al Carroll, Kansas City, J. C. Videen, Los Angeles, A. Schram, Spokane, J. Ratti, Newark, Radstad, Seattle, W. C. Owens, and J. W. Lee.

Katy Solomon, who had spoken in the jungle the night before and who seemed to exert a wonderful influence over the men, then attempted to rally the crowd and passed among them telling them to stick for $3.00 per day.[6] She was arrested and the brutality of the police at this time precipitated a near-riot in which several persons were brutally clubbed and one man was reported killed, but this was not verified.

The crowd surged around the city jail that night and listened
to songs and speeches from the prisoners within. While talking
to the crowd outside I was interrupted by the chief who informed me that I would be "fixed" unless I stopped talking.
Then we began to sing "My Country, 'Tis of Thee." The Police,
in conjunction with the fire department, laid a line of hose to
the jail with the intention of drenching us unless we desisted.
The crowd outside, however, prevented them from doing this,
with threats of retaliation. More prisoners were brought in until
Sunday night there were 34 confined in the city and county
jails.

Over twenty of us held in the city jail, a small frame building with six small cells, six bunks and six toilets, not one of
which was in working order. The food served us consisted of
rye bread, black coffee of an unusually inferior quality and
one meal of beans, too filthy to eat. Protests against this food
only resulted in more threats and no more beans. The former
chief of police had now resigned with the plea of ill-health, and
a foul mouthed "bull" whose name I did not learn, was pro-
moted to the position.

Letters given to the officers to mail were never sent and my
incoming mail was intercepted at the post office. Two rolls of
Solidarity had been sent me and of these the police kept one,
returning the other when I was released. A great many of the
prisoners were taken from the jail on Sunday night and carried
some miles out from town in an auto and brutally beaten by
thugs. The names of these upholders of law and order are not
known, but one of the deputies wore a Brotherhood of Railway
Trainmen's button, and another who had spent Saturday
night in jail with us on a charge of drunkenness, was released
Sunday. He it was who claimed to be a member of the Switchmen's Union and who wielded the club while others held the
prisoners from escaping.

At the preliminary hearing Monday, all save J. M. Lee, were
charged with violating a city ordinance prohibiting street
speaking. Lee was charged with drunkenness. (Lee was arrested
because of an altercation with a drayman who was maintaining that a workingman should be compelled to work for what-

ever the employer chose to pay. Lee asked him to carry a small parcel across the city for a dime; he refused and the crowd laughed until he did take it. Then Lee asked him to carry it back. This started a discussion which resulted in Lee's arrest. Lee is a cripple with one leg cut off, who lives by peddling.)

All of the prisoners arraigned Monday, protested their innocence, except Ratti who pleaded guilty and was sentenced to pay a fine of $25.00 or fifteen days in the jail. Radstad, Lee and others waived their right to trial by jury and were found guilty and sentenced to pay fines ranging from $5.00 to $25.00 or stay in the city jail from three to fifteen days. Carroll was given the heaviest sentence and held the longest. My case was set for September 9th, and bail set for $25.00.

As all the boys were promised freedom under suspended sentence on Tuesday I put up bond for my appearance in September and was released.

On September 3rd I was informed that my case had been dismissed from court and that it would be unnecessary for me to return to Aberdeen. As yet my bail has not been returned.

If any comment is necessary in regard to the actions of the writer or those conducting the fight, we can only state that although we had definitely decided to center in Aberdeen, yet no line of action had been agreed upon and the fight was not premeditated, and only occurred as a spontaneous revolt of the workers in Aberdeen. None of the fellow workers involved were dissatisfied with the method of procedure or the results obtained.

The writer has had several other clashes with the police in other sections in regard to public speaking and in one instance in Great Bend, Kansas, on June 13th, 1914, was threatened with bodily harm by the sheriff of the county, who also owned a farm near Great Bend, if he persisted in talking to the farmers. This man also threatened me with drowning in the Arkansas River.

Fellow-Worker Christ, now a member of the General Executive Board of the Industrial Workers of the World was with me on this occasion.

In April, 1914, I asked the Mayor of Grand Rapids, Michigan, for permission to speak on the streets of that city and was refused. Was informed that neither representatives of the Mormon Church nor of the Industrial Workers of the World could speak on the streets although almost any one else could. Upon reminding him, Mayor Ellis, that the constitution gave me that privilege, I was informed that the constitution did not apply to Grand Rapids.

Letters forwarded by William D. Haywood Relating to Free-Speech Fights, U.S. Commission on Industrial Relations, National Archives, Washington, D.C. F.A.C., Serial No. 735.

8

Kansas City Free-Speech Fight, 1914

Introduction

The outstanding free-speech fight of 1914, that in Kansas City, Missouri, erupted when local authorities attempted to negate the I.W.W.'s free-speech victory of 1911. The earlier free-speech fight began on October 6, 1911, with the arrest of Wobbly activist Frank Little for speaking on the streets; it ended on November 2, after the Wobblies threatened a mass invasion, with recognition of the I.W.W.'s right to speak on any street corner in the city.[1] But in the fall of 1913, businessmen put pressure on city officials to stop street agitation, and by the end of the year the police were ready to act. In January 1914, five men were arrested and jailed for holding street meetings. Within a week, the number in jail had grown to 50, and included Frank Little, who had headed for Kansas City with a contingent of free-speech fighters as soon as he had heard of the initial arrests. Vincent St. John immediately appealed from Chicago: "If you are foot loose make for Kansas City at once. . . . Wire the local that you are coming."[2]

This appeal attracted additional free-speech fighters and, of course, produced additional arrests. The Kansas City local indi-

cated late in February that new "jail recruits" were needed
"in order further to test the attitude of the police" and invade
the city. But none materialized. The eighty-three men found in
jail by March 1, 1914, represented the original group of Wobblies in the fight and a small number of reinforcements. They
tried to make up for their lack of numbers by addressing street
meetings as soon as they were released from prison in order to
be arrested again.[3]

To frustrate these tactics, the police and a reserve corps of
citizen police deported the I.W.W.'s as soon as they were released from jail. In addition, any man in jail, found guilty of
the slightest disturbance, such as singing or shouting at night,
was punished by being condemned to the "hole." Prisoners
sent to the dungeon were forced to stay in unheated cells,
sleep on concrete floors, and receive a two-and-a-half-inch
slice of bread, three times a day, with water. The Wobblies in
jail responded to police cruelty with a hunger strike. The
Kansas City *Journal* headlined the action as "I.W.W. Pulls Off
New Stunt," and predicted that the authorities would permit
the "hobo leaders" to starve to death before seeing them victorious. But the "new stunt" did produce results. Deportations
ceased; the authorities, for the first time, consented to meet
with a committee of the men in jail.[4]

Negotiations continued until the first week of March. On
March 4, the Kansas City authorities agreed to permit the I.W.W.
to hold street meetings without interference. The men in jail,
however, refused to call off the battle officially until the
promise had been thoroughly tested. For several nights I.W.W.
speakers addressed crowds at various street corners and no one
was arrested. The jail committee announced on March 8 that
the fight was over and wired all I.W.W. journals: "After three
months of battle with K.C. authorities the right of free speech
is established. . . . Men in jail are released in groups for fear we
may resort to a grand display. Direct Action again gets the
goods."[5]

The following two accounts of the Kansas City free-speech
fight were prepared by writers who are unknown and were submitted to the Commission on Industrial Relations.

Kansas City Free-Speech Fight
By F. W. C. DEAL

Kansas City, Mo. September 26th, 1914

Vincent St. John
Gen. Sec'y-Treas.
Chicago, Ill.

Fellow Worker:—

I see in the last Bulletin where the Industrial Commission
wants the account of Free Speech Fights. I got arrested one
night with five other fellow workers about the beginning of
January. I and the other fellow workers were taken to No. 4
Police Station, there we were searched and kept there for one
hour and then taken in a patrol wagon to No. 1 station. We were
kept all that night and the next night and the following morning, we were brought before Judge Burney and charged with
obstructing the street and blockading the sidewalks and fined
$100.00 and sent out to the Municipal Farm at Leeds, Mo.
    When we arrived there we were taken in the superintendent,
Mr. Stutzman's office and weighed, had my height taken and
then I had my supper which consisted of raisin syrup and bread
and water. After supper I was taken and put in the receiving
ward for the night. The next morning I saw the doctor and after
that I was taken in the Assistant Superintendent's office, a man
by the name of Dennison, there he read out the rules and regulations of the workhouse. At night I was taken over to the old
building which is supposed to be condemned. When I reached
there I found this place in a very bad state, foot of water was
under the beds, and one blanket to cover me over, and also the
water closet was stopped up and 83 men had to use this and
the beds were running alive with vermin, and in the morning
I was given some of that sour hash which consists of some of
the leaving of supper, bread and raisins mixed up with meat.
After breakfast was taken out to work on the country road
and at dinner time was brought in to get my dinner which con-

sisted of tough meat, and rotten potatoes and bread and water.
Now I had been in there 11 days without getting a change of
clothes or getting a bath and I was running alive with vermin.
Now when I went there I had a suit of clothes, I had this suit
all the time I was out there, they would not give the prison
outfit, and it was a summer suit and I was working outside in
the winter time. Now I stayed in there till the fight was over.
When I came out I went to Mr. Schreiber, parole officer to see
him about getting some clothes, which he would not give me.
But he said I will get your shoes repaired which he did. But I
worked in them all the time I was at the farm. Now when I
came out my teeth were on the bum and gums swollen and my
health ruined through eating that rotten food, so if this is freedom what the United States of America boasts so much about,
I do not want any of it. I am a British subject and I will still
stay one.

This is my experience of the Kansas City Free Speech Fight.

Yours for Industrial Freedom,

(signed) F. W. C. DEAL

Letters, Etc., Addressed to Vincent St. John by Various
Writers, Commission on Industrial Relations Files,
National Archives, Washington, D.C.

Free-Speech Fight in Kansas City
By WILLIAM FORD

I will give you my experience in the Kansas City, Mo., fight.
I was arrested December 3rd, 1913, and the next morning I was
arraigned before Judge Burney on the charge of obstructing the
street and blocking the side-walk, then he fined me $100.00.
That afternoon I was taken out to Leeds Farm, which is the
Kansas City workhouse. I was given a bath and some syrup
and corn meal which they called supper, then the Supt. Stutzman read the rules and regulations of the workhouse to me
and I was taken to the receiving ward till the next day when

I was brought before the doctor to see if I was in good health.
Later on I was put to work. That went on all right until one
day one of the guards named Bill Lane hit one of the boys
with a club. Then we were forced to strike and then after we
went back to work they had always given a little tobacco to
us but they shut that down. That is when bad conditions
started. We were forced to smoke anything we could get, and
the result was that I am broken down in bad health. To-day
that is what our authorities call Sanitary Conditions. Four
weeks I never had a bath and I had all kinds of vermins on me.
I scratched myself all night till I bleed then when the place got
so full of vermins that it was ready to run away they gave us
a bath and clean clothes. One Monday I was transferred to
Vincent Workhouse which is known in Kansas City Mo. as the
Woman's Reformatory. There were 52 fellow workers beside
myself sent there and they put us four in a cell. One night I
took awful sick and the fellow workers hollered for a doctor,
and they were informed that they could not get a doctor. Well
the next afternoon about 3 o'clock the doctor came. My throat
was swelled so much that I could hardly speak. He gave me
some pills.

Civilized people are trying to do good to humanity. They
have to mend their ways. I don't want to have any advice from
those kind of people.

I remain,

Yours for Industrial Freedom,

WM. FORD.

Letters from William D. Haywood Relating
to Free-Speech Fights
U.S. Commission on Industrial Relations, National
Archives, Washington, D.C. F.A.C. 11-9-14,
Serial No. 735.

Everett Free-Speech Fight, 1916

Introduction

The struggle in Kansas City was the last of the great free-speech
fights until Everett. During the Kansas City fight, recruiting
an invading army of free-speech fighters had become more and
more difficult. Organizing activities, strikes, and demonstrations by those unemployed made it impossible for workers to
respond to appeals as in the past.[1] A notice in the *Industrial
Worker* of April 29, 1916, announcing a free-speech fight in
Webb City, Missouri, and calling for "all available members,"
went completely unanswered. Most Wobblies were not interested.[2] In fact, more and more free-speech fights were being
regarded in Wobbly circles as distractions from the main task
of organizing the unorganized.

A few months later, in August 1916, the I.W.W. became involved in one of the greatest of the free-speech fights in Everett,
Washington. A drive had been initiated to organize lumber
workers, and if the I.W.W. retreated in the face of opposition
from the lumber companies in Everett, its prestige among the
workers would quickly decline. As the *Industrial Worker*
tersely stated: "Everett is a strategic point for the organization

of the Forest and Lumber Workers. Therefore, we must have free speech and full opportunity for organization in Everett."[3]

Everett, a city of about thirty-five thousand people in 1916, was a Puget Sound port from which much lumber was shipped annually. In and around the city were the sawmills, and in the surrounding countryside the woods were dotted with logging camps. Lumber interests controlled the economic and political life of the city—its stores, banks, real estate, and its government. The city's power structure was controlled by the members of the Everett Commercial Club, mill owners and business and professional men, with Fred K. Baker of the F. K. Lumber Co. as president; and representatives of the Weyerhaeuser and Jamison Mills and the Clough-Hartley Lumber Co. sat on the club's Board of Directors. The Commercial Club's chief objective was the maintenance and perpetuation of the open shop at all costs.[4]

In the spring of 1916, because of demands from war-torn Europe, the price of shingles soared, and shingle weavers demanded an increase in wages. When the Everett mill owners refused, over four hundred shingle weavers, members of the International Shingle Weavers' Union of America (an A.F. of L. affiliate), went out on strike on May 1. The police and Sheriff Donald McRae and his deputies arrested the pickets and sent them to jail. By the end of July only sixty men remained on the picket line; the rest were in jail.[5]

Late in July, 1916, the Commercial Club, bent on wiping out A.F. of L. unionism, was suddenly confronted by the activities of the I.W.W., which it feared more than the A.F. of L. On July 31 James Rowan arrived in Everett on his organizing tour for the Seattle I.W.W. local. On the night of his arrival, Rowan was pulled down from his soapbox by Sheriff McRae and taken to the county jail, but was released after an hour. He immediately returned to the street corner and resumed his speech. He was arrested a second time and locked up in the city jail. The next morning the municipal court sentenced him to thirty days in jail for peddling without a license unless he left town immediately. Rowan tried to uphold his constitutional rights but finally decided to leave.[6]

The Wobblies were now more determined than ever to hold a meeting in Everett; on August 22, James P. Thompson, national organizer and veteran free-speech fighter, came to Everett to hold such a meeting. About twenty Wobblies accompanied Thompson to Everett where he proceeded to mount a soapbox at Hewitt and Wetmore Avenues. He had spoken to a large crowd for about twenty minutes when fifteen police officers pushed through the crowd and arrested him. Rowan immediately took his place and the police promptly arrested him. Mrs. Edith Frenette, a Wobbly organizer from Seattle, called for the singing of "The Red Flag." While the crowd was singing, both she and Mrs. Lorna Mahler, wife of the secretary of the I.W.W. local, were arrested. Mrs. Letelsia Frey of Everett, who was not an I.W.W. member, began to recite the Declaration of Independence, and she, too, was pulled off the soap box. Before being silenced, however, she shouted, "Is there a red-blooded man in the audience who will take the stand?" Jack Michel, an A.F. of L. official, immediately responded and was promptly arrested. Infuriated by the continuous replacements, the police captured all the suspected Wobblies nearby and marched their prisoners through the streets to the jail. The following morning Thompson and the women prisoners were deported from Everett on the Seattle-Everett interurban railway. The rest were taken in wood carts to the city dock and sent to Seattle by steamer, the authorities taking $13 from one of the Wobblies, James Orr, to pay for the passage.[7]

Upon arriving in Seattle, the Wobblies conferred with Seattle members at a special meeting in the I.W.W. hall, and a free-speech committee was organized. The general headquarters of the I.W.W., its various branches, and the Wobbly press were notified; volunteers began immediately to conduct street meetings in Seattle to raise funds. Upon learning of these developments, the Commercial Club arranged to turn over the real power of the county and city government to Sheriff McRae and bypass Everett's mayor and police chief. Together the Club and the sheriff organized an army of several hundred deputies, who were charged with guarding the entrances to the city and patrolling the railroad yards, the streets, and the hobo jungles. The depu-

ties, recruited from Commercial Club members and the underworld, were invariably drunk. They were instructed to drive
the I.W.W. out of Everett by any methods necessary.[8]

McRae's deputies recognized no constraints when carrying
out this command. For example, when James Rowan returned
to Everett after having been thrown out, he was arrested and
jailed with thirty other Wobblies who had attempted to speak
on the streets. That same evening McRae, who had promised
to teach Rowan a lesson to keep him from returning again,
took him to the outskirts of the city and told him to "start
toward Seattle." Rowan had walked about one hundred
yards when a mob of deputies attacked and beat him on the
head with clubs and revolver butts. They dragged him into
the woods, where they beat his back to a bloody pulp. Head
and back bleeding, Rowan staggered to Seattle and had photographs made showing severe lacerations.[9]

On October 30, 1916, the Commercial Club's struggle against
the I.W.W. reached a climax. A contingent of forty-one Wobblies,
at least twice the size of any previous one, came from Seattle
on the regular passenger boat *Verona* to join the free-speech
fight in Everett. Sheriff McRae, intoxicated as usual, and about
300 armed deputies, each with an identifying white handkerchief around his neck, met the steamer at the Everett dock to
interrogate each passenger about his business in Everett. The
41 Wobblies, the majority from the harvest fields of the Pacific
Northwest, acknowledged membership in the I.W.W., and
asserted that their purpose was to participate in street meetings. After separating the Wobblies from the other passengers,
the deputies beat them with revolver butts and clubs and even
hit other passengers in their fury. A posse forced the horrified
passengers to stand quietly while the deputies loaded their
battered prisoners into trucks and automobiles. The caravan
drove to Beverly Park, an undeveloped suburb on the way to
Seattle. Here, in a cold, driving rain, the deputies formed a
gauntlet that ended in the front of the cattle guard at the inter-
urban railway track. One by one the Wobblies were taken from
the vehicles; a deputy followed each victim and beat him furi-
ously on the back to hurry him along. Just in front of the cattle

guard, six deputies were lined up, three on each side, to club
the helpless Wobbly on the face, stomach, and back and to
force him to run over the sharp blades of the cattle guard.
Eight of the most severely wounded men managed to get on an
inter-urban railway car while the others staggered back to
Seattle. Most of them went to the hospital the next day.[10]

The Everett *Tribune* featured a front-page editorial headed
"I.W.W. Entitled To No Sympathy," and argued that the
attack on the Wobblies in Beverly Park was justified if it kept
them out of Everett.[11] But the people of Everett violently dis-
agreed. Businessmen placed signs in their stores to announce
publicly "Not a Member of the Commercial Club." A committee of clergymen, labor leaders, and citizens met to discuss
how the city could be taken "out of Russia and back into the
United States." A mass meeting was planned to present the
facts to the public which had learned little of the true events
at Beverly Park from the Everett press. Reverend Oscar McGill,
a member of the committee, left for Seattle to get the coopera-
tion of the I.W.W. They agreed to hold a street meeting on the
corner of Hewitt and Wetmore Avenues on Sunday, November
5, 1916.[12]

All I.W.W. branches and locals in the region were notified of
the intention to assemble in Everett "to establish the right of
free speech. This fight must be won. All fighting members
answer this call for action." Handbills were distributed addressed
to "Citizens of Everett, Attention: A meeting will be held at
the corner of Hewitt and Wetmore Avenues, on Sunday, November 5th, 2 P.M. Come and help maintain your and our consti-
tional rights. Committee."[13]

While the Wobbly organizers in Seattle were signing up recruits for an expedition to Everett, the authorities of
Snohomish County and the Commercial Club were not idle.
New deputies were sworn in daily, and by Sunday five hundred
men were on the Sheriff's force. "At a meeting of the Commercial Club," wrote Robert L. Tyler, "the assembled deputies
were issued weapons, were regaled with speeches on the 'open
shop' and the 'I.W.W. menace,' and were told to report Sunday
for instructions when they heard the mill whistles blow."[14]

At almost the last minute, the Wobbly leaders decided to
make the journey from Seattle to Everett by boat. The inter-
urban railway could not furnish enough coaches, and the I.W.W.
could not assemble enough trucks or automobiles. Finally, it
was decided to leave on the regular passenger steamer, *Verona*,
at eleven o'clock on Sunday morning. I.W.W. members and
sympathizers pooled their money to pay the fares of all the
free-speech fighters; when the time of the steamer's departure
was close at hand, three hundred singing Wobblies paraded from
the I.W.W. hall through the streets of Seattle to Colman Dock.
About two hundred fifty boarded the *Verona*; thirty-eight
others had to wait a half hour to board the *Calista*, another
passenger boat. The funds for the passenger fares having been
exhausted, the rest of the Wobblies returned to the I.W.W.
hall.[15]

Someone, in all probability one of the two Pinkerton detectives in the Wobblies' group, slipped out and telephoned
Lieutenant Hodges of the Seattle police force. Hodges, in turn,
relayed the news of the Wobblies' departure to Everett officials. Although the I.W.W. had made its expedition public,
news of its embarkation for Everett was misleading. It was reported that a boatload of armed Wobblies had left Seattle to
avenge the Beverly Park beatings and "to invade, pillage and
burn the city."[16] At one o'clock in the afternoon, the mill
whistles blew, summoning the deputies to the Commercial
Club where they were plied with liquor and sent to wait for
the *Verona*.

At this point the Everett free-speech fight turned into the
Everett massacre and into one of the most celebrated trials of
free-speech fighters in American history. These two historic
episodes are related by men personally involved in these events.
Walker C. Smith, the official I.W.W. chronicler of the Everett
free-speech fight and massacre, described "The Voyage of the
Verona" and its tragic aftermath in the *International Socialist
Review* of December 1916, originally. His report is preceded
by an account of the brutality against the free-speech fighters
at Beverly Park by C. H. Rice, one of the Wobblies who went
through the bitter experience. The description of the imprison-

ment of 74 free-speech fighters after the Everett massacre was
written by Jack Leonard, himself a prisoner.

Terror in Beverly Park
By C. H. RICE

Two big fellows would hold a man until they were thru
beating him and then turn him loose. I was turned loose and
ran probably six or eight feet, something like that, and I was
hit and knocked down. As I scrambled to my feet and ran a
few feet again I was hit on the shoulder with a slingshot (a
club made of sapling.) This time I went down and was dazed.
I think I must have been unconscious for a moment because
when I came to they were kicking me. . . . As I was going over
the cattle guard several of them hit me and someone hollered
"Bring him back here, don't let him go over there." Then the
fellow who was on the dock, and who had been drinking
pretty heavily shouted out "Let's burn him!" About that time
Sheriff McRae came over and got hold of my throat and said,
"Now, damn you, I will tell you I can kill you right here and
there never would be nothing known about it, and you know
it." And someone said, "Let's hang him," and this other
fellow kept hollering "Burn him! Burn him!" McRae kept
hitting me, first on one side and then the other, smacking me
that way, and then he turned me loose again and hit me with
one of those "slingshots," and he started me along, following
behind me until I got over the cattle guard.

Walker C. Smith, *The Everett Massacre: A History of
the Class Struggle in the Lumber Industry*, Chicago,
1917, p. 72.

The Voyage of the Verona
By WALKER C. SMITH

Five workers and two vigilantes dead, thirty-one workers
and nineteen vigilantes wounded, from four to seven workers
missing and probably drowned, two hundred ninety-four men

and three women of the working class in jail—this is the tribute
to the class struggle in Everett, Wash., on Sunday, November 5.
Other contributions made almost daily during the past six
months have indicated the character of the Everett authorities,
but the protagonists of the open shop and the antagonists of
free speech did not stand forth in all their hideous nakedness
until the tragic trip of the steamer Verona. Not until then was
Darkest Russia robbed of its claim to "Bloody Sunday."

Early Sunday morning on November 5 the steamer Verona
started for Everett from Seattle with 260 members of the
Industrial Workers of the World as a part of its passenger list.
On the steamer Calista, which followed, were 38 more I.W.W.
men, for whom no room could be found on the crowded Verona.
Songs of the One Big Union[17] rang out over the waters of Puget
Sound, giving evidence that no thought of violence was present.

It was in answer to a call for volunteers to enter Everett to
establish free speech and the right to organize that the band of
crusaders were making the trip. They thought their large numbers would prevent any attempt to stop the street meeting
that had been advertised for that afternoon at Hewitt and Wetmore avenues in handbills previously distributed in Everett.
Their mission was an open and peaceable one.

The Seattle police, knowing that I.W.W. men had been jailed,
beaten and deported from Everett, singly and in crowds, during
the past six months, without committing a single act of personal
violence in retaliation, made no attempt to detain the men, but
merely telephoned to the Everett authorities that a large number had left for that city. Two Pinkerton detectives were on
board the Verona, according to the police and to members of
the I.W.W. The capitalist press of Seattle and Everett claim
that all the I.W.W. men were armed "to the teeth." On behalf
of the I.W.W. some have made the counter claim that the men
were absolutely unarmed, as was the case in all former "inva-
sions." Deputy Prosecuting Attorney Helsell, King County,
who is assisting the prosecutor of Snohomish County, has
stated in an interview that the number of armed workers was
between eighteen and twenty-five. This would mean that less

than ten per cent of the men were armed even were the higher figure a correct one.

Following the receipt of the telephone message from Seattle, Sheriff Donald McRae cleared the Municipal dock—owned by the city of Everett—of all citizens and employes, and after the erection of a temporary barricade of heavy timbers, the several hundred gunmen, scabs, militiamen, ex-policemen and other open shop supporters who had been deputized to do vigilante duty, were stationed at points commanding any incoming boats. These semi-legalized outlaws were provided with high power rifles, side arms and many rounds of ammunition. It has been reported that a machine gun was in readiness for service on the dock. Scabs located on the Everett Improvement dock, lying to the south of the Municipal dock, also had a part to play. The scene was set, and the tragedy of the Verona was about to be staged.

As the Seattle boat swung up to the wharf shortly before 2 o'clock the I.W.W. men were merrily singing the English Transport Workers' strike song, "Hold the Fort":[18]

> We meet today in Freedom's cause,
>   And raise our voices high,
> We'll join our hands in union strong,
>   To battle or to die.
>
> *Chorus*
>
> Hold the fort for we are coming,
>   Union men be strong.
> Side by side we battle onward,
>   Victory will come.
>
> Look, my comrades, see the union
>   Banners waving high.
> Reinforcements now appearing,
>   Victory is nigh.
>
> See our numbers still increasing;
>   Hear the bugle blow,

By our union we shall triumph
　　Over every foe.

Fierce and long the battle rages,
　　But we will not fear.
Help will come when'er it's needed,
　　Cheer, my comrades, cheer!

When the singers, together with the other passengers, crowded
to the rail so they might land the more quickly, Sheriff McRae
called out to them:
"Who is your leader?"
Immediate and unmistakable was the answer from every
I.W.W.:
"We are all leaders!"
Angrily drawing his gun from its holster and flourishing it
in a threatening manner, McRae cried:
"You can't land here."
"Like hell we can't!" came the reply from the men as they
stepped toward the partly thrown off gang plank.
A volley of shots sent them staggering backward and many
fell to the deck. The waving of McRae's revolver evidently
was the prearranged signal for the carnage to commence.
The few armed men on board, according to many of the
eye-witnesses, then drew revolvers and returned the fire,
causing consternation in the ranks of the cowardly murderers
barricaded on the dock. Until the contents of their revolvers
were exhausted the workers stood firm. They had no ammunition in reserve. The unarmed men sought cover but were subjected to a veritable hail of steel jacketed soft-nosed bullets
from the high power rifles of the vigilantes. The sudden rush
to the off-shore side of the boat caused it to list to about
thirty degrees. Bullets from the dock to the south and from
the scab tugboats moored there apparently got in their destructive work, for a number of men were seen to fall overboard
and the water was reddened with their blood. No bodies were
recovered when the harbor was dragged the next day. On the
tugboat Edison, the scab cook, a mulatto, fired shot after shot

with careful and deadly aim at the men on the off-shore side
of the boat, according to the Pacific Coast Longshoreman,
the official I.L.A. paper. This man had not even a deputy
badge to give a semblance of legality to his murders. That the
gunmen on the two docks and on the scab boats were partly
the victims of their own cross fire is quite likely.

After ten minutes of steady firing, during which hundreds
of rounds of ammunition were expended, the further murder
of unarmed men was prevented by the action of Engineer
Ernest Skelgren, who backed the boat away from the dock
with no pilot at the wheel. The vigilantes kept up their gun-
fire as long as the boat was within reach.

On a hilltop overlooking the scene thousands of Everett
citizens witnessed the whole affair. The consensus of their
opinion is that the vigilante mob started the affair and are
wholly responsible.

Many angry citizens made demonstrations against the
vigilantes as they left the dock with automobiles containing
the corpse of gunman Lieut. C. O. Curtis, who had fallen
early in the fight, and twenty wounded vigilantes, among whom
were Jeff Beard, Chief Deputy Sheriff and former Sheriff of
Snohomish county, who later died in the hospital, and
Sheriff McRae with three bullet wounds in his legs. The recovery of some of the gunmen is still in doubt.

Mrs. Edith Frenette, who was later arrested in Seattle together with Mrs. Joyce Peters and Mrs. Lorna Mahler, is held on
the allegation that she tried to throw red pepper in the eyes
of the sheriff and then drew a revolver to shoot him as he was
being removed from the dock. Mrs. Frenette was out on
$1,000 bail on an unlawful assembly charge made by the
Everett authorities.

An Everett correspondent, writing to the Seattle Union
Record, official A.F. of L. organ, makes the following statement of the temper of the people:

> Your correspondent was on the street at the time of the
> battle and at the dock ten minutes afterward. He mingled
> with the street crowds for hours afterwards. The temper

of the people is dangerous. Nothing but curses and execrations for the Commercial Club was heard. Men and women who are ordinarily law abiding, who in normal times mind their own business pretty well, pay their taxes, send their children to church and school, pay their bills, in every way comport themselves as normal citizens, were heard using the most vitriolic language concerning the Commercial Club, loudly sympathizing with the I.W.W.'s. And therein lies the great harm that was done, more menacing to the city than the presence of any number of I.W.W.'s, viz., the transformation of decent, honest citizens into beings mad for vengeance and praying for something dire to happen. I heard gray-haired women, mothers and wives, gentle, kindly, I know, in their home circles, openly hoping that the I.W.W.'s would come back and 'clean up.'

Terrorism and chaos reigned in Everett following the tragedy. Over six hundred deputies patrolled the streets. A citizen who slipped into the prohibited area claims that he overheard a group of panic stricken citizen-deputies say: "We must stick together on this story about the first shot from the boat."

Certain officials called for the state militia and, without investigating, Governor Lister ordered mobilization and soon some of the naval militiamen were on the scene. Some militiamen, knowing that the call practically amounted to strike duty *refused to go to the armory.*

The Verona, with its cargo of dead and wounded, steamed toward Seattle, meeting the Calista four miles out from Everett. Captain Wyman stopped the Calista and cried out through his megaphone, "For God's sake don't land. They'll kill you. We have dead and wounded on board now."

In Seattle large bodies of police—with drawn revolvers—lined the dock awaiting the return of the two steamers. At 4:40 P.M. the Verona reached the dock and the first words of the I.W.W. men were, "Get the wounded fellows out and we'll be all right." The four dead members, their still bodies covered with blankets, were first removed from the boat and taken to the morgue. Police and hospital ambulances were soon filled with the thirty-two wounded men, who were taken to the city hospital. The uninjured men were then lined up and slowly marched to the city jail. The thirty-eight men taken from the Calista were placed in the county jail.

A competent physician is authority for the statement that Felix Baran, the I.W.W. man who died in the city hospital, would have had more than an even chance of recovery had he been given proper surgical attention upon his arrival in the hospital.

Up to this writing no inquest has been held over the five dead fellow workers.

The Seattle I.W.W. has been denied the bodies and unless relatives come forward to claim them the men will be buried as paupers. A request that the I.W.W. be allowed to hold a public funeral for the four men met with a denial. It was claimed that the display of these men to the general public would tend to incite a riot and disorder. The even hand of capitalist justice is shown by the fact that at the same time this ruling was made the funeral of gunman C. O. Curtis took place in Seattle with Prosecuting Attorney Alfred H. Lundin as one of the pall-bearers. This funeral was held with military honors, Lieut. Curtis having been in the officers' reserve corps of the National Guard of Washington, and formerly of the Adjutant General's staff.

A hastily gathered coroner's jury in Everett viewed the bodies of gunman C. O. Curtis and Jeff F. Beard, and retiring long enough to put their instructions in writing had laid these deaths at the door of the I.W.W.—"a riotous mob on the steamer Verona." The Seattle Central Labor Council on November 8 characterized the inquest as a farce and appropriated $100 for a complete investigation. They also demanded that a fair and exhaustive inquest be held, with full examination of all available witnesses.

The men in jail were held incommunicado for several days and were not allowed even the prison bill of fare—being given only bread and coffee. Mayor H. C. Gill, being aware of the fact that the public generally were sympathizing with the men, directed that they be placed upon the regular prison diet,

and that they be allowed to see relatives and friends. He also
saw personally to the comfort of the prisoners by providing
them with 300 warm blankets and an assortment of tobacco.
In an interview which appeared in a Seattle paper the mayor
made the following statement:

> In the final analysis it will be found that these cowards
> in Everett who, without right or justification, shot into
> the crowd on the boat, were murderers and not the
> I.W.W.'s.
>
> The men who met the I.W.W.'s at the boat were a bunch
> of cowards. They outnumbered the I.W.W.'s five to one,
> and in spite of this they stood there on the dock and
> fired into the boat, I.W.W.'s, innocent passengers and all.
>
> McRae and his deputies had no legal right to tell the
> I.W.W.'s or any one else that they could not land there.
> When the sheriff put his hand on the butt of his gun and
> told them they could not land, he fired the first shot,
> in the eyes of the law, and the I.W.W.'s can claim that
> they shot in self-defense.

Speaking of the men in jail, Gill said:

> These men haven't been charged with anything. Personally
> I have no sympathy with the I.W.W.'s. The way I have
> handled them here in the past ought to be proof enough
> of that, but I don't believe I should have these men tor-
> tured just because I have them in jail.
>
> If I were one of the party of forty I.W.W.'s who was al-
> most beaten to death by 300 citizens of Everett without
> being able to defend myself, I probably would have
> armed myself if I intended to visit Everett again.

The mayor charged that Everett officials were inconsistent
in their handling of this situation. He said that they permit
candidates for office to violate the city ordinances by speak-

ing on the streets and yet run the I.W.W.'s out of town if they
endeavor to mount a soap box.

"Why hasn't a Benson supporter just as much right to speak
in the streets as a McBride or a Hughes supporter?" said Mayor
Gill.

Passenger Oscar Carlson was at the very front of the Verona
when the firing commenced. He now lies in the city hospital
with a number of serious bullet wounds. His affidavit has been
taken. In an interview he speaks of the I.W.W. attitude on the
voyage to Everett as follows:

"I never expected to have any shooting. All I heard was
'They may not let us land.' I didn't hear any threat of violence—
it seemed funny. I was not acquainted and knew but two by
sight only."

Although in a weakened condition, Carlson stated that he
saw no guns and continued the interview long enough to say,
"I tell you as it comes to me now, it seems one shot came
from the dock first, then three or four from the other side,
then all sides at once."

Ernest Nordstrom, another passenger, practically substanti-
ates all of Carlson's statement.

As was to be expected, the entire capitalist press united in
their opposition to the I.W.W.'s in this fight. Their tactics have
embraced everything from outright lies to the petty trick of
placing the words "Jew," "Irish," etc., after the names of
I.W.W. men in their newspaper references in order to create the
idea that the whole affair is the work of "ignorant foreigners."
To combat these capitalist forces there are in the immediate
vicinity three official organs of the A. F. of L., the Industrial
Worker, the Northwest Worker of Everett and the Socialist
World of Seattle. These are weekly papers, but the publicity
they have already given the case is swinging public opinion to
the side of the workers.

To arrive at an understanding of the tragedy of the Verona
some knowledge of the events that preceded it is necessary.

Everett has been in a more or less lawless condition ever
since the open shop lumber men imported thugs and scabs to
break the shingle weavers' strike of six months ago. Union

men were beaten and one picket was shot in the leg. Demands
for organization brought the I.W.W. on the scene. Headquarters
were opened and street meetings started to inform the Everett
workers of conditions in the mills and in the northwest lumber
industry generally. Obeying orders from the Commercial Club,
the I.W.W. hall was closed by the police. Speakers were arrested
and deported. Members of the I.W.W. from Seattle, some of
them striking longshoremen, aided the shingle weavers in the
maintaining of their picket line. Deportation entirely without
legal process continued for some time. On September 9 Sheriff
McRae and a bunch of vigilantes fired a volley of shots at the
launch Wonder and arrested the captain, together with twenty
I.W.W. men who were on board. Meanwhile the police were
raiding the I.W.W. hall and all of those arrested were taken to
jail, where they were severely beaten. Jury trials were denied
and finally the prisoners were turned over to the vigilante
mob, who clubbed them and illegally deported them. These
tactics continued for some time, and increased in their intensity
to such an extent that the citizens of Everett, some ten or fifteen thousand in number, gathered in a protest meeting on
September 20. There were speakers representing all factions of
the labor revolutionary movement, as well as citizens who had
come to tell of the beatings they had received at the hands of
the vigilantes.

Then, on October 30, occurred an outrage greater than all
the preceding ones—an outrage exceeded only by the wanton
murder of the I.W.W. men on the steamer Verona. Forty-one
I.W.W. men, entirely unarmed and accused of no crime, were
taken from a boat on which they were passengers, and at the
point of guns, were searched and abused by a mob of deputized
drunks. They were then thrown into automobiles and with
armed guards, who outnumbered them five to one, were taken
to a lonely country spot, where they were forced to run the
gauntlet of the vigilantes who rained blows upon their unpro-
tected heads and bodies with saps, clubs, pickhandles and
other weapons. In this mob of 200 fiends were lawyers, doctors,
business men, members of the chamber of commerce,

"patriotic" militiamen, ignorant university students, deputies and Sheriff McRae. As a result of a peaceable attempt to assert a constitutional right, forty-one members of the I.W.W. were sent to Seattle hospitals, with injuries ranging from dangerously severe bruises to broken shoulders.

The answer of the I.W.W. to this damnable act of violence and to the four months of terrorism that had preceded it was a call issued through the *Industrial Worker* for two thousand men to enter Everett, there to gain by sheer force of numbers that right of free speech and peaceable assemblage supposed to have been guaranteed them by the constitution of the United States. Then came the tragedy on the steamer Verona.

The prosecution made its first legal move on Friday, November 10, when forty-one men were singled out, heavily handcuffed and secretly transported to Everett. They are charged with first degree murder. The other men are held on the technical charge of unlawful assembly, pending the filing of more serious charges.

The defense of the men will be undertaken by lawyer Fred H. Moore, assisted by Judge Hilton,[19] Arthur Leseuer, Col. C. E. S. Wood and local Seattle attorneys, according to present advices.

The prosecution is backed by the Chamber of Commerce, the Commercial Club, the Employers' Association, the Lumber Trust and other upholders of the open shop. These men will stick at nothing to convict the prisoners so as to cover the murders committed by their hirelings.

An immediate and generous response is the only means of preventing a frame-up and wholesale conviction of these men. They have fought their class war. Are you game to back them up financially? Let your response go at once to the

DEFENSE COMMITTEE,
Box 85, Nippon Station, Seattle, Wash.

International Socialist Review, December 1916.

Jails Didn't Make Them Weaken
By JACK LEONARD

*One of the 74 Everett Victims Tells How
With Battleship and Solidarity
They Improved the Jail*

It has been suggested to me many times, that I write my personal experiences and reactions while confined in the Snohomish county and King county jails after our arrests on the first degree murder charges November 5, 1916.

The history of the events leading up to and including November 5, 1916, has been written much better than I could hope to do. The things we did to amuse ourselves; the humorous situations that arose, the bewilderment of the jailers at a group of prisoners who insisted upon and received, finally, respect from them; the lifting of authority as far as the prisoners' welfare was concerned, or the administration of all matters within the tanks and cells was concerned—these things have just been mentioned as something incidental to the trial itself.

The 74 represented a remarkable cross section of the working class, more remarkable because it was so representative. There was an Irishman from Ireland, another of Irish extraction but born in U.S.A., an English Jew, a Russian Jew and an American Jew. (All by birth, none as far as I know professing.) There were at least two from Australia. The age of the 74 ranged from a 16 year old boy to men approaching 60. There were migratory workers and resident workers; and some of them had worked at so many different jobs and at such a variety of crafts, that I honestly believe that given the tools and materials, they could have built a city complete with all utilities. In education so far as I have any knowledge none had gone to college. (Perhaps that is why Anna Louise Strong[20] said that we reminded her of college students.)

There were as many kinds of personalities and temperaments as there were individuals. This then is the group I was to spend months with, before and during the trial of Thomas Tracy.

As was customary in those days, we migrants seldom had occasion to use the names by which our births were or were

not registered, and mine had been changed from John L. Miller
to J. Leonard Miller to Jack Leonard. The last seemed to stick,
like burrs to a water spaniel.

As we were being booked at the Seattle city jail I got my first
chuckle as the booking sergeant said: "The Leonard family is
damn well represented here tonight," especially as I knew the
man's name he was registering was really Leonard and since
Leonard had become my moniker that was what I was going
to give.

Shortly after this I was shoved into what is known as a tank
with so many men that there was not enough floor space for
us all to lie down. We soon managed this by having the first
row lie down, the second row would lay head and shoulders on
the hips of the first row, the third row heads and shoulders
on the hips of the second row and so on.

The Battleship

This went on with a bread and coffee diet for a few days
until we were sufficiently organized to "Build a Battleship."
I do not know how the expression "Build a Battleship"
originated, but to those who have not participated or witnessed such a demonstration by a bunch of determined
Wobblies, I'll say but emphatically, you have missed something.

The building was not too suitable as it was built of concrete.
The jail was several floors above the street and was divided into
several tanks, so that it was hard to work in perfect concert
with all groups. First we sang a few songs to warm up. Then in
our tank we all huddled in the center and locked arms, and at
the count of three we would all jump up from the floor and of
course our combined weight would fall upon the floor at the
same time. Being one of the "constructors" I cannot say for
sure, but I have been told, that the building actually rocked
as tho it were in an earthquake. The jailers first threatened to
turn the fire hose upon us. We invited them to do so as we
intended to keep on until we furnished them with a hole in
the floor for the water to run out. They changed from an attitude of command to one of pleading. They told us of our dying fellow workers in the hospital below. We told them that

those men would be cheered rather than depressed by our
action. The jailers called the Chief of Police and the Chief of
Police called the Mayor of Seattle. The Mayor agreed that we
should have better food and tobacco be distributed, and things
arranged so that we could at least lie down and be furnished
with blankets.

Not many days afterwards we were charged by an information filed by the prosecutor of Snohomish County with first
degree murder, that is 41 of us. Later 33 more were so charged.

Three Fingers

We 74 were supposed to be the "leaders." Hell, we had already informed them at the dock in Everett on November 5,
that we were all leaders, so in order to get 74, just as many as
the Snohomish County jail would hold, they placed some one
in a padded cell—no I am not kidding— and he chose us by
sticking three fingers thru a hole for yes and two fingers for
no. Some picker, two at least were not members at all; some
had just lined up. I had been a member less than four months
and mostly by accident. Some of ability were chosen. The rest
were known because of their activities for the organization.

Now as I mentioned before we were of all temperaments
and as the information was read to the first 40, one fainted.
Some were sarcastic enough to tell the prosecutor that they
thought the charge might be something serious, some jeered,
some were indignant, but before the prosecutor could leave
we were all singing the *"Red Flag"* or *"Solidarity Forever."*[21]

A couple of nights later we were taken to Everett by inter-
urban which then ran from Seattle to Everett. The Mayor of
Seattle asked if sufficient protection had been provided for
us at Everett. I did not hear the reply. But Seattle police rode
in the car with us part of the way.

When we arrived in Everett we were placed in the upper tank
which had 40 bunks, so one of our number had to sleep in the
corridor between the cells. These cells were small, so small that
there were two bunks, one over the other hung on hinges and
chains to each wall, with an aisle just wide enough for a man
to squeeze thru. The sanitary facilities consisted of a bucket

for each four men within the cells, one toilet in the corridor,
a slop sink where we washed our faces and a shower bath.

Everett's New Jail

For some time we were all but one locked in the cell at night
with no access to the toilet. The food was even by jail standard
terrible. We were some time getting organized, but from the
first we had a jail committee which was elected every week.
This committee saw that the portion of the jail which we used
was kept clean and dished out what food was given to us.
They were the only ones who would speak to the jailers. No
one could serve on this committee the second time until each
had served upon it once. Needless to say the jailers, who had
been used to, and had encouraged the old kangaroo court
system, were puzzled. How could they play favorites, or get
stool pigeons or otherwise play one prisoner against the other,
or who could they pick for the fall guy?

Now when we entered this jail it was so new that it shone.
It was supposed to be escape proof. Hardened steel floor and
ceiling, hardened steel bars, about four inches wide and 5/8 of
an inch thick. It had a locking system which was worked by
levers from outside the corridors, but inside the building. We
could see that the jailers were proud of their jail.

Our breakfast in the morning was mouldy half cooked mush.
One morning it was so bad that it looked as if some one had
defecated into it. The committee served it into the pie pans
provided for us to eat from, and then called a meeting to see
what was to be done with it. We voted upon it and, as agreed,
one man after another took his pan and threw the contents
thru the bars at the end of the corridors and frescoed the walls
and carpeted the stairs with it. Oh, their beautiful jail.

For supper we had stew or beans. If there was ever any meat
in the stew, no one to my knowledge ever discovered it. It consisted of carrots, turnips and spuds on two occasions. We did
the same thing with the stew as we did with the mush. Then
one night they served us with sour beans, that is beans that
had been cooked and had spoiled. We did not discover this
until most of them had been eaten up. During the night we

were all seized with cramps and diarrhea. That night all of the buckets and the toilet were in constant use. All thru the next day, the jailer received such a thorough and constant cussing that they left us locked in our cells until the next morning, thereby laying keel for another "Battleship."

Taking Some Liberty

Some one found that there was about 3/4 of an inch slack in the locking mechanism. Now here is a lesson in organized or concerted action. Each four men in each of five cells on the two sides of the corridor all threw their weight against this slack, gaining a little each time, until nine of the ten doors upstairs were forced open far enough for us to get into the corridor. Then we took blankets, rolled them into a rope, and sprung the angle irons on one side of the door until they were never able to lock them while I was there.

Down stairs where the 33 others were kept, they had a bath tub. There was only a cold water tap to the tub. The water was heated by first filling the tub and then turning on the steam thru the pipe that ran down into the filled tub.

They were not able to get as many doors opened in the lower tank at first as we did in the upper tank, but those that got into the lower corridor somehow unscrewed this pipe and pried the doors to the locking system open. These doors were just above the cell doors. Then they unscrewed the bolts on the horizontal locking levers and by prying, twisting and bending, pulled the levers out of their place and onto the floor. This allowed those still in the cells to open the cell doors and come into the corridor.

You are probably asking what were the jailers doing all this time? Well the first thing that they did was to grab all the guns and run into the street. We were all locked into the corridors, but they were not sure whether we intended to stay there or not, and were not going to be present to say good-bye if we decided to leave. They didn't come back until they called the sheriff.

Time for Beef

Meanwhile some one discovered a barrel of corn beef out in the passage way, and tore a strip from a blanket and bent a nail into a hook. The hook was tied to the strip of blanket and thrown so it would catch on the rim of the barrel. The barrel was upset and the corn beef was drawn into the cell and part of it sent via the blanket strip and bent nail to the upper tank. Our sink had a steam pipe to heat water also, so when the sheriff and deputies came into their jail, we were steam cooking corned beef in the sink. The sheriff felt very badly about the damage to his brand new jail. So did the taxpayers. It cost over $800 to repair it.

This was the act by which we notified the sheriff who was actually in control. It was explained to him that if better food and treatment were not immediately forthcoming, he could expect not only a re-occurrence of what had just been done, but a more thorough job next time.

As one of the Irish put it: "We'll tear your damned jail down brick by brick and camp by bonfire till ye build another, then tear it down too until ye learn how to feed and treat us." That night we had our first meal that was fit to eat. Next morning we were served with corn flakes with white instead of blue milk and bacon, and coffee that we could drink without holding our nose.

Who Runs This Jail?

They allowed us to have a phonograph after this and I was elected to take it to the lower tank when some one wanted music, and play the records for them. I also played the records in the upper tank. One day I was called to play the phonograph in the lower tank. I called the jailer. He let me take the phonograph and records down the stairs, but said that I would not be allowed to go in. I called for the committee for that week in the lower tank and told them what the jailer said. This forced things right out in the open. The jailer was asked, but not gently, "Who in the hell do you think is running this

jail? Now you open that door and let him come in with that
phonograph, or send down to Sumner Iron Works for some
more boilermakers. If he don't come in you are going to need
them." The door was opened and I went in and stayed until
everybody had heard all the records they wished to hear. After
that it was understood by the jailers that they could either be
as decent as their jobs permitted or call the boilermakers.

There were two round steel posts running from the floor
of the lower tank thru the ceiling of the lower tank and the
floor and up to the ceiling of the upper tank. We used to sing
and march in step around these posts. I don't think the jailers
or sheriff ever realized what that was doing to their steel jail.
I wonder if they knew that soldiers marching across a bridge
are always told to break step.

Page Ripley

As I have been reading what I have just written I find a
couple of errors. We were not 74 to start with. One of our number who had been wounded on the boat Verona did not join
us until he was brought from the hospital. Another found that
he was named in the information. He went first to the chief
of police in Seattle, and then to the sheriff of King County.
Each telephoned to the Snohomish county authorities, and
got the old run around. This man accused of first-degree murder
had to pay his own fare to Everett to be arrested by the ones
who accused him! Page Mr. Ripley.

During all of this time we were not neglecting our education.
This was just after the tenth convention of the I.W.W. and
changes in the constitution were to be voted upon. The old
constitution and the proposed changes were discussed article
by article and section by section as it stood, and as it would be
after the changes were made. We called meetings with a new
chairman each time. This taught parliamentary procedure to
all of us. We exchanged our experiences in the class struggle,
in free speech fights, in the harvest fields and on the jobs
generally. We read and studied the organization literature when
it became available. We sang our songs and the popular songs
of the day, especially the verse from "Don McRae":

> "Oh Don McRae you've had your day;
> Make way for freedom's host
> For labor's sun is rising soon
> Will shine from coast to coast,
> And when at last, the working class
> Shall make the masters yield
> May your portion of the victory be
> A grave in Potter's Field."

We played games together and pranks upon each other. Oh, yes we were human beings. There were differences of opinion and a little quarreling, no one of course was allowed to strike another. These were all of a personal nature, but, let any issue arise between any one of us and the jailers, then we were at once united and all personal differences forgotten.

An amusing thought comes to me here. One of us whenever he quarreled, and he quarreled frequently, used to put the name of the one he quarreled with in a note book. He was going to fight with each as soon as we were released. I hope he kept that book as my name was in it. What a laugh we could have together, and how glad he would be to meet those same guys now!

Back to Seattle

The trial was set for March 5, 1917. As all the judges in Snohomish county had shown prejudice, the defense had obtained a change of venue to King county. In February I was transferred to the King county jail at Seattle. I was to be a witness in the trial. There were twenty-five in all who came as witnesses to Seattle. A week or so after we left Everett the jailers must have thought that because the number of prisoners left there was smaller, the spirit had changed. An argument came up between the Wobblies and the jailers. The jailers brought in the fire hose and wet down the jail. The Wobs mopped up the water with Snohomish county mattresses. Even if the jailers won, they lost.

Before we left Everett, we were taken before the judge to plead. Some of those who could raise beards, spent weeks

trimming their beards so that the shape would match the one
grown by the judge who was to hear us plead. These of course
pushed their way into the front row where the resemblance
could not be missed. The judged missed the sarcasm and seemed
to be flattered that his whiskers were a source of derision.

I am not trying to keep this article in chronological order as
I am writing entirely from memory and without notes, so if I
should remember something which I think should be inserted,
but happened previously to something already mentioned, I
can do so without rewriting the whole article.

No Kangaroo

When we arrived at the King county jail in Seattle, we were
scattered through several tanks. The first thing done by the
other prisoners was to call the Kangaroo court[22] to order. Be-
lieving in the freedom of speech and assembly even by prisoners
in jail, we listened to the whole proceedings. When they had
finished they were told firmly and with emphasis, that we as
members of the I.W.W. would neither be governed by its rules
nor be a party to it. We explained to them that we had a committee system and that so far as the I.W.W. members were concerned we intended to continue it. Seeing our determined
stand the kangaroo court waived any claim of authority so far
as we were concerned. As in all kangaroo courts, the kangaroo
judge and sheriff were inflicting fines and manual jobs on all
incoming prisoners. These fines were supposed to be equally
distributed among the prisoners, but generally the larger portions were kept by the judge and the sheriff. It was not long
until the other prisoners saw the difference between governing
themselves and being dictated to by a clique.

In Seattle some of the various religious bodies would visit
the jail. All through Sunday morning we would have to listen
to wheezy portable organs, and off key voices of men and
women in the last stages of galloping decrepitude. Then they
would tell us about sin, and its terrible results and consequences.
In fact they knew so much about sin, that we were sure they
were experts in all its branches.

After the noisy ones left, the mental healers came in. Their
theme was that everything we heard, saw, felt, smelt or tasted

was myth. The jail and its inhabitants as far as I could gather
were just conditions of the mind along with everything else.
I wonder if any of them have ever been on the wrong end of
a policeman's club. Hungry as jail grub kept us, this did not
improve our appetite, so we began to hold services of our own.
Mostly the same tunes, but oh the difference in words! There
was as much difference in the manner of singing, as there was
in the words. Our singing taught defiance, not obedience to
our masters.

Well the religionists and the jailers protested. We were asked
if we would not give to them the same rights we demanded for
ourselves. The obvious reply was that we didn't lock them up
and make them listen to us. I am not sure what the reason was
but soon after this most of us were placed in one tank, where
we could set up our committee system again.

Making Trials Cost

We had all demanded separate trials, and under the laws of
the state of Washington we were entitled to separate trials.
The state chose for its first victim Thomas H. Tracy, who had
been Secretary of the Everett Local of the I.W.W. The outcome
is history. One of the 74, a little less noble than Judas tried
to help send his fellow workers to prison. His appearance and
entrance was like the hero in a ten cent melodrama. When asked
if he had seen any one armed on the Verona, he pointed his
finger at arm's length and pointed not to Tracy but to another
of the 74 and said, "There is the man." After examination of
scores of prosecution witnesses and their cross examination by
the defense, no one was sure who had killed the deputy we
were accused of killing. Those of us who discussed it in jail
were convinced that he had stopped a bullet fired by his own
side.

The defense witnesses who were held in jail found out that
the longer the trial lasted, the more it would cost Snohomish
county. So we agreed that when we were under cross examination by the prosecution to make our answers delay the proceedings as much as possible. The prosecution helped us un-
intentionally by trying to discredit us as persons. They had no
hope of destroying the force of our testimony. Once a witness

was asked during cross examination where he had come from, when he came to Seattle. He mentioned Yakima where he had stayed one day, Spokane, several towns in Montana, North Dakota, South Dakota, Iowa and Nebraska. It all contributed to the delay. Then he was asked how he came into Omaha. "Rode in." "On what?" "On a train." "What kind of a train?" "Railroad train." "What kind of railroad train?" "Steam train." "Was it a passenger train or a freight train?" Here the defense lawyer got in an objection which was sustained. The prosecutor had learned so much geography that he must have forgotten what he wanted the jury to find out in the first place, so he excused the witness.

No Fugitives

While the trial was going on some of the prisoners in Everett were taken for a walk for exercise. On one of these occasions the deputy who was escorting them started to walk away from them. He was called back and told by the prisoners to return them to the jail as they did not know the way.

In Seattle when any of the I.W.W. prisoner witnesses were taken out of the jail for glasses, dentistry or other treatment, the deputies escorting them more than once left them in various offices in which they were being fitted or treated, knowing that none would try to escape. Why should we? Hadn't we been chosen as witnesses? We hardly thought of ourselves as individuals and gauged our actions by the value they would be to the defense, the organization and the working class. We did not feel this as those who profess religious conviction by some sort of sudden revelation, but by the association with one another and the realization that the group and the thing that the group stood for were far more important than the individual.

Acquittal

The trial finally came to an end on May 5, 1917, with the acquittal of Thomas H. Tracy. The Lumber Barons and shingle manufacturers of the Pacific Northwest had had their Roman Holiday. They had also had a belly full of murder trials. Snohomish county was broke. The I.W.W. was stronger in membership and strength on the job. It had built up a prestige with which to carry on the lumber strike of 1917.[23]

All names except those of the writer or Thomas H. Tracy have been omitted, not with any intention to slight them. Most of them need no mention for they for years at least were useful and active in the Class Struggle.

This is a story of a group. I have not forgotten the fellow worker who would rather be returned back to a prison from which he had escaped than be used by the prosecution; nor have I forgotten the lump in my throat when we tried to sing "Solidarity" for him in token of goodbye.

Industrial Worker, October 30, 1946.

Notes

Introduction

1. *Proceedings of the First Convention of the Industrial Workers of the World* (New York, 1905), p. 82. (Hereinafter cited as *Proceedings, First Convention, I.W.W.)*

For discussion of the origin and early history of the I.W.W., *see* Paul F. Brissenden, *The I.W.W., A Study of American Syndicalism* (New York, 1919); Fred Thompson, *The I.W.W.: Its First Fifty Years, 1905-1955* (Chicago, 1955); Joyce L. Kornbluh, ed., *Rebel Voices: An I.W.W. Anthology* (Ann Arbor, Michigan, 1964); Philip S. Foner, *History of the Labor Movement in the United States,* vol. 4, *The Industrial Workers of the World, 1905-1917* (New York, 1965); Melvyn Dubofsky, *We Shall Be All: A History of the Industrial Workers of the World* (Chicago, 1969); Joseph R. Conlin, *Bread and Roses Too* (Westport, Conn., 1969).

2. *Proceedings, First Convention, I.W.W.,* p. 29.

3. Ibid., pp. 4-5, 143, 153, 359, 506, 577.

4. Ibid., pp. 220, 247-48.

5. *Solidarity,* November 1, 1913.

6. *Proceedings, First Convention, I.W.W.,* p. 154.

7. Ibid., pp. 298-99.

8. Ibid., pp. 534-35.

9. Ibid., pp. 563, 575.

214   Notes

10. Ibid., pp. 170, 181-85, 193, 197-98.
11. Brissenden, op. cit., p. 42; Foner, op. cit., p. 115; *Proceedings, First Convention, I.W.W.*, pp. 520, 522.
12. Foner, op. cit., p. 39; Dubofsky, op. cit., p. 47.
13. Carleton Parker, *The Casual Laborer and Other Essays* (New York, 1920), p. 15.
14. Robert L. Tyler, "Rebels of the Woods and Fields: A Study of the I.W.W. in the Pacific Northwest" (Ph.D. dissertation, University of Oregon, 1953), p. 25.
15. Foner, op. cit., p. 116.
16. Samuel Gompers, *Labor and the Employer* (New York, 1920), p. 42.
17. Ibid., pp. 46-50.
18. *Industrial Worker*, February 26, July 30, August 6, September 10, October 15, November 9, 1910; January 19, July 20, 1911; August 11 and 22, September 26, November 7, December 12 and 19, 1912; June 5 and 12, July 17, 1913.
19. *Solidarity*, December 17, 1910; November 28, 1915; February 13, July 10, 1915.
20. Ibid., September 17, 1910; July 15, 1911; November 2, 1914; Hyman Weintraub, "The I.W.W. in California, 1906-1931" (Ph.D. dissertation, University of California, Berkeley, 1947), pp. 64-65; *International Socialist Review* 12 (February 1912): 65.
21. Tyler, op. cit., p. 18; *Solidarity*, June 4, 1910; *Industrial Worker*, June 6, 1912.
22. Donald M. Barnes, "The Ideology of the Industrial Workers of the World" (Ph.D. dissertation, Washington State University, 1962), pp. 198-99; *History of the I.W.W.* (Chicago, ca. 1913), p. 12.
23. Carleton H. Parker, "The Economic Basis of the I.W.W.," *More Truth About the I.W.W.* (Chicago, 1918), pp. 10-11; Walter V. Woehlbe, "Truth About the I.W.W." (Chicago, 1918), pp. 20-21.
24. *Proceedings of the Second Annual Convention of the I.W.W.* (Chicago, 1906), pp. 27, 304, 309-12, 610; Brissenden, op. cit., pp. 136-54; Foner, op. cit., pp. 74-78; Dubofsky, op. cit., pp. 94-108.
25. *Industrial Worker*, January, 1907; Vernon H. Jensen, *Heritage of Conflict: Labor Relations in the Nonferrous Metals Industry up to 1930* (Ithaca, N.Y.), pp. 184-87.
26. Brissenden, op. cit., p. 151; *Proceedings, Western Federation of Miners Convention, 1906* (Denver, 1906), p. 132; *Proceedings, Western Federation of Miners Convention, 1907,* (Denver, 1907), pp. 788, 799; *Proceedings, Western Federation of Miners Convention, 1908* (Denver,

1908), pp. 21-23; *Industrial Union Bulletin*, July 13, 28, August 24, November 16, December 14, 1907; January 25, 1908.

27. *Miners' Magazine*, January 9, 1908, p. 5; July 23, 1908, pp. 5, 7; July 30, 1908, p. 5; *Proceedings, Western Federation of Miners Convention, 1908*, pp. 21-23.

28. *Chicago Socialist*, October 13, 1906; *International Socialist Review* 6 (April 1906): 63; 7 (November 1906): 311-12; 8 (March 1908): 538-47.

29. William Z. Foster, "Syndicalism in the United States," *The Communist*, July, 1937, p. 1044.

30. *Industrial Union Bulletin*, November 9, 1907; February 1, March 6, April 25, May 2, 23, 1908; *Daily People*, March 13, 1908; Brissenden, op. cit., pp. 228-29; Foner, op. cit., pp. 107-12; Dubofsky, op. cit., pp. 146-52.

31. *Industrial Union Bulletin*, November 7, 1908; February 27, 1909.

32. Ibid., November 7, 1908.

33. Grant S. Youmans in William D. Haywood, "Free Speech Fights, Letters Relating to," U.S. Commission on Industrial Relations File, Department of Labor, 413 Dup, National Archives, Washington, D.C.: *Industrial Worker*, September 4, 1913.

34. *The Socialist* (Seattle), September 7, October 12, 19, 26, 1907; *Seattle Times*, October 13, 1907.

35. *Common Sense*, February 15, March 14, 21, June 27, July 25, 1908; Grace Heilman Stimson, *Rise of the Labor Movement in Los Angeles* (Berkeley and Los Angeles, California, 1955, p. 324; "A Notable Triumph for Free Speech in Los Angeles," *Arena* 11 (October 1908): 35-51.

36. *Common Sense*, July 25, 1908.

37. *New York Times*, May 9, 1912.

38. *Kansas City Star*, October 24, 1911.

39. *Solidarity*, July 25, 1914.

40. *Industrial Worker*, July 13, 1913.

41. Foner, op. cit., p. 175n.

42. *Industrial Worker*, December 28, 1911.

43. *Solidarity*, June 4, 1910.

44. *Industrial Worker*, April 25, 1912.

45. W. I. Fisher, "Soap-Boxer or Organizer, Which?" *Industrial Worker*, June 6, 1912; Grave V. Silver in *New York Call*, reprinted in *Solidarity*, March 25, 1911.

46. Reprinted in *Industrial Worker*, January 25, 1912.

47. Dubofsky, op. cit., pp. 196-97.

216 Notes

48. Selig Perlman and Philip Taft, *History of Labor in the United States, 1896-1932* (New York, 1935) p. 240.

49. Grant S. Youmans, "The Minot Free Speech Fight," in W. D. Haywood to C. McCarty, U.S. Commission on Industrial Relations Files, Department of Labor, 413 Dup, National Archives, Washington, D.C.

50. *Industrial Worker*, February 1, 1912.

51. Reprinted in ibid., December 9, 1916.

52. W. M. in ibid., June 30, 1945.

53. *Industrial Worker*, August, 1906.

54. An examination of the files of the *Mail and Empire* (Toronto) for July and August, 1906, reveals no account of the event.

55. Brissenden, op. cit., p. 387.

56. The result of a demand by a group of social workers after the bombing of the *Los Angeles Times* building in 1911 and the imprisonment of the McNamara brothers for the "Crime of the Century," for an investigation of conditions in American industry, the Commission on Industrial Relations began its real work in December 1913, "to inquire into the general conditions of labor in the principal industries of the United States . . . to discover the underlying causes of dissatisfaction in the industrial setting and report its conclusions thereon." (U.S. Commission on Industrial Relations, *Final Report*, Washington, D.C., 1915, p. 3.) Three labor representatives, three management representatives, and three representatives of the public, all appointed by President Woodrow Wilson, made up the Commission. Frank P. Walsh, known for his work in labor activities in civil and social movements as well as for his work in labor arbitration in Missouri, was chosen as both a public representative and chairman of the Commission. For the McNamara case, see Philip S. Foner, *History of the Labor Movement in the United States*, vol. 5, *The AFL in the Progressive Era, 1910-1915* (New York, 1980), pp. 7-31.

57. The son of Irish-Dutch parents, Vincent St. John was born in Newport, Kentucky, July 16, 1876, and, after drifting from job to job, settled down in Colorado as a miner; by 1901, he was president of the Telluride Local of the Western Federation of Miners and led the bitter strikes of 1901 and 1903 there. He was blacklisted but continued his union activities and supported the I.W.W. In 1906, as a member of the I.W.W. executive board, he went to Goldfield, Nevada, and organized the entire labor force. He was elected general secretary-treasurer of the I.W.W. in 1908 and led the organization during the free-speech fights and major strikes. He held the office until he resigned in 1915.

58. William D. ("Big Bill") Haywood was born in Salt Lake City, Utah,

February 4, 1869, son of a miner who died in 1872. In 1894 his family had moved to the mining town of Silver City, Idaho, where he became an officer of a local of the Western Federation of Miners; in 1900, he was elected secretary-treasurer of the union. He helped organize the I.W.W. and chaired its founding convention. After being acquitted in the famous case of Haywood, Pettibone, Moyer, involving the murder of a former Idaho governor, he continued working for the I.W.W. and the Socialist Party. Becoming disillusioned with political action, he turned more and more to direct action, and was a great leader of some of the famous I.W.W. strikes, particularly those in Lawrence and Patterson. In 1915 Haywood was elected general secretary of the I.W.W. Convicted with other Wobblies in 1917 for violating the Espionage Act, he jumped bail in 1921 to go to the Soviet Union, where he died on May 18, 1928.

Chapter 1. Free-Speech Fight in
Missoula, Montana, 1909

1. Elizabeth Gurley Flynn, "How I Became A Rebel," *Labor Herald,* July, 1922, pp. 23-25.

2. *New York Call,* October 6, 1909.

3. Frank H. Little (1879-1917), son of a Cherokee Indian mother and a Quaker father, was a member of the Western Federation of Miners by 1900 and joined the I.W.W. in 1907. Fearless and uncompromising, Little was jailed in most of the free-speech fights, and was elected a member of the I.W.W. Executive Board in 1914. While organizing copper miners in Butte, Montana, he was seized and brutally lynched by six men on the night of August 1, 1917.

4. In January 1908, during a speaking tour in the Mesabi Iron Range in Minnesota, Elizabeth Gurley Flynn met and immediately fell in love with Jack Archibald Jones, a Wobbly organizer from Bovey, Minnesota. Their married life together was hectic and brief: two years and three months. The couple had two children; the first was born prematurely and died within a few hours—probably as a result of the harsh conditions Gurley Flynn had to endure while pregnant in a Spokane jail.

5. The "Hands Off Russia" campaign was organized by all radical groups to end Allied intervention in Soviet Russia in 1918. By late 1918 the United States had approximately 7,000 soldiers on duty in Russia, and other Allied countries had intervened openly in Soviet Russia. *See* Philip S. Foner, *The Bolshevik Revolution: Its Impact on American Radicals, Liberals, and Labor* (New York, 1967).

6. Robert M. La Follette (1855-1925), governor of Wisconsin and

later U.S. senator who became the leader of the progressive forces in the Republican Party. In 1924 he was the presidential candidate on the Progressive Party ticket.

7. C. O. Young, the A.F. of L. organizer in Missoula who had refused to permit the A.F. of L. local to support the free-speech fight, wrote disgustedly to Frank Morrison, A.F. of L. secretary-treasurer: "The 'won't works' have tried the game here of filling the jails so full that the officials of the city would have to capitulate, and they have succeeded in forcing the local authorities to quit. Encouraged by their success at Missoula, they are publishing broadcast that they will do the same to any other city that denies them the privilege of using the streets for speaking." (C. O. Jones to Frank Morrison, November 17, 1909, American Federation of Labor Correspondence.) The "won't works" referred to one of the derisive distortions of the letters I.W.W. into "I Won't Work."

8. James P. Thompson, one of the I.W.W.'s leading organizers on the Pacific Coast, was involved in several free-speech fights.

Chapter 2. Free-Speech Fight in Spokane, Washington, 1909-1910

1. Testimony of William D. Haywood before the U.S. Commission on Industrial Relations, *Senate Documents*, vol. 20, no. 415 (Washington, D.C., 1916), vol. 12, p. 10573; Elizabeth Gurley Flynn, *I Speak My Own Piece, Autobiography of "The Rebel Girl"* (New York, 1955), pp. 95-96; *Industrial Worker*, February 10, 1910.

2. Fred W. Heslewood, "Barbarous Spokane," *International Socialist Review* 10 (February 1910): 711.

3. "Barbarous Spokane," *Independent* 68 (February 10, 1911): 330.

4. *Spokane Spokesman-Review*, November 3, 1909; *Portland Oregonian*, November 3, 1909.

5. *Portland Oregonian*, November 3, 1909; *Spokane Spokesman-Review*, November 3, 1909.

6. *Portland Oregonian*, November 4, 1909.

7. Ibid.

8. *Spokane Spokesman-Review*, November 5, 12, 1909.

9. Ibid., November 12, 1909; *Portland Oregonian*, November 7, 11, 1909.

10. William Z. Foster, *Pages from a Worker's Life*, New York, 1939, p. 145.

11. *Portland Oregonian*, November 7, 14, 1909; Ralph Chaplin, *Wobbly* (Chicago, 1967), p. 150; *Solidarity*, December 18, 1909.

12. Flynn, *I Speak My Own Piece*, p. 98.

13. *Portland Oregonian*, November 16, 1909.

14. Flynn, *I Speak My Own Piece*, p. 98.

15. *Solidarity*, December 23, 1909.

16. I.W.W. Circular, copy in A.F. of L. Correspondence; *Solidarity*, February 26, 1910.

17. *Industrial Worker*, February 5, 1910.

18. Ibid. Subsequently the Washington state legislature passed a law forbidding employment agencies from charging fees.

Glen J. Broyles challenges the view that the I.W.W. scored a victory in Spokane ("The Spokane Free Speech Fight, 1909-1910: A Study in I.W.W. Tactics," *Labor History* 19 (Spring 1978): 238-53.) But after insisting on this theme throughout most of the article, Broyles concludes as follows: "On May 21, 1910, the *Industrial Worker* reappeared in Spokane. The first three Wobblies were released sometime between May 7, 1910 and May 21, 1910. The Spokane I.W.W. locals began to grow again and once more free speech was allowed on the streets of Spokane." (Ibid., pp. 251-52.)

19. In I.W.W. parlance, the "home guard" referred to the factory slave who feared his wife and children might suffer if he was fired for organizing; he tended to be more cautious and less class-conscious than the migratory worker, who had no ties to family and could afford to be less servile.

20. Wobblies in the West, although lacking a formal education, often spent winters of idleness in the public libraries and became acquainted with the works of Marx and Engels, Herbert Spencer, Charles Darwin, Lewis Henry Morgan, Frederick Jackson Turner, and others. When they mounted a soapbox, they could lecture on economics, history, and politics with amazing knowledge.

21. W. F. of M. refers to the Western Federation of Miners, the militant union of miners in Idaho, Nevada, Utah, Colorado, and other western states; it helped to found the I.W.W.

22. In all, eight successive editors of the *Industrial Worker* were jailed after getting out eight successive issues. Finally, the office of the paper was raided, and it was decided late in December 1909 to transfer the paper -- masthead plates and all -- to Seattle. It was returned to Spokane in May 1910.

23. Gurley Flynn is referring to her own arrest by the Spokane police on November 31, 1909.

24. "The Red Flag" by James Connell was inspired by the London dock strike of 1899, the work of the Irish Land League, the Russian

Nihilist movement, and the hanging of the Chicago anarchists following
the Haymarket bombing of 1887. It was first published in the Christmas
1889 issue of *Justice*, a British socialist publication, and became the
official anthem of the British Labour Party. "The Red Flag" was first published in the I.W.W. press in the *Industrial Union Bulletin* of July 25,
1908, and was included in the first edition of the I.W.W.'s *Little Red
Song Book*. The book had thirty-eight songs and probably all were sung
by the Fresno prisoners. The opening verse of "The Red Flag" stated:

> The People's flag is deepest red,
>   It shrouded oft our martyred dead;
> And ere their limbs grow stiff and cold
>   Their life-blood dyed its every fold.

> *Chorus*
> Then raise the scarlet standard high
>   Beneath its folds, we'll live and die,
> Though cowards flinch and traitors sneer,
>   We'll keep the red flag flying here.

25. This statement is not accurate. Percy Bysshe Shelley (1792-1822),
one of the greatest English Romantic thinkers and poets, had two sons.
His son William, born in 1816, died on June 7, 1819. In November 1820,
he had a second son, named Percy Florence after Shelley and the city of
his birth. He was to be Mary and Percy Shelley's only surviving child.

26. The case against Elizabeth Gurley Flynn was later dismissed.

27. Ernest Untermann, associate editor of the Socialist weekly *Appeal
to Reason*, was a leading socialist writer and propagandist on the Pacific
Coast.

28. Joe Hill, the great Wobbly songwriter, summarized these sentiments
in his famous song, "The Preacher and the Slave."

29. With the railroads shut down in parts of the West owing to the
strike by switchmen, Wobblies could not and would not ride the freights to
get to Spokane. Even those trains that ran would be boycotted by militant Wobblies.

30. Wobblies who practiced passive resistance or nonresistance believed
that the Wobblies should not meet force with force but should go to jail
if arrested without offering the slightest physical resistance. This would
expose "the inner workings and purposes of the capitalist mind" and
prove that it was the capitalists and their henchmen who were guilty of
violence. At the same time, it would reveal "the fortitude, the courage,
the inherent sense of order of the workers' mind." During strikes, this

school of Wobbly thought emphasized that the workers should put their hands in their pockets and fight back through nonviolent mass picketing.

31. An effort was made to install a matron in the city jail to reform conditions publicized by Gurley Flynn, but although the City Council passed a resolution authorizing the appointment, the finance committee tabled it. However, two prison guards, denounced by the Wobblies for brutality, were discharged.

32. Fred H. Moore was one of the busiest I.W.W. lawyers and defended Wobblies in numerous trials.

33. For a summary of the type of activity he engaged in, see Leonard D. Abbott's letters in Ella Winter and Granville Hicks, eds., *The Letters of Lincoln Steffens* (New York, 1938), vol 1, pp. 336-38.

34. The reference is to Flynn's charge that she had been molested by male prison guards during her stay in the Spokane prison.

35. However, the remark is not "typical" of the I.W.W. attitude towards the black worker. See Philip S. Foner, "The I.W.W. and the Black Worker," *Journal of Negro History* 55 (1970): 45-64.

36. Turner societies were originally singing clubs of German-American workers, but became political associations under Socialist leadership in a number of cities.

37. The same, however, could not be said of the top A. F. of L. leadership. During the free-speech fight, the I.W.W. issued a circular entitled "The Shame of Spokane," appealing for financial aid. The circular was sent to many A. F. of L. affiliates as well as to socialist and progressive organizations. Moved by its detailed account of police brutalities (corroborated by reports in the press) and by the heroism of the free-speech fighters, many A.F. of L. affiliates contributed to the defense fund. Some unions wrote to President Samuel Gompers and Secretary-Treasurer Frank Morrison of the A.F. of L., urging them to take a stand officially in favor of free speech and against police brutality in Spokane. "We feel that the rights of all organized labor is at stake in the battle now taking place in our city," the Spokane Central Council wrote. "Already decent people not associated with the I.W.W. are being deprived of their right of free speech if they attempt to criticize the authorities. Certainly the American Federation of Labor cannot remain silent in the face of these facts." When more letters of this nature came to A.F. of L. headquarters, Morrison designated C. O. Young, general organizer stationed at Missoula, to go to Spokane, ascertain the facts, and report them to the A.F. of L., "so that we might be able to answer the numerous letters which reach us as to the purported treatment of said I.W.W. by Spokane authorities."

Young's report completely exonerated the Spokane authorities, and charged that the free-speech fight had been caused by the I.W.W.'s love for stirring up trouble. Spokane was "a liberal city, with the best treatment for patriotic, truly American labor of any western city," but the I.W.W. deserved no such treatment. Young urged Morrison to notify all A.F. of L. affiliates to ignore the I.W.W. circular and refrain from sending funds to assist "an un-American organization carry on their unholy work of breaking the laws and defying the constituted authority of the various communities. . . ." Morrison was more than "satisfied" with Young's report. "You need have no fear that the Executive Council will act in the matter," he assured Young, adding that he was especially happy to learn from the Missoula A.F. of L. general organizer that "the police were not brutal, but, on the contrary, were cautioned and did deal gently with every one arrested." (C. O. Young to Frank Morrison, March 28, 1910; Frank Morrison to C. O. Young, April 2, 1910, A.F. of L. Correspondence.)

The point made by the Spokane Central Council regarding the threat to the free speech of others in Spokane besides the I.W.W. was justified. A mass meeting was called during the free-speech fight at the Masonic Temple by leaders of the Women's Equal Suffrage Club, the Women's Club, several respected clergymen, and a number of socialists. It was announced as a gathering to protest the ordinance banning street speaking and police brutality against the I.W.W. At the last minute, the trustees of the Masonic Temple canceled use of their hall for the meeting. When a number of the planners of the meeting tried to gather in the streets to voice their protests, they were arrested and charged with disorderly conduct. (*Portland Oregonian*, November 4, 5, 1909; *Spokane Spokesman-Review*, November 6, 1909.)

38. Charles H. Moyer (1873-1929), president of the Western Federation of Miners, became a leading advocate of the need for a new industrial union, which led to the formation of the I.W.W. William Haywood, George Pettibone and Moyer were charged with the murder of former Idaho governor Frank Steunenberg in December, 1905. After Haywood and Pettibone had been acquitted, the charge against Moyer was dropped. Moyer soon turned against the radicals in the I.W.W., led the Western Federation of Miners out of the I.W.W., and sought to make peace with the leaders of the A.F. of L.

39. As part of the agreement ending the free-speech fight, the charges against the Wobblies imprisoned during the battle were dropped.

40. In 1907 George B. McClellan, mayor of New York City, boasted in describing his constituency: "There are Russian Socialists and Jewish Socialists and German Socialists! But thank God! There are no Irish Socialists!" Concerned lest they be overlooked, James Connolly, Tom

Flynn, his daughters Elizabeth Gurley and Kathie, and other Irish
Socialists formed the Irish Socialist Federation. Annie Gurley Flynn,
Elizabeth's mother, sewed a large green and white banner with the Irish
slogan, "Fag an Bealach" (Clear the Way) in a field of harps and sham-
rocks. To paraphrase Connelly's viewpoint, the Federation was formed
"not out of national sentiment but in estimation of the needs of a socialist movement growing in a cosmopolitan environment." Fifteen-year-old
Kathie Flynn became secretary of the Irish Socialist Federation.

James Connolly, the Irish revolutionary who was later martyred during
the Easter uprising in 1916 in Ireland, then lived in New York and published *The Harp* to publicize the struggle for Irish freedom and efforts to
organize dock workers within the I.W.W. It was through Connolly that
Elizabeth Gurley Flynn learned of the work of the I.W.W.

41. The son of an Irish railroad car washer, William Zebulon Foster
(1881-1961) was born in Taunton, Massachusetts; apprenticed to an
artist in 1891, he learned the art crafts of modeling and stonecutting;
he quit art work in 1894 and for the next few years was employed as an
industrial worker in a number of occupations, including sailor, railroader,
and homesteader. He joined the Socialist Party in 1900 but was expelled
nine years later when the party split in Washington led to the formation
of the United Wage Workers of Washington. Following the Spokane free-
speech fight, Foster joined the I.W.W. but left the Wobblies after a trip
to Europe convinced him that the correct strategy involved "boring-
from-within," in keeping with syndicalist principles. He led the historic
steel strike of 1919 and was a leader of the Communist Party until his
death. A leading theorist on trade union tactics and strategy, Foster
headed the Trade Union Educational League. He was the Communist
Party candidate for president in 1924, 1928, and 1932.

42. "The Pinkerton Agency," "Pinkerton Police," and "Pinkerton
strikebreakers" were names applied to the detective organization founded
by Allan Pinkerton (1819-1884), a Chartist who came to America in
1842 and settled in Chicago, where he set up the detective agency. The
Agency was mainly associated with anti-labor and anti-union activities
and was involved in the case of Haywood, Pettibone, and Moyer, as well
as in numerous strikes including the Homestead Strike of 1892.

43. Libby Prison was, after Andersonville, the most notorious of the
Confederate prisons during the Civil War. Tremendous overcrowding and
food shortages caused much suffering among the inmates who were Union
army commissioned officers.

44. "Soap-boxers" were I.W.W. street-corner speakers who stood on
a box to address the audience.

45. John Pancner (sometimes spelled Panzner) was a miner who participated in the I.W.W.'s first successful strike at Goldfield, Nevada in 1906, and thereafter worked and organized in logging camps and sawmills in California, Oregon, and Washington for several years. Although he was involved in a number of free-speech fights, he began to urge that they be dropped because they were destructive to the organization; defense money for those jailed took funds better spent on constructive organization on the job, and the jailings, beatings, and bread-and-water diets were ruining the health of those in the movement.

46. Here Pancner is using the term "trade unions" to mean craft unions.

47. Walter T. Nef was a "shovel man" on a construction job and a sawmill worker in Oregon who organized lumber workers in the Duluth-Superior logging camps and later was elected secretary-treasurer of the I.W.W.'s famous Agricultural Workers Organization 400.

48. The United Wage Workers of Washington was formed by Dr. Herman F. Titus, one of the founders of the Socialist Party in Seattle. In 1909 Titus became disillusioned with the Socialist Party, viewing it as an organization of "petit-bourgeois" farmers and "reformers," and organized the United Wage Workers to be composed exclusively of proletarians, "as defined by the *Communist Manifesto*." Titus published *The Socialist* until the split, after which he changed its name to *The Workingman's Paper*.

Chapter 3. Fresno Free-Speech Fight, 1910-1911

1. *Industrial Worker*, May 28, June 4, 1910; *Solidarity*, August 27, 1910; Hyman Weintraub, "The I.W.W. in California, 1906-1931" (Ph. D. dissertation, University of California, Berkeley, 1947), p. 25; *Oakland World*, December 31, 1910.

2. *Solidarity*, August 27, 1910.

3. Ibid., August 20, September 5, 1910; *Industrial Worker*, October 26, 1910.

4. *Industrial Worker*, November 2, 9; December 15, 1910; *San Francisco Call*, December 10, 1910.

5. *Industrial Worker*, January 26, 1911.

6. *San Francisco Call*, March 2, 1911; *Industrial Worker*, March 16, 1911; *The Agitator*, March 15, 1911.

7. Hyman Weintraub, "The I.W.W. in California, 1906-1931" (Ph.D. dissertation, University of California, Berkeley, 1947), p. 274.

8. Following the aborted Portland to Fresno trip, several short accounts appeared. See *Industrial Worker*, April 6, 1911.

9. Clyde also wrote a short piece about the trip for *Solidarity*, April

18, 1911, which is reprinted in Joyce L. Kornbluh, ed., *Rebel Voices: An I.W.W. Anthology* (Ann Arbor, Michigan, 1964), pp. 100-2. His fuller account reprinted here apparently was written at the request of Socialist Labor Party leader Daniel De Leon. This is based on information given by Clyde's widow to Charles P. LeWarne, who obtained the manuscript of Clyde's account and published it. See *Labor History*, 14 (Spring 1973): 266.

10. This was the address of Local 432, the largest and the leading I.W.W. local of Pacific Northwest lumber workers.

11. According to the *Portland Oregonian* the Wobblies whom the paper described as "vagrants" broke seals on the freight cars and climbed aboard while railroad agents watched helplessly. *The Seattle Daily Times*, in a dispatch from Portland, reported that the men had "captured" the freight train as it left the yard. The *Oregonian* listed about 150 men, whom, it said, were mostly aliens. (*Seattle Daily Times*, February 16, 1911; *Portland Morning Oregonian*, February 17, 1911.)

12. On February 18, 1911, the *Portland Morning Oregonian* published an extensive account of the Steinman interview. It noted that "individual members" had claimed on several occasions that the real destination was Mexico, where other I.W.W. members were contributing to the rebel cause. In fact, some of the I.W.W. marchers went on to lower California, where they joined General Pryce's force of socialist insurrectionists and fought in the Mexican Revolution. For the role of the I.W.W. in this movement, see Lowell L. Blaisdell, *The Desert Revolution: Baja, California, 1911* (Madison, Wisconsin, 1962.)

13. "Mulligan" was stew in I.W.W. parlance.

14. "The Eight-Hour Day" was written by Richard Brazier and was published in the third edition of the I.W.W. songbook. Sung to the tune of "Silver Threads among the Gold," the first chorus declared:

> Arise, then, throw your chains asunder,
> stand up for the eight-hour day,
> Then you workers who now hunger
> will have work and get more pay.

15. Clyde is referring to the agreement reached between the Wobblies in prison and Fresno city authorities and the rescinding on March 2, 1911, of the ban against street meetings.

16. In 1911 the I.W.W. initiated a drive to line up the working class in a national demonstration for the eight-hour day to take place in a year, on May 1, 1912—May Day. Clyde is a year ahead of the selected date, but since the I.W.W. annually celebrated May Day as labor's day, he may have been referring to local activities in support of the eight-hour day.

The Portland, Oregon, locals had already launched a campaign for the
eight-hour day in January, 1911. (*Industrial Worker*, January 15, 1911.)

17. Militant strikes of the Western Federation of Miners and the
Industrial Workers of the World took place in the Goldfield and Cripple
Creek mining districts.

18. The origin of "making a battleship" is not precisely known, but it
is believed to be derived from the practice of banging tin cups and plates
on the prison bars to make a terrible racket, as when the Wobblies also protested conditions in jail by yelling, singing, and piling up mattresses to protect themselves from hosings. For a description of a "battleship," see
pp. 200-202.

19. District industrial councils were made up of representatives from
all industrial union locals within a given area. These councils provided a
direct link with the general organization. However, those Wobblies who
favored decentralization opposed the formation of such district councils.

20. The reference here is to acceptance of the Wobblies' demand that
they not be required to leave the city as part of an agreement ending the
free-speech fight.

Chapter 4. Aberdeen Free-Speech Fight, 1911-1912

1. Weintraub, op. cit., p. 274; *Industrial Worker*, November 30, 1911.

2. Quoted in Richard Connelly Miller, "Otis and His *Times:* The
Career of Harrison Gray Otis of Los Angeles" (Ph.D. dissertation, University of California, Berkeley, 1961), p. 437.

3. Robert L. Tyler, "Rebels of the Woods and Fields: A Study of the
I.W.W. in the Pacific Northwest" (Ph.D. dissertation, University of Oregon,
1953), p. 35; *Industrial Worker*, November 23, 1911, February 1, 1912.

4. *Portland Oregonian*, November 23-24, 1911; Tyler, op. cit., pp.
36-37; *Industrial Worker*, December 14, 1911.

5. *Portland Oregonian*, November 25, December 4-5, 1911;
Solidarity, January 6, 1912; *Industrial Worker*, November 23, 1911; *The
Agitator*, December 1, 1911.

6. *Portland Oregonian*, December 4-5, 1911; *Solidarity*, December
16, 1911; *Industrial Worker*, December 14, 1911; Tyler, op. cit., p. 35.

7. *Industrial Worker*, February 1, 1912. Tyler calls the Aberdeen
free-speech fight a failure for the I.W.W., but his treatment of the battle
ends with December 1911, the period of the temporary victory for the
authorities and the citizen police. (op. cit., p. 51)

8. *Industrial Worker*, January 25, February 29, 1912.

9. Ibid., January 25, February 29, 1912; *New York Call*, February 11, 1912.

10. "Workers of the World Unite. You have nothing to lose but your Chains," the slogan that closed the *Communist Manifesto* by Karl Marx and Friedrich Engels.

Chapter 5. San Diego Free-Speech Fight, 1912

1. Ernest Jerome Hopkins, "The San Diego Fight," *The Coming Nation*, May 4, 1912, pp. 8-9; *Solidarity*, February 17, 1912; *Industrial Worker*, February 29, 1912; Rosalie Shanks, "The I.W.W. Free Speech Movement in San Diego, 1912," *Journal of San Diego History* 8 (Spring 1973): 26-28.

2. *Solidarity*, February 17, 1912.

3. *San Francisco Call*, February 10 and 19, 1912.

4. Reprinted in *Report of Harris Weinstock, Commissioner to Investigate the Recent Disturbances in the City of San Diego and the County of San Diego, California to His Excellency Hiram W. Johnson, Governor of California* (Sacramento, 1912), pp. 17-19.

5. Fred H. Moore and Marcus W. Robbins to Governor Hiram W. Johnson, April 3, 1912, Hiram Johnson Papers, University of California Library, Berkeley; *Industrial Worker*, March 7, 1912; *Oakland World*, March 23, 1912; *Solidarity*, June 1, 1912.

6. *Industrial Worker*, April 11, 1912; *San Diego Free Speech Controversy: Report to the San Francisco Labor Council by Special Investigating Committee* (San Francisco, Calif., April 25, 1912), pp. 3-4.

7. *Report of Harris Weinstock*, pp. 32-33.

8. *Industrial Worker*, June 13, August 8, 1912; *San Diego Sun*, June 14, 1912; Weintraub, op. cit., p. 38; Shanks, op. cit., pp. 31-32.

9. *Industrial Worker*, June 5, 1913; Shanks, op. cit., pp. 32-33; Richard Drinnon, *Rebel in Paradise: A Biography of Emma Goldman* (Chicago, 1961), p. 136; George Edwards, "Free Speech in San Diego," *Mother Earth* 10 (July 1915): 182-85.

10. "Casey Jones—the Union Scab" was Joe Hill's first known song, written when he was working in 1910 as a longshoreman in San Pedro. It is a parody of the original Casey Jones song, which had appeared two years before. Written to support workers on strike against the South Pacific Line and to denounce the railroad's importation of scabs, the famous ballad dealt with a scab who "got a wooden medal for being good and faithful on the S.P. line." It told of the I.W.W.'s sabotage of Casey Jones's engine, his trip to heaven where he even "went scabbing on the

angels," his descent into hell, and the ignominious tasks assigned him there:

> "Casey Jones," the Devil said, "oh fine;
> Casey Jones, get busy shoveling sulphur;
> That's what you get for scabbing on the J.P. line."

The song was an immediate success. Printed on colored cards which were sold to help the strike fund, the song helped keep the strike alive. Within a few months it was being sung by workers in many parts of the country where migratory laborers had carried it.

11. On the night of May 4, 1886, a bomb was thrown into a group of policemen who had begun to disperse a small crowd of workingmen at a protest meeting in Chicago's Haymarket Square. One policeman was killed instantly, and several others died later. The police opened fire, and several workers were killed and hundreds wounded. Hysteria swept the city and the nation. Eight anarchists, leaders of the movement for the eight-hour day, were indicted although there was no evidence linking them with the bombing. They were tried and convicted solely on the basis of their opinions. Seven were condemned to death, the eighth to fifteen years in prison. Four were hanged on November 11, 1887, and one committed suicide in prison or was killed by the police.

12. In the summer of 1911, a great wave of industrial unrest broke out in Great Britain and flowed over into Ireland. Two gigantic national strikes of transit workers and railway men in Britain heralded the dawn of a new day for labor. The first of these began with the seamen's and firemen's strike which broke out in Hull in the middle of June 1911 and which, by the end of the month, had crippled every port in Britain. This was only the beginning of a sympathetic strike movement in the waterside trades. Dockers, coal-fillers, and carters were soon out in sympathy with the seamen and firemen, demanding an improvement in their own wages and conditions also.

The second great national strike was the railway strike called in August 1911. This, too, ended in a victory for the strikers, and ushered in a wave of strikes which continued throughout 1911 and into 1912.

Chapter 6. Denver Free-Speech Fight, 1913

1. *Industrial Worker*, May 29, June 5 and 12, July 3, September 4, 1913; *Solidarity*, June 4, October 18, 1913; January 31, 1914; *Philadelphia Public Ledger*, June 6, 1913.

2. *Industrial Worker*, January 9, March 6, March 27, 1913.

3. *Solidarity*, April 26, May 3, 1913.

4. *Industrial Worker*, May 8, 1913; *Solidarity*, June 7, 1913.

5. Carl Browne had been first lieutenant to General Coxey on his famous march to Washington in 1894. He led a march in California of I.W.W. members to support unemployed workers during the depression that began in 1913.

6. "Mr. Block" and "The White Slave" were songs by Joe Hill.

7. The usual account of Wobblies in the commercial press described them as overwhelmingly foreign agitators.

Chapter 7. Two Free-Speech Fights in the Dakotas— Minot, North Dakota, 1913 and Aberdeen, South Dakota, 1914

1. *Industrial Worker*, May 29, June 5 and 12, July 3, September 4, 1913; *Solidarity*, June 4, October 8, 1913.

2. "Jungle" was the meeting place, usually near railroad tracks, for hoboes where they prepared their food and slept.

3. In 1910 Jack Johnson, black prizefighter, defeated Jim Jeffries, "the great white hope," in their heavyweight championship bout.

4. The Aberdeen *Sunday American* of July 19 also published the call, which went: "The fight is on in Aberdeen. Send 200 rebels at once. Signed. W. D. King."

5. Gamblers and holdup men preyed on lumber and harvest migrant workers, and the I.W.W. made it a practice to expose their nefarious activities.

6. In its issue of July 19, 1914, the Aberdeen *Sunday American* had the following account:

> The crisis of yesterday's gathering was reached when Katy Solomon, a notorious I.W.W. agitator and nicknamed, "Queen of the Tramps," was arrested when she attempted to speak to the crowd. The woman seemed to have a stronger influence over the men and several of them attempted to prevent Officer Kirley from arresting her. The crowd made a rush for the station door, but several officers who were on guard used their clubs so effectively that the rush was abruptly stopped. . . .

> The principal theme of the speakers is that the wages of $2.50 a day, which has been offered for harvest hands is not enough, and the men were encouraged to demand $3 a day or refuse work. The

slogan "$3 and 10 hours," was the watch-word and whenever it was heard cheers followed. Katy Solomon, the I.W.W. leader, went among the crowd yesterday afternoon telling the men to demand from $3 to $20 a day. She also spoke in the jungles Friday night, to a large and attentive audience.

Chapter 8. Kansas City Free-Speech Fight, 1914

1. *Kansas City Journal*, October 30, 1911; *Industrial Worker*, November 16, 1911; *Solidarity*, October 28, November 9, 1911.
2. *Kansas City Journal*, December 12-13, 1913; *The Wooden Shoe*, January 22, 1914.
3. *The Wooden Shoe*, January 29, 1914; *Solidarity*, February 28, March 7, 1914.
4. *Kansas City Journal*, February 18, 22, 1914; *Solidarity*, March 7, 1914.
5. *Solidarity*, March 14, 1914.

Chapter 9. Everett Free-Speech Fight, 1916

1. *Solidarity*, March 7, 1914.
2. One of the major objections to the free-speech fights was that while they attracted widespread attention and even aroused sympathy among many who were otherwise hostile to the doctrines and activities of the I.W.W., they interfered with the effective conduct of strikes. Wobbly organizers objected that strikes were lost because they were allowed "to degenerate into a free-speech fight," and charged that this was precisely what the employers wanted. Free-speech fights, it was further charged, did not result in any organizational growth in the community affected. For one thing, agitation or "soap boxing" were viewed by these critics as a limited means of reaching the mass of the workers, the majority of whom did not congregate at street corners. Then again, invading free-speech fighters scattered as soon as they were released from jail, and some of the most competent organizers, like Frank Little, went on to participate in other free-speech battles. (W. I. Fisher, "Soap-Boxer or Organizer, Which?" *Industrial Worker*, June 6, 1912; Grace V. Silver in *New York Call*, reprinted in *Solidarity*, March 25, 1911.)
3. *Industrial Worker*, September 16, October 2, 1916.
Yet as if to assure skeptical Wobblies that Everett did not signify a return to the old pattern, the *Industrial Worker* noted: "This is not a free-speech fight. It is a fight on the part of the bosses for the open shop and

the destruction of all unionism on the Pacific Coast." (September 16, 1916.)

4. Robert Edward Hull, "I.W.W. Activity in Everett, Washington, from May 1916 to June 1917" (M.A. thesis, State College of Washington, 1938), pp. 12-15; *Everett Tribune*, May 15, 1916.

5. *The Shingle Weaver*, April 29, July 22, 1916; *Everett Tribune*, July 22, 27, 1916.

6. *Everett Tribune*, April 4, 1917; Walker C. Smith, *The Everett Massacre: A History of the Class Struggle in the Lumber Industry* (Chicago, 1917), pp. 35-36.

7. *Everett Tribune*, April 5, 6, 10, and 13, 1917; *The Shingle Weaver*, August 26, 1916; David C. Botting, Jr., "Bloody Sunday," *Pacific Northwest Quarterly* 49 (October 1958): 164-65.

8. Smith, op. cit., p. 44; Botting, op. cit., p. 165; Robert L. Tyler, "I.W.W. in the Pacific N.W.: Rebels of the Woods," *Oregon Historical Quarterly* 40 (March 1954): 14.

9. *Industrial Worker*, September 16, 1916; *Everett Tribune*, April 4, 1917; Smith, op. cit., pp. 58-59.

10. Smith, op. cit., pp. 72-77; Botting, op. cit., p. 168; *Everett Tribune*, March 28, April 15 and 22, 1917.

11. *Everett Tribune*, November 6, 1916.

12. *Everett Tribune*, April 17, 1917.
Reverend McGill proposed at first that the meeting be held in a tabernacle in Everett, but Herbert Mahler of the Seattle I.W.W. local countered with the proposal that in order to make a test case of the constitutionality of an Everett ordinance banning street-speaking, it be held at the corner of Hewitt and Wetmore; Reverend McGill agreed.

13. Smith, op. cit., p. 80.

14. Captain Harry Ramwell, "History of Everett's Troubles with I.W.W.," *Everett Tribune*, November 25, 1916; Tyler, "I.W.W. in the Pacific Northwest," p. 15. See also *Everett Tribune*, November 4, 1916.

15. *Everett Tribune*, March 23, 1917; Smith, op. cit., p. 84; *Industrial Worker*, November 18, 1916.

16. Ramwell, op. cit.; Smith, op. cit., p. 85.

17. In the I.W.W. the primary example of working-class power was the revolutionary industrial union. Industrial union locals were combined into national industrial unions and thence into industrial departments of related industries, which departments, taken together, composed the general organization—the One Big Union. In the eyes of many commentators, the One Big Union was synonymous with the I.W.W. This was certainly true for many Wobblies who signed their letters, "Yours for the O.B.U."

18. "Hold the Fort" was popularized in the United States first by the Knights of Labor. See Philip S. Foner, *American Labor Songs of the Nineteenth Century* (Urbana, Illinois, 1975), pp. 122-24.

19. Judge O. N. Hilton was another lawyer who devoted much time to defending the I.W.W. He was the lawyer in the case of Joe Hill.

20. Anna Louise Strong was a militant correspondent and labor poet on the staff of the *Seattle Union-Record.*

21. "Solidarity Forever," written to the tune of "John Brown's Body" by Ralph Chaplin, the artist, poet, and leader of the Chicago section of the I.W.W., was published for the first time in *Solidarity,* January 9, 1915, and was originally known as "Wage Workers Come Join the Union." It rapidly became the most famous I.W.W. and probably the most famous American labor song, and even today one hears the stirring words at union meetings and on picket lines:

> It is we who plowed the prairies, built the cities where
>   they stand;
> Dug the mines and built the workshops, endless miles of
>   railroad laid
> Now we stand outcast and starving, 'mid the wonders
>   we have made.
> But the union makes us strong.
>
> Solidarity forever!
> Solidarity forever!
> Solidarity forever!
> For the union makes us strong.

22. A "kangaroo court" was a court stacked against the working class by its very composition, with a jury usually composed of anti-labor business groups or farmers.

23. On November 5, 1916, the date of the *Verona* battle, the Seattle district had only two paid officials, Herbert Mahler, secretary of Local 432, and J. A. McDonald, editor of the *Industrial Worker.* By July 4, 1917, thirty people were employed by the district, and were working day and night to take care of the constantly increasing membership, especially the newly organized lumber workers. Referring to the effect of Tracy's acquittal and the release of the other prisoners, the *Seattle Union Record* declared: "It is the first victory of the kind ever achieved by labor on the Pacific Coast, previous trials without exception having been decided against the workers." Quoted in Harvey O'Connor, *Revolution in Seattle: A Memoir* (New York, 1964), p. 55. For the effect of the acquittal on the growth of the Seattle local, see *Industrial Worker,* May 19, 1917; Smith, op. cit., p. 291.

For additional accounts of the Everett Free-Speech Fight and the
Everett Massacre, *see also* Norman H. Clark, *Mill Town: A Social History
of Everett, Washington* (Seattle, 1970); Norman H. Clark, "Everett,
1916, and After," *Pacific Northwest Quarterly* 57 (1966): 57-64;
David C. Botting, Jr., "Bloody Sunday," ibid., 49 (1958): 167-72;
Robert Edward Hull, "I.W.W. Activity in Everett, Washington from May,
1916 to June, 1917," M.A. thesis, State College of Washington, 1938;
Donald M. Barnes, "The Everett Massacre: A Turning Point in I.W.W.
History," *Organon* 1 (Winter 1969): 35-42, and William J. Williams,
"Bloody Sunday Revisited," *Pacific Northwest Quarterly* 71 (1980):
50-63. The last-mentioned study includes the text of the investigation
of the Everett shooting conducted by the Seattle office of the Steamboat-
Inspection Service. The investigation, however, does little to settle the
controversy over what happened when the Wobblies tried to land in
Everett.

Index

About the Editor

PHILIP S. FONER is Professor Emeritus of History at Lincoln University in Pennsylvania. His many books include *Labor and the American Revolution* (Greenwood Press, 1976), *American Socialism and Black Americans* (Greenwood Press, 1977), and *The Democratic-Republican Societies, 1790-1800* (Greenwood Press, 1976).